POWER
and the
PRESIDENCY

POWER
and the
PRESIDENCY

Edited by
Philip C. Dolce
and George H. Skau

Charles Scribner's Sons · New York

Copyright © 1976 Philip C. Dolce and George H. Skau

Library of Congress Cataloging in Publication Data

Main entry under title:

71421

Power and the presidency.

"An outgrowth of a 54-program CBS television series
entitled 'The American presidency: the men and the
office.'"
   Bibliography: p.
   Includes index.
   1. Presidents—United States—History—Addresses,
essays, lectures.   2. Executive power—United States—
History—Addresses, essays, lectures.   I. Dolce,
Philip C   II. Skau, George H
JK511.P7   353.03   76–6969
ISBN 0–684–14603–7
ISBN 0–684–14602–9 pbk.

1 3 5 7 9 11 13 15 17 19 C/C 20 18 16 14 12 10 8 6 4 2

Printed in the United States of America

TO OUR WIVES AND CHILDREN
Patty and Susan Dolce
Anne, John, Peter, and Marianne Skau

CONTENTS

PREFACE

The role of the Chief Executive has been central to an understanding of American historical development since the time of Washington. Within our flexible constitutional system, the Presidency has become increasingly instrumental in shaping the nation's destiny. This is especially true in our own age as domestic and international problems seem to demand vigorous executive leadership. To many, the President is the most visible symbol of the nation.

The Founding Fathers realized that the Presidency would occupy a central position in the affairs of the country and hoped that the office would be filled by "honest and wise men." How well this hope has been fulfilled is a matter of opinion, for the men who have occupied the executive office have been diverse in background, outlook, and ability. This diversity is obvious in the essays comprising the first two sections of the volume. The trend in these essays points toward increased Presidential authority especially in foreign affairs.

However, a clear understanding of the executive office requires more than an analysis of Presidential administrations. Therefore, we have included a section on key issues which evaluates different phases of the office and also includes essays on areas in which Presidential power has not been fully utilized or effective. The essays in the last section analyze the Presidency from the nomination process to the restrictions inherent in the office. The limitations of space forced a certain degee of selectivity and therefore we do not pretend that this volume is all inclusive. Yet we believe that an essential understanding of the Presidential office and the men who occupied it can be achieved by reading these specially commissioned articles and interviews.

This volume is an outgrowth of a 54-program CBS television

series entitled "The American Presidency: The Men and the Office." Most of the essays have been substantially revised for this publication. Since a study of the executive office transcends any one discipline, we have attempted to combine the expertise and perspectives of historians, political scientists, journalists, and actual participants in the historical process in order to present the reader with a multidimensional view. In doing so, we have refrained from any attempt to reconcile opposing interpretations presented by the contributors. Due to the fact that these essays are primarily designed for students and a general audience, citations have been omitted. In most cases, however, documentation can be found in major works previously published by the contributors.

We would like to express our appreciation to all the contributors for their participation in this project; they deserve full credit for the merits of this volume. A very special note of gratitude belongs to Mary Christiano and Mary Darragh, who provided indispensable assistance in the preparation of the manuscript. Naturally, the perseverance and support of our wives and children were essential.

Philip C. Dolce
George H. Skau

PART I

THE PRESIDENCY
from GEORGE WASHINGTON
to WILLIAM McKINLEY

1

THE FOUNDING FATHERS
and the CREATION of the
EXECUTIVE BRANCH
by Robert F. Jones

Napoleon Bonaparte is supposed to have said that constitutions should be short and obscure; the United States Constitution is certainly short—some forty-five hundred words as it came from the convention in Philadelphia in 1787—and on many points, it is also obscure. One of the more obscure portions is Article 2, describing and defining the powers and duties of the Presidency.

Of course, there are clear precedents in America's colonial and revolutionary history for several of the powers which the President exercises today; the reasons why the President does not have certain powers, or must share them, also go back to those same periods. One type of executive familiar to most adult Americans in 1787 was the royal governor of colonial days. He had represented royal power and was the point at which the colonists came into touch with the London government. Although he theoretically exercised unlimited powers, colonial assemblies controlled taxation and appropriation, gaining a fair degree of freedom for themselves and often frustrating the work of the governor. In the ten years before the outbreak of the War of American Independence in 1775, attempts by the governors to enforce unwelcome British policy served to confirm the colonists' view of them as agents of a foreign and uncontrollable power.

When the colonies formed states between 1776 and 1780, they remembered these conflicts, and the constitutions of only New

York, Massachusetts, and New Hampshire permitted strong executives. Generally the governor was limited to a one-year term, had strict limits on reeligibility, and was elected by the legislature. In his deliberations and the execution of his office, he was also limited by a council chosen by the legislature. There was no general grant of executive power; the judiciary was as powerless as the executive, leaving the legislature unchecked by anything other than what their respect for the state constitution might impose on them. Only lip service, if that, was paid to the principle of the separation of powers.

New York, in its 1777 constitution, was the first state to break from this pattern. Its governor, indefinitely reeligible for office, was elected by the people for a three-year term. He enjoyed extensive, well-defined powers, including the right to convene and adjourn the legislature and to advise it of the condition of the state and recommend matters to its attention. With the participation of councils drawn from the judiciary and the state senate, he had the rights of appointment and veto. Along with the judiciary, the executive gained in stature, thus translating the principle of separation of powers from theory into fact. In New York, in good part because of the governor's independent position, the constitution became the controlling document that it should be. This constitution worked extremely well, not the least because the first governor, George Clinton, was an effective, popular executive who was elected for six successive terms. New York's practical demonstration of the benefits of an independent executive became a model for the Philadelphia convention and one of the most significant influences on it. Massachusetts and New Hampshire gave their executives some of the sources of independent power enjoyed by Governor Clinton.

From the experience of the Continental Congress came an object lesson on the necessity for an independent national executive. Originally a kind of committee of ambassadors from the various colonies, the Congress never entirely lost this character. Even after the ratification of the Articles of Confederation in 1781, it lacked the power to enforce its decisions, and the Articles did not provide for a strong, independent executive. With the end of the War of American Independence in 1783, the Congress lost whatever informal power the war had given it. It was powerless to compel the states to execute the treaty of peace with Great Britain, to contribute to the support of defense forces, or to provide for the payment of debts incurred during the war. Although the plight of the United States, even its economic difficulties, was probably not as serious as they thought, many people felt that the country was undergoing a crisis and that a stronger national government could rescue it. In February 1787 the Congress formally summoned the states to a convention for "the sole and express purpose of revising the Articles of Confederation . . . [to] render the federal constitution adequate to the exigencies of Government and the preservation of the Union."

By Friday, May 25, delegates from eight states had gathered in Philadelphia. Before they adjourned in September, every state except Rhode Island, stubbornly insistent on going its own way, would be represented at one time or another. Meeting in the Old State House, where the Continental Congress had sat during the war and where the Declaration of Independence had been approved, the convention elected George Washington as its president. It was an index of his own feelings about the seriousness of the situation the country faced that he had left Mount Vernon and resigned himself to spending an uncomfortable summer in Philadelphia. Since the convention did almost all of its important deliberating in committee, his presidency was largely honorific. Washington's real contribution to the convention was his inestimable prestige among the people. His presence lent a kind of legitimacy to the meeting that even the formal approval of the Congress had not been able to impart. Similarly, Benjamin Franklin, then serving as president of the Executive Council of Pennsylvania, lent primarily his prestige to the meeting. Old and in failing health, he was carried from his nearby house in a sedan chair, borne by convicts from the old Walnut Street Prison; most of his contributions to the debate had to be read for him by one of his Pennsylvania colleagues. James Madison, of the Virginia delegation, has often been called the Father of the Constitution for his forthright advocacy of a strong central government clearly superior to the states. Although this is true in a general sense, Madison came to Philadelphia with a very hazy conception of the office of the executive. Far more important to the formation of the executive in the new government were James Wilson and Gouverneur Morris, both of Pennsylvania.

Wilson, born in Scotland, was a lawyer and constitutional theorist, and the one most concerned with creating a strong, independent executive. Morris, a member of a wealthy landholding family in New York, had come to Philadelphia during the war and assisted Robert Morris (no relation) in supervising Congressional finances during the early 1780s.

James Madison. *Colonial Williamsburg*

At the outset, the convention decided to keep its debates secret, to vote by states (one vote to a state), and to scrap the Articles and draft a new frame of government. Debate on the executive opened on the first of June and continued for a week until the office was fairly well filled out. In this first round, after considerable debate, the framers at Philadelphia decided on a single executive, serving for one seven-year term to which he had been elected by the legislature; his salary was to be fixed and not changed during his term of office. He was to execute the national laws and appoint all officers not otherwise provided for. He was given the veto power, but his veto could be overridden by a two-thirds' vote of the legislature. He could be impeached for malpractice or neglect of duty, with the trial being conducted by the national judiciary.

Although the office of the executive had been partially filled in, it still differed markedly from what would finally be adopted. When the Convention reassembled on August 6 after a short recess, the title of President was used for the first time and he gained the right to inform the Congress of the state of the union and recommend matters to their consideration. He also became commander in chief of the armed forces and was to conduct correspondence with foreign governments, but the treaty-making power resided entirely with the Senate. He was still to be elected by the legislature for one seven-year term and could be impeached for treason, bribery, and corruption; the impeachment trial would be held by the Supreme Court.

During this phase of the debate on the Presidency, the convention encountered the problem of detailing several essential points. In the process, the framers decided for a joint ballot, rather than separate voting by both houses of the Congress in the election of the President. Immediately, the small states lost the advantage their equal representation in the Senate gave them; for they were certain to be overwhelmed by the large state delegations in the House of Representatives. Now the small states might be readier to agree to some other mode of selecting the President. Morris proposed election by electors chosen by the people and the small states of New Jersey, Delaware, and Connecticut joined Pennsylvania and Virginia in a yes vote, only to lose by one. Then, on the abstract question of election by electors, chosen by an unspecified mode, there was a tie vote and New Jersey moved that the matter be put over. The presentation of any kind of an alternative to joint legislative election which would give the small states a significant voice could well gain their assent.

On August 31, the convention referred some difficult points, including several on the Presidency, to the Committee on Postponed Matters. In its report of September 4 the Presidency appears for the first time in a recognizable form. The President was to be elected for a four-year term, with no mention of eligibility for a second term, by electors chosen as the state legislatures would provide and in proportion to the size of the Congressional delegations of the various states. Although on the surface this would favor the large states, few delegates anticipated that the so-called Electoral College, because of the size of the United States and the likelihood that after Washington there would be no men with a national reputation, could do more than indicate suitable candidates. If no one received a majority in the Electoral College, then the Senate would select from among the candidates with the five highest vote totals. There the small states could have their say. With the sole dependence on the legislature for his election being removed, the trial of impeachments could be moved from the Supreme Court to the Senate with the grounds for impeachment remaining treason or bribery.

In deliberating on the committee's draft, George Mason of Virginia objected to limiting the grounds for impeachment so stringently, remarking that a President could subvert the Constitution without resorting to such crimes. He moved that "maladministration" be added. When Madison objected to the vagueness of that term, Mason substituted "other high crimes and misdemeanors" and the motion carried. This committee also gave the President the treaty-making power and the power to appoint important officials, but only with the consent of the Senate, a two-thirds' majority being specified for approval of treaties. No one was completely happy with the new scheme of election, but, as Wilson noted, "It is in truth the most difficult of all on which we have had to decide," confessing that he had never been able to make up his own mind on it. When the objection was made that selection by the Senate in case of an inconclusive election gave it too much power, that part of the election was moved to the House but with the voting to be done by state delegations, each state having one vote, thus preserving the small-states' advantage.

Throughout the convention, Wilson, Gouverneur Morris, and a few others, with the later addition of Madison, had worked to ensure the independence and strength of the Presidency. Perhaps nothing worked toward this goal so much as the election of the President by a body other than the legislature. The Electoral College, although clumsy, gave the President a separate source of power even if he had to be selected by the House. The legislators could only choose from among those the College had marked out for election. Further, the system has shown itself to be sufficiently flexible to permit the evolution of what is, in effect, a direct popular election. Direct election was supported by few in the convention; most delegates thought the size of the United States made an intelligent choice by the people from among candidates from different parts of the country impossible.

A few last-minute touches remained. For example, it was only after the Committee on Style had drafted the Constitution into its present form that the Senate lost the unfettered right to appoint the Secretary of the Treasury. And it was the Committee on Style, whose most active member was Gouverneur Morris, which drafted the vesting clause—"The executive Power shall be vested in a President of the United States of America" (Article 2, Section 1) —giving the President a general grant of executive power according to the Constitution, not according to the laws of Congress.

Obscure points abounded. The delegates had argued interminably over the question of eligibility for a second term and then did not mention it at all. One prescient member pointed to the vagueness of the clause regarding presidential disability and asked plaintively what it meant. No one answered him, for no one knew. Whether or not the Vice-President becomes President when he succeeds to the office was also not stated. The Convention may well have expected him to become acting President, but it did not say so. In 1841 John Tyler convinced the nation otherwise and a significant precedent was set. Similarly, nothing was said about the power of the President to remove ministers appointed with the consent of the Senate. This had to be settled by a combination of Congressional debate, Presidential action, and Supreme Court decision.

All in all, the Presidency as it emerged from the convention was quite strong enough. It combined, as Alexander Hamilton described it in *The Federalist* number 70, unity, duration, competent powers, "adequate provision for its support," "due dependence on the people," and "due responsibility." More picturesquely, Clinton Rossiter has described the President as being similar to a lion in a large reservation. In the reservation, the lion reigns supreme, but around it runs a strong, well-secured fence making it unlikely that he will ever break out.

There are various similarities between the powers provided for the governor of New York in that state's 1777 constitution and those given to the President of the United States. Other, less obvious, influences were also working. Frequent references to the necessity of an effective separation of powers indicate not only that the delegates were thinking of the recent example of the states but also that they had been reading their Montesquieu and their Blackstone. Their desire to prevent the arbitrary exercise of unfettered executive power and opportunity for corruption show the influence of English radical writers such as Trenchard and Gordon, the authors of *Cato's Letters*. The strength of the office reflected a desire for a national executive who would not be as powerless as the average state governor. Finally, the confident expectation that George Washington would be the first President convinced some delegates that the further definition of the office could safely be left to its first occupant. Benjamin Franklin said as much during the convention, and later Pierce Butler of South Carolina admitted the effect of Washington's anticipated election on himself and other delegates.

During the ratification controversy, as the states were considering the new frame of government, the Presidency came in for its share of criticism by the Antifederalists, as opponents of the new Constitution were labeled. Several states submitted, along with their instruments of ratification, possible amendments to the Constitution. Virginia, New York, and North Carolina all suggested a check on the reelection of the President. More generally, those who opposed the Constitution feared that the President would be an irresponsible executive, the first step toward a monarchy. The idea of a strong republican executive did not occur to them. They also viewed the Senate as a kind of executive council because of its connection with the President in foreign affairs and its role in the appointment of important officials. To them, this connection also violated the principle of the separation of powers. On a less creditable level, some Antifederalists feared that the lack of a religious qualification for Presidents would permit a "Papist" or a "Mahometan" to occupy the office, perhaps even the Pope. One imaginative critic combined the power of Congress to locate the capital city wherever it pleased with the possibility of the Pope as President and foresaw a country governed from Peking, China, by a Pope who, naturally, would be a tyrant.

In countering these criticisms of the office, the Federalists repeated much of what had already been said in the convention and also pointed to the various ways in which the President's apparently unfettered power was checked. Richard Neustadt in his study of the modern Presidency has pointed to the fact that, rather than illustrating the separation of powers, the Constitution actually put into effect a system of separated institutions sharing powers. Some defenders of the new frame of government made this point implicitly when they pointed to the limitation on each power of the

Signing of the Constitution. Painting by Howard C. Christy. *Library of Congress*

President, especially the Senate's participation in the treaty-making and appointive power, in addition to the Congress's control over taxes, appropriations, and all other points of legislation. The Antifederalists' most serious criticism, the lack of a bar to reelection, a criticism concurred in by Thomas Jefferson, would be handled for one hundred and fifty years by the two-term tradition begun by Washington and confirmed by Jefferson himself when he retired in 1809.

For the immediate future, however, the location of the fence, marking off the domain of Mr. Rossiter's lion, remained in some areas uncertain. The work of surveying the field of Presidential power would be started, fittingly enough, by an ex-surveyor, George Washington.

2

GEORGE WASHINGTON
and the ESTABLISHMENT
of a TRADITION

by Robert F. Jones

The men who began the federal government in 1789 had several advantages; one of the most significant was that George Washington was to be the first President. Washington's difficulties as commander of the Continental Army during the War of Independence had convinced him of the need for a strong central government. Now he was to be given the opportunity to help create that government. In 1789, as at the Constitutional Convention in 1787, Washington's major contribution would be made simply by being there. His prestige among the people and the confidence they placed in his judgment and integrity gave the new government a kind of legitimacy before it had even begun.

The President-elect was welcomed to New York City, the first seat of the new federal government, on April 23 by a delegation led by George Clinton, governor of New York and a leader of the opposition to the new Constitution. Even Clinton, however, was gracious and apparently sincere in his welcome. The inauguration took place at Federal Hall, the refurbished New York City Hall, on April 30 before a crowd numbering several thousands. Robert R. Livingston, chancellor of the State of New York, administered the oath of office since federal judicial officials had not yet been commissioned. Afterward, Washington delivered his inaugural address to the Congress. It was brief, some two thousand words, pious, and general, and it contained only one specific statement: a request to the House of Representatives that it fix his compensation according to his wartime practice of receiving compensation for his expenses instead of a salary. (Congress did not heed this request and set a salary of twenty-five thousand dollars from which the President would have to pay expenses. Actually this barely sufficed for Washington, although his successor, John Adams, managed to save money.) Senator William Maclay of Pennsylvania, who had come to New York ready to be scandalized by the luxurious and unrepublican character of the city and had not been disappointed,

Inauguration of George Washington. *Library of Congress*

noted how nervous and uncomfortable the new President was while speaking, and the Senator wished that Washington could have been first in speechmaking as in everything else. After the speech, the Congress adjourned for a thanksgiving service at St. Paul's Church and a banquet that evening.

The novelty of the office (Washington was the only elected head of state in the European world at that time) meant that even some admittedly trivial details had to be settled. For example, what to call the President? A Senate committee solemnly deliberated on how to address their reply to the inaugural address and came up with "To His Highness, the President of the United States of America and Protector of their Liberties." Maclay scoffed at this as representing the hidden desire of the Vice-President, John Adams, and others to convert the infant government into a monarchy, but he could not prevent the Senate from approving it. Fortunately the House stood firm, and the Congress's reply was addressed simply "To the President of the United States." Washington was usually addressed as "His Excellency" as he had been during the war; "Mr. President" evolved later. Those who desired a plain, republican tone for the new government were not pleased when Washington decided to hold an afternoon reception, a "levee," once a week at which he could meet the public. He was criticized by some for copying this custom of European monarchs. To Senator Maclay, "Nothing is regarded or valued at such meetings but the qualifications that flow from the tailor, barber, or dancing master." The levees, however, did fulfill their intended goal of relieving the President of a constant round of time-wasting visits and were continued. Washington also started a series of dinners designed to bring every member of the Congress to his table at least once during a session. Here Maclay was struck by the excellence of the meal but also by the stiffness of the President as a host. Washington always found it difficult to relax except with a few intimate friends, and this was reflected in the formal, stately tone of the social life of his administration. It was very much a reflection of the man himself.

All was not levees and excellent, even if dull, dinners. Much remained to be done to convert the Constitution into a working government. Washington had to make appointments to the Cabinet and lesser offices of government. In doing this he kept in mind competence as well as geographical distribution. He did not want any section to feel that the government was being unduly influenced by men from another area, for the bonds of loyalty were still slim enough to be strained by such considerations. His Vice-President was from Massachusetts as was the Secretary of War, Henry Knox, Washington's chief of artillery during the war and the man who had filled the same position for the old Congress. Alexander Hamilton, the Secretary of the Treasury, was a New Yorker who had served on Washington's staff during the war. The State Department was not filled until March 1790 when Washington convinced his fellow Virginian, Thomas Jefferson, to take the post. Edmund Randolph, the Attorney General, was also a Virginian. In lesser appointments, Washington also followed the rule of Senatorial courtesy, withdrawing one nomination when the Senators from the appointee's home state objected even though he could see nothing wrong with the man. All of his close associates were already known to the President, and he confidently expected a harmonious relationship within his official family.

George Washington and his Cabinet (left to right, Washington, Henry Knox, Alexander Hamilton, Thomas Jefferson, Edmund Randolph). *Library of Congress*

None of these early department heads administered large bureaucratic organizations. The Treasury Department eventually employed close to a thousand persons to collect the revenue, but only about thirty or so were located in the capital. Other offices employed fewer than a dozen full- and part-time clerks and were located in private houses when the government moved to Philadelphia in the fall of 1790. One house sufficed for all but the Treasury. It was government on a very small scale indeed. For his office the President used a room on the second floor of his house, which meant that all visitors had to go through or by the family living quarters to meet with him.

Washington supervised the operations of government rather closely, conferring with department heads on an almost daily basis. He read all mail going out over a Secretary's signature along with the letter that inspired it. Thus he kept himself informed of all important business of the executive departments. In return, he gave his Secretaries a rather free hand and insisted that all business pertaining to their departments be routed to them. He once rebuked the French minister gently but firmly for trying to contact him directly, rather than through the Secretary of State. He viewed his Secretaries as his subordinates, however, a view concurred in by the Congress. When the State Department was being debated by the House, some members took exception to a clause permitting the President to discharge the Secretary without Senatorial consent. As a result of the complex debate that followed, the clause was deleted but with the clear implication that the President enjoyed that right as part of the general grant of executive power. It was his responsibility to see to the careful administration of government business; the Congress should hold the executive, not the Secretary, directly responsible for failure.

Washington used his Secretaries for a variety of functions, frequently calling them together to deliberate on significant matters but sometimes contenting himself with written advice from them. He did not believe in overspecialization and sometimes asked a Secretary to draft a state paper outside his department, especially if he was following that person's advice. At the same time, if he asked for a Cabinet vote, Washington almost always followed the majority, even when it differed from his view of the problem. This was partly the result of having two Secretaries with very different views, Hamilton and Jefferson. When a consensus could be reached, it reflected their conflicting opinions and was generally a compromise between them.

Washington also sought advice from outside the circle of his

Secretaries, frequently calling on John Jay, then Chief Justice of the Supreme Court, for advice on foreign affairs and James Madison, then a Representative from Virginia, for domestic problems. But no matter who advised him or who wrote the state paper expressing the solution of the particular difficulty, Washington took full responsibility for the decision. He understood fully the implications of the motto Harry Truman had on his desk, "The buck stops here."

In his relationship with the Congress, Washington was not nearly as flexible as with his Secretaries. He considered the Constitution to be a fairly detailed guide and adhered rigidly to the concept of separation of powers. While he took advantage of his constitutional prerogative of suggesting topics for Congress's legislative action, thereafter he would not comment on them or attempt to direct the Congress's deliberations. When the Congress presented him with a finished bill, the only question he asked was whether or not it was constitutional. He did not consider himself to be entirely passive in legislative matters. When one of Hamilton's reports urged the Congress to enact a complicated system of preferential tariffs and bounties in order to promote the industrialization of the country, Washington never supported it, because he doubted both the constitutionality and effectiveness of the suggested plan.

The first President began the practice of serving as the principal author of foreign policy. Taking literally the clause of the Constitution that bound the President to seek the "advice and consent" of the Senate to all treaties, the President and his Secretary of War visited the upper house in the summer of 1789 with draft instructions for commissioners who were to negotiate treaties with the southern Indians. When the Senate refused to deliberate in his presence, Washington reportedly said that he would be "damned if he ever went there again." No President ever has gone "there" again, and the Senate found itself in a position where it could only agree or disagree with a treaty that the executive had negotiated with a free hand.

More substantial problems only served to further the President's primacy in the area of foreign affairs. In the spring of 1793, Great Britain entered the wars of the French Revolution and the conflict moved out onto the Atlantic and other seas where American vessels pursued a growing commerce. Although no one in the Cabinet wanted to see America involved in the war, Alexander

Hamilton urged the President to proclaim American neutrality immediately, a neutrality which, because of British command of the seas, would most benefit that nation. Jefferson wanted a delay in any announcement of American policy in the hope that the warring nations might grant favors in return for American neutrality. He also had a constitutional objection: if the Constitution gave only the Congress the power to declare war, could the President, on his own, declare neutrality or no war? Washington decided that his prerogative in foreign policy justified an announcement of American intentions. Out of deference to Jefferson's feelings, his pronouncement, drafted by Attorney General Randolph, did not contain the word neutrality; rather it enjoined "friendly and impartial" conduct by American citizens toward the belligerents. The message, known nevertheless as the "Neutrality Proclamation," contained another problem. The President had ordered all federal officers to enforce the proclamation, but there was no federal law describing what constituted neutral behavior for the individual citizen. Could the President, by executive fiat, make law in this regard, and, if he did, would it serve as a precedent in other areas? Fortunately, before serious difficulties developed, the Congress passed a neutrality law in 1794. Nevertheless, the proclamation was a significant precedent supporting the idea that the President was the chief author of American foreign policy.

An incident stemming from foreign affairs also served to mark out one of the unofficial prerogatives of the President. In 1796, the House was considering an appropriations bill needed to execute the Jay Treaty. The opposition utilized this as an excuse to force reconsideration and possible repudiation of the treaty by passing a motion calling on the President to deliver all documents connected with negotiation of the treaty. After consultation with his Cabinet, Washington refused, stating that, since the House had no constitutional role to play in ratifying treaties, it had no basis for its request other than that of a consideration of a possible impeachment. Since the resolution did not express that purpose, the House had no right to make the request. (Presumably, if the House had been considering impeachment, the President would have complied with the request.) Beyond that, the circumstances of diplomatic negotiations required confidentiality. Although Republicans in the House were angry at the President's denial, Washington began to execute the treaty, after which the House passed the appropriations bill by a narrow margin. Thus, this first assertion of executive privilege was concurred in, although grudgingly, by the Congress.

In the main, however, Washington saw himself as a magistrate, as the officer charged with executing the law that the Congress had made. This was clearly the case in the circumstances surrounding his suppression of the Whiskey Rebellion during the summer of 1794. Ever since the enactment of the first federal excise tax on "spiritous liquors of domestic manufacture," farmers in western Pennsylvania and Virginia had been protesting the levy. Various changes in the law in 1792 had made it more, not less onerous, and Washington recommended to the Congress that the law be revised. Before changes enacted in 1793 could take full effect, the frontier exploded into open resistance. After terrorizing several excisemen and burning the house of the chief collector of the excise for western Pennsylvania, John Neville, the rebels collected at Braddock's Field near Pittsburgh and vowed defiance to the government. When other attempts to settle the dispute failed, Washington, who had already consulted his Cabinet, reluctantly called out the militia of Pennsylvania and neighboring states. In his role as commander in chief, he led the troops as far as Bradford. There General Henry Lee assumed nominal command, while Secretary of the Treasury Hamilton went along as the unofficial representative of the civil power. When the troops arrived in the rebellious area, resistance collapsed and the leaders fled. Later, after several of those involved in the disturbances had been convicted of treason, Washington pardoned them.

Although the President has often been accused of being a tool of Hamilton in this incident, it being assumed that the Secretary was bent on demonstrating the ability of the federal government to enforce its laws, Washington was in command of the situation. He saw the issue as one of resistance to duly constituted authority. Earlier resistance to British policy was not a fair parallel since the colonists had not been represented in the Parliament; the whiskey rebels were opposing a law enacted by a Congress in which their representatives sat. Washington regarded petitions to lawful authority as the only proper way to present grievances to the government. He blamed the Democratic-Republican Societies, voluntary political-action groups that had recently sprung up in the area of the rebellion and elsewhere, for much of the disturbance. In his view such groups posed an improper barrier between the citizen and his government. To him, the Constitution defined individual freedom and imposed responsibilities as well as guaranteed rights. Washington recognized no legitimate role for political groups of any kind.

Yet his administration was much bothered by such political opposition. Originating in very different views of the proper role of the federal government, political opposition to administration policies appeared during his first term. Washington was very disturbed when the conflict invaded the Cabinet and quarrels between Hamilton and Jefferson began to turn Cabinet meetings into disputations. His anxiety mounted when the dispute became public, and he requested both men to bury their disagreement in the interest of unity. His appeals were ineffective. Jefferson resigned at the end of 1793.

By the end of 1795 Washington's original Cabinet had disappeared. Their successors were not men of equal talents. After four others had declined, Washington asked Timothy Pickering to take on the State Department, while the amiable but incompetent Baltimore physician James McHenry took his place at the War Department. Oliver Wolcott, Jr., was a respectable administrator of the Treasury, but he lacked the fire and ability of his predecessor. Charles Lee of Virginia became Attorney General. More important than their general lack of talent was the fact that they were all of one political philosophy. Washington no longer had any close associates from the opposition, no ready way to receive different advice. Wolcott and McHenry took their cues from Hamilton, who was practicing law in New York City. Added to this, Washington now began to correspond with his ex-Secretary of the Treasury frequently, thus sometimes receiving Hamilton's advice directly, sometimes through his present Cabinet. Although Washington never abandoned his resolve to be an impartial first magistrate, he could not help but be influenced by the one-dimensional advice he was receiving from those around him.

Even the Farewell Address would not be free of the effects of this gradual closing off of diverse opinions. When the time came to announce his decision to retire, Washington turned to Hamilton for help in drafting his final message. By late summer it was finished. It was published in a Philadelphia newspaper in September 1796. In the address Washington issued his famous advice against permanent alliances, indeed, against even feelings of persistent enmity or favoritism toward foreign nations; he also warned his fellow Americans "against the baneful effects of the Spirit of Party" and foreign influence in the domestic affairs of the country. Divorced from the circumstances in which they were made, his remarks have become part of a catechism of American ideas on political parties and foreign policy.

If one remembers that it was a persistent Federalist charge that Republicans were the dupes of the French, especially in their opposition to Jay's Treaty, and that the only permanent alliance the United States then had was with the French, Washington's remarks seem to lose some of their nonpartisan aura. He did not see the situation in these terms though, and he sincerely advised his fellow citizens according to his best judgment. Washington had intended to conduct an administration free of partisanship on his part and was convinced that he had done so. As he saw it, any errors that might be attributed to him, and he had never claimed infallibility, could be due to a variety of factors, never to what could be called political considerations. However, he did not appreciate how much the development of political parties had changed the Presidency. The office he had expected to fill was that of a chief magistrate, impartially executing the laws passed by a Congress of the first citizens of their respective states, but the office had already begun to evolve into the modern Presidency, where its occupant is also the leader of his party. Unconsciously, Washington had become a Federalist.

Despite this unwitting lapse into partisanship, Washington contributed much to the Presidency. He had gotten the administrative machinery of the federal government running after the various executive departments had been created by the Congress; his appointments to office, from the Cabinet level down almost always went to the best-available candidates; and he had given the example of a hard-working, intelligent administrator. In trying to conduct national affairs impartially he had succeeded more often than he had failed. And he had kept the Presidency independent of the Congress without riding roughshod over the rights of that body. His Cabinet, as it was first staffed, had functioned as an effective advisory body without either hindering the President or permitting him to hide his actions behind a cloak of collective responsibility. The deterioration of his administration in its last years was due largely to events beyond his control and understanding. He had tried to be, and to a large extent succeeded in being, what the framers at Philadelphia had hoped the President would be—as Clinton Rossiter put it, "a strong, dignified, largely non-political chief of state and government." He left behind the image of the ideal President, the standard which most of us use consciously or not when we measure the work of the later occupants of the office.

3

THE EMERGENCE of POLITICAL PARTIES and THEIR EFFECT on the PRESIDENCY

by Robert V. Remini

Americans have long shared a conceit about the nation's Founding Fathers—those extraordinary men who met in Philadelphia in 1787, disobeyed their explicit instructions from the states to amend the Articles of Confederation, and instead hammered out the Constitution as the organic instrument for the governance of the American people. The conceit presumes genius as the guiding force of that noble document, a genius which in one stroke solved the problem of creating a central government that could function side by side with the governments of the several sovereign states that comprised the Union. Indeed, there was genius, much of it borrowed overseas but nonetheless adopted with imagination and skill to the unique American scene.

The basic document as originally written, however, contained serious flaws that in time probably would have made it unworkable. It failed to provide institutional means to break deadlocks when disagreements over issues were so serious as to threaten the stability of the government. The Founding Fathers were astute enough to recognize that there would be disagreements but they chose to believe that such controversies would be temporary rather than permanent divisions. They belonged to the Age of the Enlightenment and they were convinced that men of reason, intelligence, and good will could come together and resolve whatever problems divided them.

But men are not always enlightened and they can sometimes surrender themselves to passion rather than reason. Fortunately, within a relatively short time, political parties developed to repair the failure—and the Constitution itself was later amended to recognize the existence of a party system of government. The evolution of political parties had much to do with the ultimate success of the Constitution. It made workable a system that inherently tried to keep everything in balance but that at the same time ran the risk of negating all positive action, of producing a stalemate principally between the executive and legislative branches. Political parties became the means by which serious disagreements over grave issues could normally be kept from jeopardizing the safety of the Union. Only once did the system fail. The issue was slavery and it took a bloody conflict to resolve it.

The Founding Fathers failed to take cognizance of parties because they had an intense horror of them. They looked upon political parties as the instruments of dissension and discord. In the *Federalist* papers, James Madison and Alexander Hamilton worried about their effects upon the political life of the nation. In his Farewell Address, George Washington warned his countrymen against the disruptiveness of parties, arguing that they were factions of artful men intent on subverting the will of the majority to gain their own selfish ends. John Adams, the second President, echoed Washington's sentiments and declared that "division of the republic into two great parties . . . is to be dreaded as the greatest political evil under our Constitution."

Despite these fears and warnings, a two-party system did develop within a few years of Washington's inauguration as President. Washington brought into his Cabinet two highly intelligent, individual, and opinionated men who fundamentally disagreed on the direction the government should take and competed with one another to gain a commitment from Washington to their point of view. Thomas Jefferson as Secretary of State and Alexander Hamilton as Secretary of the Treasury represented two conflicting philosophies of government. Hamilton insisted on a broad definition of federal powers in order to inaugurate a fiscal program that would unite private interest to public duty. He understood that only a government that guaranteed the financial interests of its constituency was likely to succeed. Jefferson, on the other hand, emphasized the need and value of local autonomy in order to preserve individual freedom, and he took great exception to Hamilton's concept of expanding federal power.

The speed with which Hamilton succeeded in dominating Congress and in convincing President Washington to adopt his fiscal policies only hastened the arrival of the party system. In Congress the leading opponent of Hamilton's policies was James Madison. Repeatedly Madison spoke before the House of Representatives to attack Hamilton's schemes; together with John Beckley, the clerk of the House, he formed an opposition composed of Southern politicians and politicians from the middle Atlantic states which eventually became known as the Republican party. Those sympathetic to Hamilton's policies and program called themselves Federalists.

Throughout Washington's administration and all through the administration of John Adams, the contest between Republicans and Federalists intensified. Then, in 1800, Thomas Jefferson challenged Adams's bid for a second term. A near war with France, the XYZ Affair, passage of the Alien and Sedition Acts, and higher taxes diminished Adams's popularity and brought about his defeat and the defeat of the entire Federalist ticket.

When the electors finally cast their vote, Jefferson and his running mate, Aaron Burr of New York, both received seventy-three electoral votes. Adams had sixty-five votes and Charles C. Pinckney sixty-four. The Constitution, unaware of political parties, made no distinction between President and Vice-President and simply stated that the person with the highest majority of electoral votes would be President and the person with the next highest vote would be Vice-President. Burr, of course, had not been intended by the Republican party to stand as its Presidential candidate. But there he was. He had as many electoral votes as Jefferson and he would not back off. He felt he had as much right to the Presidency as Jefferson—and according to the Constitution, he did.

The Presidential election of 1800 was far different from the first one held in 1789 because of the existence of fully organized political parties. Now one man was selected to be a candidate for Vice-President, not a contender for the Presidency. In any event, since no one had a majority of electoral votes, the election went to the House of Representatives. After many ballots and a good deal of political maneuverings the House in February 1801 elected Thomas

Jefferson the third President of the United States. Clearly something had to be done to prevent this from happening again, and so in 1804 the Twelfth Amendment was adopted. It required that the electors cast separate ballots for President and Vice-President. It seems like a small matter, but the amendment in fact grafted the party system into the Constitution. For the future it meant that the President and Vice-President would normally represent the same party. If a majority of Congressmen elected to the House and Senate were also from the President's party—as they were in 1800—there was the clear prospect that the executive and legislature could work together, rather than check one another, to provide the country with purpose and strong, united direction.

Jefferson as President assumed the role of party leader, the first such President to do so, but he was very careful to preserve the separation of power between the executive and legislative branches at least in appearance. So conscious was he of this separation that he abandoned the practice established by Washington and continued by Adams of appearing personally before Congress to read the President's annual message. Jefferson was content to have a clerk do his reading for him. For more than a hundred years Presidential messages were droned out to the Congress by some clerk with practically no one paying much attention. Not until Woodrow Wilson became President was the earlier practice revived. Despite Jefferson's concern for the separation of powers, he nonetheless made his influence felt in Congress because he was the head of the party and exercised influence through Republican members of Congressional committees. Thus, in appearance, he preserved the separation, but because of the party system he was able to bridge it.

The arrival of parties did not mean that the checks and balances conceived by the framers of the Constitution were done away with. Instead of undue checking power between the coordinate branches of government, political parties allowed coordination among the branches while serving as a check upon each other. A degree of checking remains among the three branches—enough to prevent any one branch from unduly intimidating the others—but the best check now is the party system. Alexis de Tocqueville observed in his book *Democracy in America* that most Americans are essentially conservative in their politics. They demand change but abhor revolution. Thus, with a two-party system as it emerged, change could be achieved through regular shifts in administration from one party to another, all obtained through nonviolent party contest.

The value of a two-party system even after it had been in operation for a dozen years was not readily seen at the time, not even by Thomas Jefferson. It was his hope that the Federalist party would shrivel and die, thereby leaving the Republicans in unchallenged control of the government. And this in fact did happen.

Election Day at the State House, Philadelphia, 1816. Painting by John Lewis Krimmel. *Historical Society of Pennsylvania*

After the War of 1812 the Federalist party went into a long decline and finally disappeared. Now only one party controlled the government in the period known as the Era of Good Feelings, and some men actually thought that without party rivalry there would be political peace.

But political wrangling did not end. In fact it seemed to get worse. To some extent it was really an Era of Ill Feelings. During it a new generation of political leaders was just beginning to appear.

These were men born during or immediately after the Revolution, who were still children when the Federalist and Republican parties were established. They arrived to take the place of the Founding Fathers, most of whom were dead or very aged. This new generation of politicians included such distinguished men as Henry Clay, Daniel Webster, John C. Calhoun, Thomas Hart Benton, and Martin Van Buren. Van Buren particularly represented a political

Martin Van Buren. *Library of Congress*

astuteness that marked this generation as more mature in understanding the merit of a system of party government. Men like Van Buren were a new breed of politician, professionals who believed in organization and whose leadership developed naturally because of their liking for people and their enjoyment of political association and political contest. They had the good sense not to confuse political conflict with personal antagonism. These politicians detested the single-party structure of the misnamed Era of Good

Feelings and attributed all the animosity of that period to the lack of a two-party system. Modern government, they contended, demanded well-functioning political parties openly arrayed against each other. Van Buren claimed that democratic principles in government were impossible without party politics; others declared that parties not only preserved liberty by allowing for opposition but also inhibited governmental corruption by providing the means for periodic reexamination of the conduct of public business.

Obviously, this new generation had come a long way from the stance of the Founding Fathers. For them the two-party system meant stability both in government and in society. It is not surprising, then, that the one-party rule of the Era of Good Feelings quickly ended. Van Buren, with the help of several other politicians including John C. Calhoun and Thomas Hart Benton, organized a party in support of Andrew Jackson's bid for the Presidency. This party, called Democratic-Republicans, eventually came to be known simply as the Democratic party. The opponents of Jackson and his party, such as Henry Clay, Daniel Webster, and John Quincy Adams, were called National-Republicans and later took the name "Whigs" to express their opposition to the assertion of strong executive leadership by Andrew Jackson.

This full evolution of national political parties had an enormous effect on the Presidency, particularly on the choice of Presidential candidates and the way they were presented for election to the American people. The framers of the Constitution, in writing the document, had endeavored to protect the executive branch from popular, democratic control. In providing an electoral system, they expected thoughtful and dedicated men from the different states to select the President from a number of possible contenders, each of whom had previously earned a national reputation as a wise and just man devoted to public service—just as the Founding Fathers had been. This is why there had been no clear distinction between electing the President and Vice-President. Both were expected to have the highest qualifications for the office.

With the evolution of national parties the selection of candidates required something more than a reputation for wisdom, justice, and public service. It required party identification. Consequently, party regulars in Congress held nominating caucuses to select their candidates. That is how Presidents Jefferson, Madison, and Monroe were selected by the Republican party. Later, by the time of Andrew Jackson, the caucus method of nomination was criticized as undemocratic. It was replaced briefly by nominations of favorite sons by state legislatures. But during the election of 1832, when Jackson was reelected for a second term, the parties introduced the national nominating convention system as a more democratic method of selecting party candidates. The system continues to this day.

When the Constitution was adopted, the state legislatures chose the Presidential electors—and it is the electors, it must be remembered, who actually elect the President. But this mode slowly changed. New states entering the Union provided universal white manhood suffrage in their constitutions; soon the older states revised their constitutions and extended the franchise, eliminating property qualifications to vote or hold office. At the same time Presidential electors were now chosen by popular vote instead of by the state legislatures. Only South Carolina refused to permit the selection of electors by popular vote.

The arrival of the mass electorate to national politics precipitated many changes. For one thing it encouraged politicians to find new and exciting ways of interesting the masses in the party's slate of candidates. They looked for very attractive and charismatic figures to run for President, military heroes and Indian fighters like Andrew Jackson and William Henry Harrison. And this new generation of politicians devised more sophisticated techniques of campaigning to catch the voters' attention.

The noise and nonsense so characteristic of American electioneering came into vogue during the Jacksonian period. Parades, barbecues, songs, buttons, and other paraphernalia were used extensively to encourage people to vote. Probably the most notorious campaign of this type occurred in 1840 when General William Henry Harrison, noted for his victory over the Indians at Tippecanoe Creek, defeated Martin Van Buren, who was running for reelection. This was the famous Log Cabin Campaign and it is remembered for such gems as "Tippecanoe and Tyler, Too," "Van Van Is a Used Up Man," and expressions such as "OK," "booze," and "Keep the ball rolling."

The arrival of the mass electorate to national politics not only encouraged the hoopla of song and slogan and other nonsense, but it also necessitated greater organization to mobilize and direct these increased numbers. When Andrew Jackson was elected President in 1828 the number of voters who appeared at the polls increased by more than three hundred percent over the previous election. And those numbers kept getting larger with each successive election. What the politicians did was to structure a pyramid of state committees from local groups in the wards and precincts through county and state organizations. At the very top they introduced the national nominating convention.

Changes in the style and character of elections introduced in the Jacksonian period caused great concern among thoughtful men who feared that the nation would fail to obtain the services of its best citizens. Prior to the arrival of the mass electorate, the Presidents had included such statesmen as Washington, Adams, Jefferson, and Madison. Now the country would go through a list of lesser talents, such as John Tyler, Zachary Taylor, Millard Fillmore, Franklin Pierce, and James Buchanan, while a Henry Clay and a Daniel Webster were repeatedly rejected by the electorate. Fortunately for the future, the parties were also able to produce such distinguished men as Abraham Lincoln, the two Roosevelts, and Woodrow Wilson.

The emergence of political parties not only created party government under the Constitution and assisted in advancing democracy within the country by encouraging the mass electorate to exercise the franchise, but it also had a profound effect on the office of the Presidency itself. The President became both the head of the executive branch and leader of the party. The first six Presidents usually acted in a manner that accorded Congress an equality of power. However, starting with Andrew Jackson the President began more and more to assert his role not simply as head of the executive branch but as leader of the government. By the skillful use of his position as head of the party he persuaded Congress to follow his lead, thereby allowing him to assume greater control of the government and to direct and dominate public affairs. He was the one person who would define national issues, set national policy, and direct the party in its commitment to and implementation of issues and ideas.

Jackson chose to destroy the Bank of the United States, the successor to the Bank initially suggested by Alexander Hamilton as part of his fiscal policy. He took the Bank issue to the people in the Presidential election of 1832 and asked the electorate to decide the question by their vote. If they voted for him they would in effect be voting against the Bank; if they voted for Henry Clay, the candidate of the National-Republicans, they would be voting for the Bank. Jackson was overwhelmingly reelected President and he chose to regard the vote as a mandate from the American people to destroy the Bank. Probably the people intended no such thing; they reelected Jackson because they were devoted to him and wanted him at the head of their government. Jackson went even further than simply destroying the Bank. He informed Congress that he considered himself the true and sole representative of all the people and stated further that his responsibility lay with the American people. Indeed he felt he was the tribune of the people. Both Clay and Webster strongly denounced what they called his "revolutionary ideas." They felt that in a democracy the legislature was the true representative of the people, not the executive. "If Jackson," said Webster on the Senate floor, "be allowed to consider himself the sole Representative of all the American people, then I say that the government has already a master. I deny the sentiment, therefore, and I protest the language; neither the sentiment nor the language is to be found in the Constitution of this country."

So his enemies called him "King Andrew the First." But it did them no good. His party in Congress, the Democrats, followed his lead, and the American people supported his contentions. There was enormous arrogance and presumption in Jackson to assert himself as the spokesman of the American people. Nevertheless, the strongest, most effective, and best Presidents have been those who saw their role as the instrument of popular will.

Today the system of American party government normally depends on strong executive action to accomplish the purposes of democracy. Since the office did not come equipped with the necessary powers under the Constitution, they had to be added through a historical process by the forceful action of vigorous Presidents whose position within the government and relation to the American people was strengthened by the rise and development of political parties. It does not mean that because a President establishes national goals and priorities the Congress must be spineless and bow down in obedience to the executive will each time it is expressed. Strong Presidents should not mean weak Congresses. The Founding Fathers believed men could be reasonable and work out their difference of opinions for the benefit of the whole nation. But men like Martin Van Buren, who was a little more realistic about the modern world, saw that true cooperation and accommodation could best be attained through the party system.

4

ANDREW JACKSON
and the STRONG
PRESIDENCY

by Edward Pessen

On March 28, 1834, the Senate voted to censure Andrew Jackson, seventh President of the United States, for assuming "upon himself authority and power not conferred by the Constitution and laws, but in derogation of both." Behind the censure resolution stood a new political party, the Whigs, led by Jackson's long-time foe, Henry Clay. Taking their name from the famous English political party, the better to dramatize their opposition to the man they called "King Andrew," the American Whigs charged the President with executive tyranny. Jackson was infuriated by what he called the "imputation upon his private as well as public character." His fear that the insult would "stand forever" in the Senate's journals turned out to be groundless, however. Three years later a pro-Jackson majority physically "expunged" the censure resolution from the official Senate journal. Even before his friends in the Senate moved to change the record, the American people acted to vindicate Jackson by electing Martin Van Buren, his hand-picked successor, to the Presidency. And subsequently most historians and political scientists came to regard Andrew Jackson as one of slightly more than a handful of great Presidents. What the Hero's opponents derided as "executive tyranny" has come to be viewed as the strong Presidency.

There can be little question that the Whig denunciation of Jackson was in large part partisan politics, a transparent attack by the "outs" on the "ins," with the end in view of influencing public opinion in their own favor. It is likely however that some anti-Jacksonians were sincerely shocked by Old Hickory's transformation of what they had regarded as an essentially passive office. In Jackson's tenure the Presidency attained a power and thrust not hinted at in the language of Article 2 of the federal Constitution which defines the scope of the office; the *limited* scope, according to Alexander Hamilton's essays on the Presidency in the classic *Federalist* papers. The political scientist Herman Finer has described the dozen or so features of the strong Presidency. These include the Chief Executive's control over the executive apparatus, the patronage he disposes, his accessibility to the public, and his influence as party leader. It is no exaggeration to say that Andrew Jackson, better than any of his predecessors, initiated and manifested these powers. In the process he substituted what the great constitutional historian Edward S. Corwin called Presidential domination for the legislative supremacy that had prevailed before Andrew Jackson's ascent to the highest office.

What accounted for Jackson's bold and innovative administration of the Presidency? Although it is impossible to answer this question definitively, certain things are clear. Jackson was not impelled to his dynamic leadership by theories absorbed either from extensive reading or reflective thinking about the high office. The Hero of New Orleans was not a man of philosophical bent, nor was he a widely read man. Some admirers of Jacksonian Democracy have suggested that Old Hickory found it necessary to resort to bold tactics that transformed the Presidency because the "aristocracy" against which he and his followers waged political war were too well entrenched to have been dislodged from their positions of power by traditional or orthodox means. The problem with this theory is that much recent evidence indicates that the policies and programs of Jacksonian Democracy were neither antiaristocratic nor anticapitalistic, and hardly of such a radical nature as to demand a new type of Presidential leadership for their execution. Probably the best explanation lies in Andrew Jackson's own personality and character.

The seventh President was a dominating man who seems to have believed that his purposes were identical with the nation's purposes, that his enemies were evil men, that the means he chose to realize his goals or to flay the obstructionists who would oppose them were appropriate means—even if neither precedent nor constitutional language upheld them. The historian John William Ward has suggested that this man came to personify to his countrymen the forces of Nature, Will, and Providence. At times he appears to have personified them to himself as well. Andrew Jackson did not bear tolerantly opposition to his wishes even in

Major General Andrew Jackson. *Library of Congress*

what might appear to have been small things. When the women of the families of his first Cabinet members persisted in isolating Peggy Eaton, the wife of his friend and Secretary of War, John Eaton, a woman Jackson insisted was as pure as the driven snow, he unceremoniously dismissed the entire Cabinet! Jacksonians then and later insisted that there was more to the "Eaton malaria" than met the eye; the social snubs cloaked the sinister political designs of the Vice-President, John C. Calhoun. Even if this interpretation were valid, however, it would hardly detract from the audacity of Presidential action to remove an entire Cabinet on the basis of a surmise about the motives of some of its members. (Critics have pointed out that Jackson had contempt for and rarely met with his Cabinet, much preferring to get his advice from his cronies in the "kitchen cabinet," men whose "appointments" required no approval from the Congress.)

One of the chief means by which Jackson transformed the Presidential office was his use of the veto power. The essential point is not that he vetoed more bills than had all of his predecessors combined. More striking were the justifications he gave for his vetoes. Jackson repudiated Congressional measures not only because of their alleged unconstitutionality but also on the grounds of expediency and his simple opposition to them. What one modern constitutional authority calls this "resounding exercise of executive authority" infuriated Democratic worshipers of precedent as well as Whigs. It is true that in requiring no reasons for a veto, the Constitution in effect gives the President carte blanche in exercising the power. The Founding Fathers in discussing the matter at the Constitutional Convention and the authors of *The Federalist* in writing about it had assured the nation that this "monarchical" power would be rarely used and then only to guard against Congressional attempts to weaken or destroy the Presidency and legislation flagrantly at odds with the meaning of the Constitution. The rare application of the veto power by the first six Presidents showed their acceptance of this theory. But self-imposed restraints had no significance, let alone attractiveness, to Andrew Jackson. In applying the veto power as he did and winning acceptance for his usage, Jackson added to the executive power of the President a legislative power that made him the equal not of two-thirds of Congress, as some scholars have written, but of close to one-sixth of Congress (or the difference between the bare majority needed to pass a bill and the two-thirds needed to override a veto). The smaller fraction represents a substantial enough accretion to Presidential power.

Jackson's most famous veto was the one written for him in 1832 by his adviser Amos Kendall rejecting the bill to recharter the second Bank of the United States after its charter would run out in 1836. Historians have described the ensuing conflict between the

President and the many supporters of the Bank as the "Bank War," perhaps the most significant, certainly the most dramatic, issue of Jackson's two administrations. It was above all in the course of waging that war that Jackson spoke and acted to magnify the powers of the Presidency. Among other things, the veto message in holding the second Bank unconstitutional in effect repudiated previous Supreme Court decisions and the actions of the Washington and Madison administrations in sponsoring the first and second Banks. As he made clear on many occasions, Old Hickory did not feel bound by precedent.

In conducting the struggle against "Biddle's Bank"—Nicholas Biddle was the president of the second Bank—Jackson and his supporters went over the heads of the Congress to appeal directly to the people. For the first time the claim was made that the President, as the choice of the whole nation, better and more directly represented the people than did the members of Congress. Deciding not to wait until the charter of the second Bank ran out, Jackson in 1833 prepared to deposit federal monies thereafter in a number of state banks (most of them led by Democratic bankers). His argument that the second Bank of the United States was an "unsafe" depository ran directly counter to the findings of a Congressional committee and has not been credited even by historians sympathetic to Old Hickory. For that matter his Secretary of the Treasury, Louis McLane, balked at "removing the deposits," arguing that "no adequate reason existed for the removal." To Andrew Jackson, however, the fact that he himself had decided on a policy was reason enough to execute it, despite the fact that his stated reason seemed to be at variance with his actual motive. It is likely that he wanted to "get" Biddle and the Bank for reasons having little to do with the Bank's alleged weaknesses as a federal depository. The President promptly removed McLane to the State Department, replacing him with William J. Duane. When Duane too proved recalcitrant, refusing to obey Jackson's directive that he order the removal of the deposits, he too was kicked out. His replacement was the complaisant Roger B. Taney, who as a reward for doing his master's bidding, was shortly afterward named Chief Justice of the Supreme Court.

A President *does* have the right and the power under the Constitution to appoint and to dismiss members of his Cabinet. The

Cabinet is, after all, an agency of the executive office. But Cabinet members are not mere puppets. Duane had been in the right in insisting that he, not the President, had the responsibility for the deposits. According to the clear language of the law establishing the second Bank, "The deposits of the money of the United States . . . shall be made in said bank or branches thereof, unless the Secretary of the Treasury shall at any time otherwise order and direct." The high court later ruled that an appointed official was not a mere creature of the Chief Executive. But to Andrew Jackson, Supreme Court decisions that he opposed were a matter of indifference.

Certainly he refused to enforce the Court's 1832 decision in the case of *Worcester* v. *Georgia*. Jackson may never have made the remark attributed to him that "John Marshall has made his decision, now let him enforce it"; what is more significant is that Jackson acted on that principle. Despite the fact that the Court ruled that Georgia lacked authority to extend its laws over Indian lands in the face of the national government's exclusive jurisdiction over those lands, Jackson refused to interfere with Georgia's claims to the lands in question, professing that the federal government was too weak to protect the Indians' rights. Jackson's subsequent words and actions made clear that he would not rest until the southern tribes were removed west of the Mississippi on one pretext or another. But his claims of federal impotence against aggressive state demands, demands that ran afoul of federal treaties, encouraged Southerners, particularly in John Calhoun's South Carolina, to think that the seventh President was so ardent a champion of states' rights that he would also tolerate that state's nullification of the tariff law that they opposed. The nullifiers did not know Andrew Jackson.

The same man who had blown hot and cold with regard to the tariff, who had spoken against "partisan appointments" and loose construction of the Constitution yet had made partisan appointments and signed into law internal improvements that were the epitome of loose construction, now showed that he could reverse himself too over the issues of states' rights and national power.

Whether or not his own previous policies may have given encouragement to the Calhounites, the fact remains that Jackson handled the issue of nullification decisively, even masterfully, once it arose. Rejecting as preposterous South Carolina's claim that as a party to the "compact" creating the Constitution she had the right to "nullify," or rule as not binding on her, laws she judged to be opposed to her interests. Old Hickory resolved the issue with a blend of bluster and guile. At the same time that his proclamation to the people of South Carolina warned that federal troops would invade the state unless it backed down, he worked behind the scenes to support an acceptable compromise that finally induced the South Carolinians to retreat from their original posture. Jackson's firmness in responding to this threat of secession compares most favorably with Buchanan's irresolution during the secession crisis that a generation later split the Union in two.

Andrew Jackson was a masterful politician in the sense that he could justify opportunistic policies in terms that seemed democratic and lofty. Artful rhetoric claiming that a Jacksonian action was in the interests of the common man won readier acceptance for measures that were in fact strengthening his own and his party's power. Thus in his first annual message he spoke of turning federal offices over to ordinary men so long as they had good sense. In fact Jackson appointed uncommonly wealthy and socially prestigious men, little different from the type of men the allegedly aristocratic John Adams had appointed to high civil-service posts a generation earlier, with the exception that the Jacksonian appointees were good Democrats. In the judgment of scholarly authorities, the "spoils system" popularized by the Jackson administration impaired the efficiency, the prestige, and the morale of the civil service. Corruptionists appointed to the customs collectorship of New York City and land offices throughout the country absconded with millions of dollars of the "people's money." Perhaps the most significant political effect of the spoils system was its enlargement of Presidential power, in the authoritative Leonard D. White's words, "to proportions hitherto unknown or unthought of." According to Edward Corwin, the new system compelled not only jobholders but Congressmen who hoped to secure federal appointments for their constituents "to submit to political blackmail." It filled government offices with an informal private army whose political souls—like part of their pocketbooks, since they were expected to make large "donations"—belonged to the party leader, the President, who had appointed them.

Andrew Jackson at times displayed an imperiousness, even a contempt for law, that is no less disturbing for anticipating the arbitrariness that characterized many of the actions of strong Presidents who followed him. Almost single-handedly he provoked a war crisis with France that was occasioned not by the substantive matter in conflict—French foot dragging in paying an international debt—but by the President's intemperate manner in dealing with the issue. On the basis of no constitutional warrant whatever, he dispatched troops to break a strike of workers against a corporation

King Andrew the First.
Library of Congress

that happened to be headed by his good friend John Eaton. In 1835 he conspired with his new Postmaster General, Amos Kendall, to prevent the delivery in the South of antislavery literature that Jackson as a great slaveowner personally abhorred, even inviting violence against Southerners who chose to accept or receive these "incendiary" pamphlets. In the case of *Kendall* v. *Stokes* the Supreme Court said of one of Jackson's attempted usurpations that if carried out it "would be clothing the president with a power entirely to control the legislation of Congress and paralyze the administration of justice." Nor does this brief catalogue exhaust the list of what have been called Jackson's "bold innovations."

He was a forceful leader who in a sense simply realized the potential latent in the executive office. The strong Presidency he did so much to create is, however, a mixed blessing. That it has gone over well both with scholars and the general public is hardly proof that it is in the national interest, for all the undeniable light it throws on the popularity of political father figures. It has been used to lead the people to disaster as well as toward admirable goals. The clearest things about it are that it has upset the constitutional balance of power among the judicial, legislative, and executive branches of government, and that it appears to have been particularly congenial to men of Napoleonic, if not messianic, character.

5

ABRAHAM LINCOLN
and USE of
the WAR POWER
by John A. Carpenter

For practically the entire time Lincoln was President the nation was at war. It was not a constitutionally clear-cut conflict but a civil war which left in question the exact powers that the Chief Executive might exercise. It is even possible to state that during Lincoln's four years in office he was as much the commander in chief as he was the civilian President.

Lincoln himself seemed to be aware of the distinction and each time he extended his power he carefully related the action to his duty as commander in chief to suppress rebellion. He exercised questionable executive authority throughout the war, but perhaps the best illustration of this was during the period from the attack on Fort Sumter, April 12, 1861, to the meeting of the special session of Congress on July 4 of that same year.

Lincoln's assumption of executive authority stemmed from his belief that the Constitution gave him, and not Congress, authority to act in time of emergency. At one point in the war, Lincoln commented, "As commander-in-chief of the Army and Navy, in time of war, I suppose I have a right to take any measure which may best subdue the enemy." Among his acts of doubtful constitutionality was the enlargement of the regular army, under normal conditions wholly within the province of Congress. Further, Lincoln declared a blockade of Southern ports and authorized the transmittal of two million dollars from the Treasury to certain individuals in

New York for emergency purposes. Spending public funds without authorization from Congress was, to say the least, highly irregular, but Lincoln believed the emergency to be such as to excuse this departure from normal practice. Lincoln also suspended the writ of habeas corpus without the approval of Congress, and proceeded to order the arrest of persons engaged in aiding the Confederacy.

When Congress met in July, it in effect ratified all of Lincoln's actions. In 1863, Congress formally passed a law which stated that "during the present rebellion, the President . . . is authorized to suspend the privilege of the writ of *habeas corpus.*" That came two years after the start of the war, and in the intervening time, Lincoln had authorized and ordered the arbitrary arrest of thousands of persons. These persons might be tried by a military commission or they might not be tried at all. Most frequently they simply were held for an indefinite time and then released with no charges ever having been brought against them. These arrests could occur anywhere, at least after September 1862, when Lincoln decreed that martial law was applicable wherever there was interference with the prosecution of the war.

One of the noteworthy examples of arbitrary arrest early in the war was the case of a secessionist-minded Marylander, John Merryman. Merryman was imprisoned at Fort McHenry despite the issuance of a writ of habeas corpus signed by Chief Justice Roger B. Taney, who was on circuit duty at the time. The local military commander refused to surrender the prisoner. Unable to have a writ citing the general for contempt delivered to the fort, the Chief Justice accused the President of violating the Constitution and there the matter rested. In a short time Merryman was released and charges of treason brought against him in a Maryland civil court were ultimately dropped. The Merryman case was fairly representative of numerous others—arrest by military authorities, detention for a relatively short time, and then release.

Not so typical was the celebrated case of Clement L. Vallandigham, one-time Congressman from Ohio and leader of the opposition to the war in the Middle West. Vallandigham had lost his seat in Congress in the 1862 midterm elections, but he continued to speak out against the Lincoln administration and the war.

The military commander of the Department of the Ohio in 1863 was General Ambrose E. Burnside, who had issued an order stating that public expressions of sympathy for the Southern cause would not be allowed and that offenders would be subject to punitive action by military commission. When Vallandigham proceeded to make a speech critical of the Lincoln administration and the war, Burnside ordered him arrested. Soldiers routed the Copperhead leader out of his home in Dayton in the early hours of the morning and sent him under arrest to Cincinnati. A military commission found him guilty of disloyal utterances and sentenced him to imprisonment for the duration of the war.

The President was now in the embarrassing dilemma of having either to approve the sentence and possibly make a martyr of Vallandigham or to free him and thus display weakness as well as refusal to support a subordinate. Lincoln partially escaped the dilemma by commuting the sentence to banishment to the Confederate lines in Tennessee. This was done, but the Ohioan did not stay long in the Confederacy. He ran the blockade, made his way to Canada, and ran for the governorship of Ohio in absentia. At length he returned to the United States unmolested, and took an active part in the Democratic convention of 1864. The Supreme Court refused to accept jurisdiction in this case, maintaining that Congress in the Judiciary Act of 1789 had not intended that the appellate jurisdiction of the Court be extended to cover the decisions of a military commission.

The possibility that the Supreme Court might rule against the President in his policy of suspension of the writ of habeas corpus in areas where the civil courts were functioning and where there was no military action in progress constantly worried Lincoln and his Attorney General, Edward Bates. Although the Court never did rule on the constitutionality of that policy during the war, it did decide a case about a year after the fighting had stopped and it decided against Lincoln. Charged with plotting to aid the Confederacy, Lambdin P. Milligan had been tried by a military commission, convicted, and sentenced to be hanged. The case was taken to the Supreme Court, where on April 3, 1866, the majority of the Court ruled that his trial had been illegal, since the civil courts were operating at the time and there was no actual military activity in the locality.

By the time the Court had so ruled, Lincoln had been dead for almost a year. That a similar decision would have been rendered during the war is highly unlikely; even if it had been, there is reason to believe that Lincoln would have found some way to circumvent it.

The Lincoln government also cracked down on opposition newspapers. Papers were seized outright, editors were arrested, and their publications denied the use of the mails—all without the specific sanction of Congress. Strictly from the standpoint of the

Lincoln and his Cabinet. *Library of Congress*

rights of the people under the Constitution and especially the Bill of Rights, the record of the Lincoln administration is anything but admirable. The safety of the nation, however, seemed to depend on the suppression of subversive activity.

Actually, nothing approaching a reign of terror existed during the war years. Not many newspapers were seized, there were no mass executions, no brutal suppression of the civil liberties of the average citizen. Lincoln tempered his harsh decrees by a leniency which softened their impact considerably. The right of dissent was never suppressed and the very fact that a national Presidential election was held in 1864, an election which conceivably could have been won by the opposition Democratic party, is proof of the comparative moderation of the Lincoln administration.

Lincoln as Commander-in-Chief. *Library of Congress*

Lincoln's relationship with his subordinates in the executive branch is another instructive exercise in determining the locus of executive authority during the Civil War. While Lincoln had little desire to involve himself in the every-day problems of any of the departments, the War Department excepted, he nonetheless let it be clearly understood that he was the leader of the executive branch of the government. On April 1, 1861, Secretary of State William Seward had informed the President that he was prepared to assume the direction of the administration. Lincoln's firm reply made it quite clear that the President was, in fact, the head of the administration and Seward soon settled down to become an exceptionally fine Secretary of State.

Treasury Secretary Salmon P. Chase also gave Lincoln considerable difficulty because of his inordinate ambition. In what is referred to as the Cabinet crisis of 1862, Lincoln boldly put Chase down and emerged the unchallenged leader of the administration.

Lincoln likewise kept a firm hand on his military subordinates. It was he who appointed and removed the top commanders, and who frequently decided basic strategy. General George B. McClellan, to be sure, went his independent way, but Lincoln, aware of his insubordination and lack of common courtesy, chose to tolerate these actions in the hope that McClellan would bring victory. When even Lincoln had taken all he could of the general's dilatory ways, he summarily relieved him of command.

Lincoln looked beyond military considerations and pointedly made sure that leading Democrats received important commands. In Ulysses S. Grant (nominally a Democrat at that time) he found a general who loyally accepted Presidential decisions even when they interfered with his own military plans.

As for the Congress, Lincoln, in true Whig fashion, scarcely interfered with that body, maintaining correct relations with almost all the leading Republicans and dutifully signing virtually every bill placed before him. Most of the important legislation of the war years, such measures as the Homestead Act, the chartering of the transcontinental railroad, and the banking and tariff acts, were enacted through the initiative of Congressional leaders.

Lincoln was not nearly so reluctant to exercise his powers as commander in chief. The emancipation of the slaves is an excellent example of this. Under the Constitution, as it was generally understood at the time, the federal government had no right to interfere with slavery in the states. Thus the only way to deal with the problem in the slave states themselves would be through the power of the President as commander in chief in time of war.

This interpretation did not deter Republicans in Congress from acting. Under the logic of military necessity, Congress passed confiscation acts which authorized not only the confiscation of rebel property, but also the liberation of slaves being used directly for the Confederate war effort. The act of July 17, 1862, went so far as to declare freedom for slaves of any person engaged in rebellion against the United States. Lincoln had conscientiously tried to persuade the loyal slave states to institute their own plans of compensated emancipation financially assisted by the federal government. If the states themselves undertook to adopt a plan of emancipation no one could label it unconstitutional. Unfortunately for the President, the loyal slave states rejected his proposal.

Lincoln and his generals. *Library of Congress*

Frustrated by shortsighted slaveholders in the border states, forced into taking executive action in order to forestall further Congressional intrusion into the emancipation question, and thinking of the growing pressure from antislavery sentiment in the North, as well as of the international and military advantages to be gained from emancipation, Lincoln in the summer of 1862 decided to issue an emancipation proclamation based on his authority as commander in chief in time of war. The source of the authority was of the utmost importance to Lincoln, and the legalistic motivation, as opposed to one that was humanitarian, explains the frigid tone of the proclamation, which Richard Hofstadter described as having "all the moral grandeur of a bill of lading."

Much has been made of the fact that the Emancipation Proclamation did not apply to the border slave states or to certain areas in the seceded states controlled by federal armies. Since the proclamation was a war measure, however, Lincoln did not believe he had authority to decree the end of slavery in the border slave states as a military act. Even this careful and legal approach to the question did not forestall bitter denunciation of the proclamation as an unconstitutional usurpation of power.

A similar constitutional question arose about a plan of reconstruction. The Constitution is silent on this subject, and it is possible to read into it what one seeks to find there. The adherents of Presidential as well as Congressional reconstruction discovered constitutional provisions that seemed to bear out their claims.

Lincoln fully believed that reconstruction belonged under the aegis of the executive branch. Again, as with the Emancipation Proclamation, he founded his conviction on the war powers of the President. In addition, his whole conception of the rebellion dictated his approach to reconstruction. To him, and to the government of the United States, officially, the conflict in progress was not a war, but an insurrection of individuals against the United States. It logically followed that the only way the insurrection could end would be for the rebels to lay down their arms and for the President to exercise his constitutional pardoning powers to restore these individuals to full citizenship.

It was this kind of reasoning that lay behind Lincoln's plan of reconstruction formally announced in a proclamation of December 8, 1863. The opening sentence of the proclamation makes direct reference to the President's "power to grant reprieves and pardons for offenses against the United States." Nonetheless, Lincoln was careful to acknowledge "that whether members sent to Congress from any State [reconstructed under the foregoing plan] shall be admitted to seats, constitutionally rests exclusively with the respective Houses, and not to any extent with the Executive." He concluded with the admission that other modes of reconstruction could be as acceptable as the one he had just put forward.

Certain Republican members of Congress argued that Congress alone could formulate plans for reconstruction. These views were incorporated in the Wade-Davis bill, a measure sponsored by Senator Benjamin Wade of Ohio and Representative Henry Winter Davis of Maryland and passed in the final hours of the session on July 2, 1864. Among other things, this measure prohibited slavery in any reconstructed state. Denying that Congress had constitutional authority to act in this area, Lincoln refused to act on the bill and imposed a pocket veto. There the matter of reconstruction rested during the remainder of the war, and the executive-legislative impasse carried over into the Johnson administration to become one of the major problems of the postwar period.

Lincoln's conception of the Presidency, therefore, had two facets. His Whig background inclined him to be a passive President. Had he served in peacetime it seems likely he would not have given any direction to Congress nor would he have made much use of the veto power or assumed any unusual authority. But taking office as he did, at a time of grave crisis, he believed that he had the constitutional power to act decisively, without necessarily having to gain Congressional sanction prior to his actions. Thus it would seem that Lincoln did not set precedents for the future, except in wartime.

There was, indeed, justification and explanation for what Lincoln did, and as long as the power was in the hands of an Abraham Lincoln the fundamental rights of the citizens were safe in the long run. He had no dreams of grandeur and no ambitions to subvert the Constitution with the aim of becoming a despot. Yet his avowed policy to use any means necessary to achieve his ends, laudatory as those ends were, when pursued by a President lacking the judgment, the restraint, the humanity, and the common sense of Lincoln makes one realize how fragile is the fabric of democratic government and how vulnerable the rights of the citizens. The Constitution makes no guarantee that in time of emergency the country can always count on having an Abraham Lincoln as President.

6

THE PRESIDENCY in the GILDED AGE: FROM RUTHERFORD B. HAYES to WILLIAM McKINLEY

by Richard Harmond

Despite recent events the Presidency remains the most power-ful branch of the governmental system. It is taken for granted that the President is, among other things, chief of state, head administra-tor, chief legislator, leader of his party, global potentate, and formulator of national goals.

It was quite otherwise in the last quarter of the nineteenth century. Although the Presidency recovered from the crises of the stormy Johnson-Grant years, the President was not looked upon, for instance, as the leader of public opinion or as chief legislator. Until the very end of the century, when foreign affairs became prominent, the balance of power in government clearly remained with Congress. Congress did not even pay much attention to Presidential messages. Most of the major domestic legislation of the era, as well as the decision for war in 1898, originated with Congress.

Why Congress should have so dominated the government was a matter of conjecture among contemporaries, as well as later students. Some found the explanation in the personalities and philosophy of the men occupying the Presidency, for the Chief Executives of the Gilded Age lacked personal drive and magnetism. But there is at least equal substance to the argument that the Presidency failed to become the commanding branch of government because of circumstances. The late-nineteenth-century political environment was not conducive to Chief Executives of initiative and authority.

Despite their limitations, the Gilded Age Presidents exhibited certain abilities. They were experienced politicians and honest, hard-working Chief Executives. Rutherford B. Hayes, for example, after serving with distinction in the Union Army, was elected to Congress and then to three terms as governor of Ohio. Victor in the

Rutherford B. Hayes is declared President after the disputed election of 1877. *New York Daily Graphic,* March 3, 1877

disputed Presidential election of 1876, he was dubbed "His Fraudulency" and "Rutherfraud" B. Hayes by opposition Democrats. Hayes, however, was a deeply religious man of abstemious habits (he avoided the use of tobacco and liquor, and refused to serve wine at White House functions), and he established a tone of respectability and moral rectitude about the executive office. He appointed an outstanding Cabinet, made some progress in civil-service reform, battled spoilsmen in his own party, and, in general, restored public respect for government—a respect that had been badly eroded during the previous Grant regime.

Similarly favorable judgments can be made of the Presidents who followed Hayes. James A. Garfield, a genial and warm-hearted man, with a background of some seventeen years in Congress, was assassinated within six months of assuming office, but in that short time he strengthened the Presidential appointing power. After a fierce row, his choice for the important post of collector of the Port of New York won out in the Senate over the candidate of Roscoe Conkling, the powerful and imperious Senator from New York.

Little was expected of Garfield's successor, Chester A. Arthur, since he was known as a machine politician, but Arthur turned his back on his spoilsman past. In 1882 he vetoed a pork-barrel river-and-harbor bill favored by politicos, and the following year he threw his support behind the Civil Service Reform Act. A "man of surpassing sweetness and grace," according to a newspaperman, Arthur was also an excellent administrator. His successor, Grover Cleveland, was the single Democratic President of the Gilded Age. A former sheriff of Erie County, mayor of Buffalo, and governor of New York, Cleveland was determined to follow his conscience rather than the path of expediency and set a record unequaled until Franklin D. Roosevelt for the number of vetoes he issued.

The other two Presidents of the Gilded Age make an interesting contrast in personality types: the reserved and frosty Benjamin Harrison, and the amiable and compassionate William McKinley. Harrison, a former Senator and member of a famous family—his great-grandfather was a signer of the Declaration of Independence and his grandfather a President of the United States—was a diligent President. He was a dour sort of person, but as a contemporary remarked, "Everybody respects Harrison's ability and integrity." During a busy four years he signed into law measures dealing with trusts, free silver, veterans' pensions, and the tariff. McKinley, who brought a wealth of political experience to his high office (he had spent thirteen years in Congress and served a term as governor of Ohio) was, by any reckoning, a conscientious and capable Chief Executive. He was also the only President of the period to supply Congress with any sort of effective leadership. Most importantly, though, he presided over the United States when for the first time in its history the nation began to take an active leadership role in world affairs.

Hayes and his successors were prepared to defend their office against Congressional encroachments. Hayes, for instance, resisted unprecedented efforts of a Democratic Congress to force him to accept legislation that would have nullified his authority under existing statutes to dispatch troops to the South to protect voters at the polls. To achieve this purpose Congress attached "riders" to money bills. The President could not veto part of a bill, and it was assumed that, since he dared not risk losing the money needed to pay the army and judges, he would be compelled to accept the appropriation bills with the riders. But Hayes refused to allow Congress to legislate in this way. This "new doctrine, if maintained," wrote Hayes, will mean that "the Executive will no longer be . . . an equal and independent branch of the government." Six times he vetoed appropriation bills with the offending riders. Eventually Congress capitulated and passed the money bills minus the riders. The action of Hayes was defensive in nature, but nonetheless significant.

The Gilded Age Presidents also reasserted the right of the President to appoint and remove important officers without untoward Congressional interference. This right had seemingly been settled before the Civil War, but under the terms of the Tenure of Office Act, passed by the Reconstruction Congress in 1867, Senate authorization was required for the removal of Cabinet and other officials whom the Senate had originally approved. Over the years, in the words of Congressman James A. Garfield, this act had "virtually resulted in the usurpation, by the Senate, of a large share of the appointing power," seriously crippled "the just power of the executive," and "placed in the hands of senators and representatives a power most corrupting and dangerous." President Hayes and his successors resisted this "usurpation." After a long encounter with the Senate, Hayes reestablished the right of the executive to choose his own Cabinet officers without consulting the upper house. Hayes, as well as Garfield, also battled for the President's right to select lesser officers, and in 1887 Cleveland persuaded Congress to repeal the Tenure of Office Act.

Merely upholding the traditional prerogatives of the office was hardly the mark of strong Presidential leadership. Unlike a Theodore Roosevelt, a Woodrow Wilson, or a Franklin Roosevelt, the late-nineteenth-century Presidents did not broaden the limits of their office in domestic affairs. Unlike a Jackson, a Lincoln, or the two Roosevelts, Hayes and his successors never rallied the nation behind some important cause. And unlike a Jefferson, a Teddy Roosevelt, or a Wilson, the Gilded Age Presidents failed to provide Congress with energetic, positive, and creative leadership.

In part, these failings were a matter of temperament. Since Washington, the great Presidents have been ambitious for, and have relished the challenge of, the executive office. This was not so with the Gilded Age Presidents, for they did not really seem to take to the job. Even McKinley, who had at first enjoyed the post, was soon overwhelmed by burdens and responsibilities. In the trying days before war with Spain in 1898, the harried McKinley was unable to sleep, even with the aid of narcotics. The following year a close friend reported in his diary, after a chat with McKinley, that the "President talked of his renomination and reiterated his intense desire to retire to private life. Nothing but the strongest sense of duty will lead him to stay in office another four years."

The Gilded Age Presidents seemed incapable of rousing public opinion behind their programs. Except for McKinley, they stirred little popular enthusiasm. Arthur, as a White House servant observed, "was not a generally popular man." Cleveland preferred to do what he thought was right, rather than cultivate public esteem. He certainly did not add to his popularity when in his first term he vetoed a bill providing free seeds for drought-stricken Texas farmers, remarking that such federal aid "weakens the sturdiness of our national character." Nor did he endear himself to Civil War veterans by vetoing dozens of private pension bills, and the Dependent Pension Bill of 1887 (which provided aid to most of those who had served in the Union forces). As for Harrison, known unaffectionately as "the human iceberg," he was in the words of a contemporary "a stranger to the art of popularizing himself." He "was the only man I ever saw," wrote one who knew Harrison, "who could do another man a favor in such a way that all the sweetness and appreciation and sense of gratitude was gone from it." McKinley was by all odds the most well-liked of the Gilded Age Presidents, but, preferring caution to boldness, he failed to mobilize this popular good will behind his programs. He was an "ear-to-the-ground" follower rather than a "nose-in-the-wind" leader of public opinion.

If they lacked colorful and dynamic personalities, these Presidents were also restrained in the exercise of forceful leadership by the commonly held belief that Congress made the laws and their job was to execute them. The Republicans inherited this view from the Whigs, but even Cleveland, a Democrat, subscribed to it. "It don't look as though Congress was very well prepared to do anything, but maybe it will get into shape," he wrote in late 1883. "If a botch is made at the other end of the Avenue, I don't mean to be party to it." "I did not come here to legislate," he insisted on another occasion. It is true that Cleveland called upon Congress, in December 1887, to take up the question of tariff reform, but then, typically, he sat back and left the matter in the hands of the legislators. Early in his second term, though, Cleveland did turn legislator, bringing great pressure on Congress to repeal the inflationary Sherman Silver Purchase Act. After a bitter row, Congress passed the repeal measure in the summer of 1893. It was a costly victory, though, for Cleveland had alienated the silver Democrats, thereby badly splitting his party and impairing his own ability to govern.

Unlike his predecessors, William McKinley was able to develop a constructive relationship with Congress. Nevertheless, even he had occasional problems with that independent-minded body. Despite his arguments and use of patronage Congress never gave him the kind of tariff bill he wanted, but at least it gave him some legislation; his requests in other areas were simply ignored.

To explain the status of the late-nineteenth-century Presidency simply in terms of the personal limitations of the men who held the office, or their Whiggish philosophy, is insufficient. The reigning climate of opinion, as well as the political stalemate of the era, also inhibited the emergence of expansive Presidential leadership.

Until the end of the century, the American people were not ready to accept any significant enlargement in the size and scope of the federal government. Today, in the era of the institutionalized Presidency, the Chief Executive can draw on the talents of hundreds of men and women to help him do his job. He can turn for assistance and information to the Office of Management and Budget (an agency that alone employs over six hundred people), the White

House staff, and a variety of Presidential advisory groups. In 1871 Congress appropriated $13,800 for a Presidential staff of seven people. Over the years there was a modest growth in staff, though if a citizen rang up the White House in the mid-1880s, the likelihood was that President Cleveland would answer the phone. Even by the end of the century, the White House staff consisted of only about eighty people, and this total included messengers and doorkeepers.

Lacking any real administrative staff, the Gilded Age Presidents were not only overworked, but distinctly limited in the range of concerns with which they were able to deal. They did not, for example, prepare a federal budget. Congress dealt with the various bureau chiefs concerning the amounts and uses of appropriations for the federal administration. Since the Presidents did not control the finances of the federal bureaucracy, they had little influence over it. In government, as elsewhere, power will be found where the money is.

These Presidents also faced the problem of an evenly divided electorate from the mid-1870s to the mid-1890s. Election campaigns were exciting and colorful, and a higher percentage of eligible voters turned out to vote than would in the twentieth century. Yet until McKinley no party or Presidential candidate received a clear-cut mandate from the people. No President from Hayes to Cleveland won reelection after serving a term in office; none carried a majority of his own party into both the House and Senate during his full four years in office.

Under these circumstances, it was difficult for a President to steer a program through Congress. Moreover, because the electorate was so closely split, the parties tended to avoid controversial issues for fear of alienating any important segment of the electorate. As Rutherford B. Hayes shrewdly remarked, "We are in a period when old questions are settled, and new ones are not yet brought forward. Extreme party action, if continued in such a time, would ruin the [Republican] party. Moderation is its only chance. The party out of power gains by all the partisan conduct of those in power."

The turning point in Gilded Age politics came when this stalemate was broken mainly as the result of the depression of 1893. It was Cleveland's, and the Democratic party's, misfortune to be in power when the political upheaval occurred. Cleveland was reelected in 1892 with the largest plurality of any Presidential candidate in the period. What is more, he could anticipate Congressional support, as the Democrats won majorities in both the House and Senate. But the depression of 1893 rudely shattered this promising situation.

Not long after Cleveland's inauguration in March 1893, the country underwent a severe economic downturn. By the winter of 1893–94 more than two and a half million people—almost twenty percent of the labor force—were unemployed. "Armies" of the jobless sprang up, while savage labor unrest erupted in the nation's cities and mill towns.

Even under the best of circumstances Cleveland would have received some blame at the polls from those forced to endure these hardships. His reactions, however, made the defeat a massive one. In 1893 he split his party on the silver issue. Then, in the spring of 1894, a ragged army of about five hundred, led by "General" Jacob S. Coxey, descended on Washington, D.C., to induce Congress to issue $500,000,000 in greenbacks for the building of roads. The administration met this "living petition" with brutality, as Washington police clubbed some marchers and arrested the leaders for trespassing on Capitol grounds.

Even more damaging was the President's response to the Pullman strike. Against the protests of Governor Altgeld of Illinois, Cleveland ordered troops into Chicago in May 1894 to ensure order and to "remove obstructions to the United States mails." Added to the subsequent imprisonment of the popular leader of the American Railway Union, Eugene V. Debs, this episode earned Cleveland the hatred of labor. The workers secured a measure of revenge in the Congressional elections of 1894 when they dealt the Democrats the most shattering defeat in American political history.

Two years later the Democratic party repudiated Cleveland and his policies and nominated William Jennings Bryan. McKinley decisively defeated the "Boy Orator of the Plains," and the Republicans took control of Congress. From 1897 to 1911, in fact, the GOP dominated the federal government.

With the stalemate shattered, the Republicans in charge of Congress, and the new President on friendly terms with party chieftains, the situation at last seemed ripe for the appearance of creative leadership in domestic affairs. But McKinley was not the figure to fill that role. A man of traditional thinking, he was too cautious to plot new goals for the nation.

Toward the end of his first term, however, McKinley's initiatives in foreign policy enhanced executive authority at the expense of Congress. It was largely his decision to acquire the Philippines. Bypassing the Senate through the device of executive agreements, he and his Secretary of State, John Hay, promulgated

William McKinley delivers his inaugural address. Former President Grover Cleveland is on the left. *Library of Congress*

the Open Door policy for China. Without consulting Congress, he dispatched five thousand American troops to China in 1900 to help put down the Boxer Rebellion: for the first time a President employed armed forces against a sovereign state without Congressional authorization. By waging war and acquiring an empire, McKinley had, quite unintentionally, begun to tip the governmental balance once more against Congress. It remained for future Presidents to build on this base.

PART II

THE PRESIDENCY
in the CONTEMPORARY AGE

7

THEODORE ROOSEVELT and the MAKING of the MODERN PRESIDENCY

by Richard Harmond

Theodore Roosevelt was among the handful of twentieth-century Presidents who added new dimensions to the authority and responsibilities of the executive office. To be sure, Roosevelt built on the foundations laid by the Gilded Age Presidents, particularly the initiatives taken by William McKinley in foreign affairs. But Roosevelt changed the office, where his predecessors merely held it. Not only did he invent the "stewardship theory" of the Presidency, but, in a very real sense, he developed the modern roles of the President as leader of public opinion and chief legislator. Moreover, he added several cubits to the role of the President as world leader.

There is, of course, no way to predict, or prepare for, the appearance of such a "maker and shaker." But Roosevelt's accomplishments, as can be seen today, were the result of a special historical blend of the potentialities of the executive office, the tumult of the times, and, above all, the man himself.

Born in 1858 of "substantial stock," Roosevelt was a sickly youth who had to overcome his early affirmities to become an athletically inclined, nature-loving young man. After graduating from Harvard, Roosevelt served two terms in the New York State Legislature, tried his hand at ranching in the Badlands, wrote several books (including *The Winning of The West*, still well worth reading), and ran unsuccessfully for mayor of New York City in 1886. Restless and ambitious, TR subsequently accepted the posts of United States civil-service commissioner and then of New York City police commissioner.

In 1896 Roosevelt actively campaigned for the GOP and McKinley and was rewarded with the post of Assistant Secretary of the Navy. Anxious to get into the thick of the battle against Spain in 1898, Roosevelt resigned from the government and organized the "Rough Riders." After a stint in Cuba, he returned home a hero. Elected governor of New York in 1898, he clashed with the Republican boss of New York, Tom Platt, and the "Easy Boss" saw to it that TR was booted upstairs as McKinley's running mate in 1900. McKinley defeated William Jennings Bryan in November, but ten months later the popular President fell before an assassin's bullet—and the "damned cowboy," as Mark Hanna, McKinley's friend, referred to Roosevelt, was then President of the United States.

Roosevelt was a man of boundless energy. Henry Adams ascribed to him "the singular primitive quality that belongs to ultimate matter—the quality that medieval theology assigned to God—he was pure act." Not only did he have a dynamic personality, but he also possessed a pronounced flair for self-advertisement. He was, in truth, something of an exhibitionist. He loved to be at the center of things. The quip about Roosevelt wanting to be bridegroom, bride, and preacher at a wedding certainly hit the mark.

Some of Roosevelt's biographers have suggested that his love of attention, his apparent search for approval, stemmed from a sense of insecurity. Whatever the reasons, his love of the spotlight redounded measurably on the executive office; by drawing attention to himself, he focused attention on the White House. He hunted bears in the Far West; played tennis (probably the first President to do so); took jujitsu lessons in the White House; tramped exhausted generals and ambassadors through Rock Creek Park; went horseback riding in the afternoon; caused an uproar in the South by inviting the Negro leader Booker T. Washington to the White House; denounced Jack London and other "nature fakers" for their "grotesque" depictions of animal life; antagonized the British press and Congress over the "simplified spelling" that he ordered used in government documents.

Beyond entertaining and exciting the public, Roosevelt knew

how to use the press to achieve his political goals. Taking advantage
of the customary drabness of Monday-morning papers after a quiet
Sabbath, he shrewdly released news items on Sunday so as to
dominate the front pages of the next-day's newspapers. He established an excellent relationship with newspapermen. For the first
time in the history of the Presidency, Roosevelt provided special

Theodore Roosevelt
addresses a rally. *Library of
Congress*

quarters in the White House for correspondents. He gave reporters
background briefings, floated trial balloons, and used the technique
of news "leaks." By virtue of these contacts, as well as his dynamic
personality, Roosevelt made news and inspired headlines.

More than that, TR, in the press, as well as on the stump,
consciously strove to cultivate public opinion. He seemed to know
instinctively what the bulk of the population wanted. Consequently,
the American people came to applaud his views on important issues
of the day—like the trusts and railroad regulation—as expressions of

desirable public policy. In effect, Roosevelt transformed the Presidency into the spokesman for public opinion. Or, as Roosevelt himself conceived of his role, of all elected officials the President alone, he wrote, "is or ought to be peculiarly the representative of the people as a whole."

If Roosevelt looked upon the President as spokesman of the people, he also saw the Chief Executive as "a steward of the people." The Gilded Age Presidents had held that the Chief Executive could do only that which the Constitution specifically empowered him to do. But Roosevelt, who unlike his predecessors enjoyed the office—"I love the White House; I greatly enjoy the exercise of power," he wrote once—took a much broader view of Presidential authority. "My view," he explained,

> was that every executive officer, and above all every executive officer in high position, was a steward of the people. . . . My belief was that it was not only his right but his duty to do anything that the needs of the Nation demanded unless such action was forbidden by the Constitution or by the laws. Under this interpretation of executive power I did and caused to be done many things not previously done by the President and the heads of Departments. I did not usurp power, but I did greatly broaden the use of executive power.

Many contemporaries considered the stewardship principle revolutionary in nature. But this did not deter Roosevelt who, being a man of action, was not one to develop a theory, however controversial, and let it go at that. To inform himself on the "state of the union," for instance, he appointed "voluntary unpaid commissions" (such as the Commission on Inland Waterways, the Commission on Country Life, and the Commission on National Conservation) to investigate particular situations or problems and report their findings to the President. Roosevelt was the first President to use such volunteer commissions on a large scale. When the practice was denounced as "unconstitutional" and Congress passed a law forbidding it, Roosevelt declared that he would ignore the restrictive statute. Congress, he asserted, could not "prevent the President from seeking advice" or volunteers from giving their service to the country.

Again, acting as steward of the people, TR bent the law in the field of conservation. Although the statutes authorized the withdrawal of public lands from private use only when minerals had been discovered thereon, Roosevelt withdrew lands for any number of other purposes, including the establishment of forest and bird preserves. In all, he added 125 million acres to the reserved national forests. It was one of his most significant achievements. But

The President's Dream of a Successful Hunt. *Library of Congress*

Western interests and conservative-minded contemporaries considered Roosevelt's actions high-handed, perhaps even illegal. As far as TR was concerned, though, he was satisfied that he had acted for the national good.

Probably the most striking illustration of Roosevelt as the steward of the people was his handling of the coal strike of 1902. In May of that year, fifty thousand miners walked off their jobs, demanding union recognition and a pay hike. With winter approaching, and the mine owners refusing even to deal with the United Mine Workers Union, Roosevelt summoned both sides to the White House to confer with him in early October. When that failed, he let it be known that he was prepared to send in troops to dispossess the operators and run the mines. At this threat, the mine owners agreed to binding arbitration. Roosevelt appointed the Anthracite Coal Strike Commission to arbitrate the issues dividing the parties, and the miners returned to work. The public was grateful, and the press praised the President for his skill in handling the affair. More importantly, Roosevelt had set precedents that enhanced Presidential authority. For the first time a President called the parties in a labor dispute to the White House; named an arbitration panel; and planned to use troops, not to break a strike, but to seize and operate an important industry.

The nation was ready for such leadership in the early years of this century. People were relatively prosperous, but the country was in turmoil nonetheless. Western and Southern farmers harbored serious grievances against the railroads; small businessmen and others demanded a solution to the trust problem (the years from 1897 to 1904 constituted the greatest period of business consolidation in American history); labor was in a militant mood; and crusading journalists like Ida Tarbell and Lincoln Steffens had begun their assault on business abuses and political corruption. By the year Roosevelt moved into the Presidential office, the people had already elected to office progressive-minded mayors like Hazen S. Pingree (Detroit), Josiah Quincy (Boston), "Golden Rule" Jones (Toledo), Seth Low (New York), and Tom Johnson (Cleveland). Moreover, the Wisconsin electorate had placed "Fighting Bob" La Follette in the governor's chair.

Why Roosevelt reacted to these currents of criticism and discontent as he did remains a subject of debate. Some historians argue that he was essentially a conservative, who was chiefly interested in heading off socialism and other radical movements with his own loudly proclaimed but quite restrained brand of reformism. Other scholars stress Roosevelt's part in arousing the popular demand for reform; his genuine sympathy for the poor and downtrodden; his sincere desire to curb the abuses of big business; and his abhorrence of the "dull, purblind folly of the very rich men, their greed and arrogance."

Whatever Roosevelt's motives, he asserted the claim of the President to be chief legislator. He outlined his goals in speeches to the country and messages to Congress. Then—and here Roosevelt was distinctly an innovator—he sent drafts of bills to the legislative branch. Finally, by one means or another, he worked to get his bills through Congress. A "good executive under the present conditions of American political life," he wrote once, "must take a very active interest in getting the right kind of legislation."

THE BREAK IN THE COAL STRIKE.—A HISTORIC MOMENT

Dealing with the coal strike. Theodore Roosevelt meets with Elihu Root and J. Pierpont Morgan. *Harper's Weekly, Oct. 25, 1902.*

Roosevelt, a superb politician, suited his approach to the situation. He would flatter and cajole legislative leaders and even cooperate with opposition Democrats when the situation called for it. He could be flexible, but he was not above threatening Congress. A case in point was the pure-food-and-drug legislation of 1906. Bills to regulate the drug and food industry, including the meatpackers, had been pigeonholed in Congress for some time. Then in 1906 Upton Sinclair's novel *The Jungle* appeared. It described in gory detail the filthy conditions in Chicago's meatpacking houses. Roosevelt's subsequent independent study of the packing houses sustained Sinclair's findings. Since Congress had shown little disposition to legislate in this area, Roosevelt threatened to publish the entire report unless Congress acted promptly. When the legislative branch still proved dilatory, he released the first part of the report, privately threatening to publicize the more explosive second part. Opposition collapsed, and on June 30, 1906, a chastened Congress passed the Meat Inspection Act and the Pure Food and Drug Act.

Roosevelt was also ready to circumvent Congress. When it failed to respond to his request for legislation to regulate big business (for instance, by the federal licensing of corporations), Roosevelt reinvigorated the Sherman Antitrust law. Though known to history as "the trust buster," TR much preferred federal supervision to the dissolution of giant corporations.

In the area of foreign affairs, Roosevelt believed that the days of old-fashioned isolation were at an end, and that the United States must exert itself in the "larger world life, in which, whether we will it or not, we must take an ever increasing share." In practical terms this meant, first of all, building up the American Navy and constructing an isthmus canal to increase the efficiency of the Navy. Moreover, not least to protect the canal, Roosevelt aimed at establishing American hegemony in the Caribbean. In the Far East, where the American people would not support the use of force, he sought to protect American interests—particularly the Philippine Islands (acquired from Spain in 1898) and the Open Door in China—by balancing Russia off against Japan.

As far as the Caribbean basin was concerned, he achieved his purposes, though at the cost of alienating Latin-American opinion. In an episode that did little credit to him, Roosevelt, as he later put it, "took" the Panama Canal Zone. With the canal site secured, the President moved energetically—and with little assistance from Congress—to promote order and stability in the Caribbean, even to the point of sending armed forces into Caribbean countries without Congressional authorization. When Santo Domingo proved unable to pay its foreign debts, Roosevelt signed an executive agreement with the ruler of that tiny country to manage its customhouse. Since the Senate at first refused to ratify the agreement, Roosevelt "put the agreement into effect, and I continued its execution for two years before the Senate acted; and I would have continued it until the end of my term, if necessary, without any action by Congress." Of another foreign-policy decision TR made, he wrote, "I should not dream of asking the permission of Congress. . . . It is for the enormous interest of this government to strengthen and give independence to the Executive in dealing with foreign powers."

Roosevelt was just as active in the Far East. Under his direction, representatives of Russia and Japan met at Portsmouth, New Hampshire, in August 1905 to negotiate an end to the Russo-Japanese War. Roosevelt's efforts in bringing the war to an end helped him to win the Nobel Peace Prize in 1906.

In the years that followed, the President's major problems in the Far East revolved about a resurgent Japan. To impress Japan with American naval might, he decided in 1907 to send the American Navy on a world cruise. When Congress balked (arguing that such a move would leave the eastern seaboard undefended) and threatened to withhold the necessary funds, Roosevelt answered that he would send the fleet anyway; if it ran out of fuel in midocean, that would be Congress's responsibility. Needless to say, Congress supplied the necessary funds.

In other dealings with Japan, TR sidestepped the Senate and again resorted to executive agreements. In the Gentlemen's Agreement of 1907 Japan and the United States agreed to restrictions on the migration of their nationals to each other's shores. More importantly, in the famous Root-Takahira Agreement of 1908, the United States and Japan agreed to observe the Open Door in China, support the status quo in the Pacific, and respect each other's territorial possessions in the Far East. To the extent that such agreements mean anything, Roosevelt had succeeded in protecting American interests in the Far East from the threat of Japanese expansion.

Shortly before he left office in 1909, Roosevelt summarized his expansive view of the President as chief diplomat. The "biggest matters," he wrote, "such as the Portsmouth peace, the acquisition of Panama, and sending the fleet around the world, I managed without consultation with anyone; for when a matter is of capital importance, it is well to have it handled by one man only."

Clearly, Theodore Roosevelt is not an easy figure to evaluate.

Controversy swirls about his personality, his stability, his love of display, and his outsized drive for power. Historians argue, too, about his accomplishments as a progressive reformer. And serious questions can be raised about some of his activities in the foreign area, particularly in Latin America. But there is little debate about what he did for the Presidency. By the time his exciting and controversial seven years in office were over, future Presidents could lay strong claim to the roles of chief legislator, expounder of public opinion, world leader, and, if they chose, steward of the people. Few Presidents have done more to enlarge the Presidential domain. How enduring or desirable that legacy might be is another question.

8

WOODROW WILSON'S
IMPACT on the
AMERICAN PRESIDENCY

by George H. Skau

Unlike most occupants of the White House, Woodrow Wilson
had written a great deal about the American Presidency before he
assumed the office. In fact, he wrote more about the Presidency,
before assuming the Presidential powers and duties, than any other
Chief Executive in the nation's history.

Wilson was born on December 29, 1856, in Staunton, Virginia,
the son of a Presbyterian minister. He went north to attend the
College of New Jersey, now Princeton University, from which he
was graduated in 1879. He attended the University of Virginia Law
School, but unhappy with law, he decided to study political science
and history at Johns Hopkins University, where he took his Ph.D. in
1886. After brief teaching stints at Bryn Mawr and Wesleyan,
Wilson returned in 1890 to Princeton, where he remained until he
entered politics in 1910 with a victory in the New Jersey
gubernatorial race. As a reform governor he commanded a great
deal of national attention and in 1912 the Democrats nominated
him as their candidate for President. During the subsequent
campaign Wilson spoke out in favor of progressive reforms,
including regulation of competition through antitrust legislation,
tariff reform, and currency and banking reform. With the national
groundswell for progressive legislation underway and helped by the
split in the Roosevelt and Taft wings of the Republican party,
Wilson was elected the first Democratic President in the twentieth

century. At the same time the Democrats gained a better than two-to-one majority in the House of Representatives and a workable majority in the Senate. Wilson could also count on the support of progressive Republicans. The stage was set for vigorous implementation of domestic reform, but was Wilson the person who could provide the necessary Presidential leadership?

Interested in history and political science, young Wilson had always admired political leadership and statesmanship. At first, in the post–Civil War era, he found his heroes across the Atlantic. Inspired by the writings of Walter Bagehot, an English political economist, and the oratory and parliamentary leadership of William Gladstone, one of England's greatest prime ministers, Wilson felt that the British-cabinet form of government might be adaptable to the American constitutional system. Congress dominated the United States government for most of the latter decades of the nineteenth century and strong leadership in the executive branch was dormant and virtually nonexistent. The British system hopefully would provide greater cooperation and closer liaison between the executive and legislative branches of government, generate more open discussion and debate, and ultimately lead to more responsible leadership within the party and governmental structures.

The difficulties of implementing such a system caused Wilson to drop his cabinet proposal by the time his book *Congressional Government* was published in 1885. Industrial and political developments within the United States at the turn of the twentieth century made him reconsider his earlier ideas of the Presidency. Impressed by Grover Cleveland's second administration and the growing importance of foreign problems, Wilson came to realize that these events would have an important and enduring impact on the American Presidency. Another factor, less apparent in his writings, but perhaps most important of all, was the example set by Theodore Roosevelt. He had revitalized the Presidential office and made the Presidency more responsive to the people.

In his last scholarly book, *Constitutional Government in the United States*, published in 1908, Wilson, recognizing Roosevelt's energetic stewardship of national affairs, said that the President, if a capable and resourceful individual, could be head of his party, spokesman of the nation, and even leader of the Congress. Wilson had come to the conclusion that the President of the United States could and should exercise responsible leadership within the American constitutional system.

In the years before he came to the White House, he had shown that he was capable of such leadership but only under certain conditions. When obstacles arose and personalities clashed over issues, he revealed temperamental characteristics—intransigence, refusal to compromise on principles, and failure to treat his opposition tolerably—which hindered or prevented strong leadership.

At first Wilson was successful as a Presidential leader. He dramatized his power over Congress by calling it into special session in 1913. He reinstituted the Presidential practice, not utilized since John Adams's Presidency, of addressing Congress in person, symbolizing the coordination and cooperation he established between the two branches of government. More than any other of his predecessors, he exerted exceptional leadership in Congress by working through the Democratic majority. At times, he seemed to be acting as a prime minister. He not only initiated legislation but guided it through Congress. He met with Congressional leaders and the party caucus, sent letters to wavering Congressmen, kept in close contact with floor managers, utilized the influence and patronage of Cabinet officers, sought expert advice, and talked to the nation. When necessary, he pressured, persuaded, mediated, promised, and threatened. This display of Presidential leadership of Congress and party was unprecedented in American history.

Wilson was at his best in 1913 and 1914. In less than two years as President, he had been able to get four major pieces of progressive reform legislation through Congress. His greatest single legislative achievement was the Federal Reserve Act. It established the Federal Reserve System, which provided for public supervision of banking functions. The Underwood Tariff was the first major tariff reduction legislation since 1846. The two other reform measures, namely, the Federal Trade Commission Act, which established a commission to prevent unlawful suppression of competition, and the Clayton Antitrust Act, which improved upon the Sherman Act, while important, did not entirely fulfill the hopes of their progressive advocates. By 1916, however, he had enacted substantial segments of both the Democratic and Progressive platforms of 1912; his conversion to Theodore Roosevelt's New

Nationalism was based on changing circumstances and his recognition of the political advantages of adopting a more progressive stance. He was narrowly reelected on a progressive platform in 1916.

Foreign affairs dominated Wilson's attention and challenged his concept of leadership especially during his second administration. His ideas on foreign policy were rooted in certain basic

PRESIDENT WILSON
"The challenge is to all mankind. The wrongs against which we now array ourselves cut to the very root of human life."

Woodrow Wilson. *Library of Congress*

principles. His strong Presbyterian faith molded his policies. He believed in Divine Providence and felt that God utilized both men and nations in His plan. Moreover, Wilson believed in the capacity of the people to rule themselves. He strongly felt that democracy was the most advanced and Christian form of government and that all people when properly directed were fitted for self-government. Finally, Wilson believed that America had a special mission in world affairs. The nation's emphasis on freedom and equality fitted it for leadership in moral purposes and in advancing world peace and unity.

Wilson's sense of moral idealism was the touchstone of his policies. An intense activist who strove for complete solutions, Wilson took personal responsibility for the conduct of American diplomacy. Believing that he was personally responsible to the people, he recognized wide Presidential latitude in his conduct of foreign affairs and was reluctant to delegate authority. He demanded a strong sense of loyalty from his subordinates and he expected those under him to support his decisions.

In his relations with other nations, especially those in the Western Hemisphere, Wilson displayed what has been called "missionary diplomacy." His well-meaning but misguided righteousness continued the United States policy of intervention in this hemisphere. His ill-fated intervention in Mexico seemed to have taught Wilson the lesson that genuine revolutions cannot be controlled by an outside military force.

After the outbreak of war in Europe in the summer of 1914, Wilson attempted to maintain American neutrality and at the same time protect America's neutral rights and freedom of the seas. Unsuccessfully attempting to mediate a European peace, he agonized over the proper response to Germany's submarine policy. Finally, feeling he had no alternative, he asked Congress for a declaration of war against Germany in April 1917. In his war message, he proclaimed that often quoted idealistic slogan, "the world must be made safe for democracy." Once the United States entered the world conflict, Wilson, as a wartime President, asked for and received sweeping powers over the nation's resources and economy. The Lever Act of 1917 and the Overman Act of 1918 gave him wide executive powers.

As commander in chief during the war, Wilson was convinced of the necessity of establishing a just and lasting peace when hostilities ended. His peace aims and program were stated in his famous Fourteen Points address on January 8, 1918. The last—but to Wilson the most important of the Fourteen Points—called for the formation of a general association of nations, or the League of Nations, as it became known.

With Congressional elections upcoming, Wilson, seeking a vote of confidence, made the unfortunate decision to appeal to the people to elect a Democratic Congress. The voters, influenced more by local, sectional, and domestic issues, elected a Republican Congress. Unfortunately for Wilson, the Democrats and the kind of leadership Wilson believed in, the Republican bare majority in the Senate proved to be of paramount importance in the crucial days ahead. It foreshadowed the future frustrations of an idealistic determined President trying to lead the nation from a war to a new kind of international cooperation and peace.

While the President was still the leader of his party, the Democratic party was the minority party and therefore Wilson was not the leader of Congress. Republicans, who had been the target of Wilson rhetoric, would now be in a commanding position. Although the situation called for bipartisanship and cooperation it was unlikely that Wilson would adapt to a Republican-controlled Congress.

Unfortunately for Wilson, when the new Congress met in 1919, the Republican majority leader and chairman of the Senate Foreign Relations Committee was Senator Henry Cabot Lodge of Massachusetts. The highly educated patrician had served over three decades in Congress, mostly in the Senate. Lodge, like Wilson, could be intensely partisan on issues. Lodge was anxious to preserve the equality of the Senate in the treaty-making process.

The militant Lodge considered Wilson too weak and timid in foreign relations. Lodge once wrote to Theodore Roosevelt that he never expected to hate anyone in politics with the hatred he felt toward Wilson. Convinced that Wilson was egotistical, unprincipled, and narrow-minded, Lodge became a caustic critic of Wilson's foreign policy, including his peace program. While Lodge had spoken in favor of some kind of united nations in 1915 and 1916, he became increasingly skeptical of such an international organization after that time. While his strong sense of nationalism repelled him against any surrender of American sovereignty, no doubt Wilson's championing of the League helped prejudice Lodge against it.

As majority-party leader, Lodge was determined to preserve party harmony. He hoped, no doubt, that the Republicans would recapture the White House after eight years of Wilson. Thus Lodge's emphasis on national sovereignty, his desire to keep the Republican party together for the election of 1920, and his hatred of Wilson all helped to explain his resistance to Wilson's League.

After the war ended on November 11, 1918, President Wilson made some momentous decisions whose wisdom has been widely disputed. Although the United States would be facing the thorny problem of demobilization now that the armistice had been signed, Wilson decided that his personal presence at the Versailles Peace Conference was necessary to bring about a just peace and the establishment of the League of Nations. He ignored advisers and friends who thought that he might have more influence if he remained at home. Convinced of the righteousness of his cause, he was determined to go to Paris. He told his secretary, Joseph Tumulty, that he believed in Divine Providence and that the trip would either be the greatest success or the supremest tragedy in all history.

The President soon made another decision—the selection of the other peace commissioners to go with him to Versailles. This fateful decision was a notable tactical mistake on Wilson's part. Overlooking tradition, political realities, and expediency, Wilson did not appoint any Senators as peace commissioners. This is somewhat understandable, since Lodge would have been an obvious selection and Wilson felt that Lodge was unprincipled and not to be trusted. But if not Lodge, then certainly some representative of the Republican party seemed an obvious choice. Although a number of Republican leaders were considered by Wilson he simply felt that he would not be able to trust them completely and he dared not risk division or obstruction within his own delegation. He appointed men upon whom he thought he could rely—Colonel Edward House, his close adviser, Secretary of State Robert Lansing, General Tasker H. Bliss, and Henry White, a career diplomat who was a nominal Republican. Wilson's decision to go to Paris as chief diplomat and his selection of peace commissioners helped to create a partisan approach on the issues of the peace treaty and the League.

Republican leaders, particularly Lodge and Theodore Roosevelt, did not feel that they had to rally behind Wilson as he left for Paris. Embittered by his appeal for a Democratic Congress, his decision to go to Paris, and his selection of peace commissioners, they expressed their lack of support both privately and publicly. They criticized Wilson's Fourteen Points; they would only accept a League with reservations. Pointing out that Wilson had been repudiated at the polls, they felt that Wilson no longer had the right to speak for the American people. They also claimed that the newly elected Congress more truly represented the will of the American people.

Despite the breakup of national unity since the Congressional elections of 1918, Wilson remained determined to seek the objectives for which he believed America had fought. He wanted to ensure a just and lasting peace based on the Fourteen Points; he felt the way to do this was to make the Covenant of the League of Nations an integral part of the peace treaty; he considered the United States's participation in the international organization to be of critical importance. These goals, he felt, could be obtained only through his Presidential leadership. With the Republicans controlling the Senate, Wilson knew that his ability to dominate or lead Congress had greatly diminished. No doubt his distrust of Lodge in particular led Wilson to hope that he could take the initiative in treaty making, gain the support of the people, and virtually force the Senate to accept the peace treaty he had negotiated.

The President and a large group of advisers left New York on December 4, 1918. After a triumphal tour of Paris, London, and Rome, Wilson had to negotiate the terms of the peace treaty with Lloyd George of England, Georges Clemenceau of France, and Vittorio Orlando of Italy. These European leaders displayed ample skepticism of Wilson's Fourteen Points.

Finally, after months of discussion, debate, and compromise, the Treaty of Versailles, including the Covenant of the League of Nations, was signed by Wilson and the other Allied leaders in late June of 1919. The President, fatigued by the endless conferences and tired of compromise, was anxious to be home and obtain the ratification of the treaty, which he would ardently defend. As he was leaving France, Colonel House urged the President to deal with the Senate in conciliatory manner. However, Wilson was convinced that he was right and that the American people would vindicate him; he felt that the Senate would ratify the treaty, which he formally presented to them on July 10, 1919. In an eloquent moralistic plea he exclaimed, "The League of Nations . . . was the only hope for mankind. . . . It has come about by no plan of our conceiving, but by the hand of God who led us into this way. . . . America shall in truth show the way."

In the weeks that followed, the President, attempting to line up

Senatorial support for the treaty, conferred with Senators of both parties. He hoped to discuss the treaty with every Senator not opposed to it or determined to weaken and emasculate it. He was particularly anxious to gain the support of the Republicans who were mild reservationists. On August 19, 1919, he met with the members of the Senate Foreign Relations Committee at the White House. Wilson underwent interrogation by the committee but his

The Big Four at Versailles—Vittorio Orlando, Lloyd George, Georges Clemenceau, and Woodrow Wilson. *U.S. Signal Corps—Library of Congress*

attempt at conciliation was not successful. Lodge held the Republicans in line and won a tactical advantage in successfully obtaining incorporation of reservations by a majority vote rather than the two-thirds which Wilson had sought. While he still hoped to have the treaty passed as submitted, the President was prepared to accept interpretative reservations which would not require the renegotiation of the treaty. While not publicly admitting this, Wilson did give to Senator Gilbert Hitchcock, the Democratic leader in the Senate, four reservations and told him to use them, if necessary, on his own. He asked Hitchcock to keep the authorship secret lest the opponents of the League increase their demands.

Meanwhile, prolonged hearings were held on the treaty by the Senate Foreign Relations Committee. This committee, under the leadership of Henry Cabot Lodge, was composed of ten Republicans and seven Democrats. Lodge had stacked the committee with staunch critics of the League, a move which brought criticism not only from Democrats but also from moderate Republican Senators and former President Taft. Feeling that keeping the treaty in committee was one of their strongest weapons, Lodge was able to gain more support for amendments and reservations.

Among the provisions of the League Covenant which Lodge objected to was Article 10. A great deal of the controversy centered around this important article, the cornerstone of the proposed new collective-security system. It guaranteed the territorial integrity and political independence of member nations. It also provided for the League Council to act in an advisory capacity in case of aggression or threat of aggression. Lodge was anxious to protect America's national sovereignty and especially to limit its obligations under Article 10.

Wilson, realizing that the opponents of the League were making headway in the debate in the country, decided to appeal to the people. Although warned by his physician, Admiral Cary Grayson, that a prolonged speaking tour would endanger his health, he was determined to go to the people for support. Wilson should have realized that an appeal to the people might have an adverse effect on the Senators who ultimately would vote on the treaty.

During his ill-fated tour in September 1919 the embattled President explained and defended the Versailles treaty; he devoted his supreme effort to the defense of the League of Nations; he repeatedly exclaimed that the controversial Article 10 was the "heart" and "backbone" of the whole Covenant and the very foundation stone of the new system of worldwide security. The extensive speaking tour which covered over eight thousand miles in twenty-two days finally took its toll. After his speech at Pueblo, Colorado, on September 25, 1919, Wilson, on the verge of a breakdown, reluctantly and with a sense of disappointment, agreed to cancel the remainder of the tour and go back to Washington. On October 2, 1919, a few days after his return to the White House, he suffered a thrombosis, caused by a clot in an artery in the brain. This stroke paralyzed the left side of Wilson's face and body. For a couple of weeks the President was a very sick man; his life hung in the balance and at one point it seemed that death was imminent. However, his strength gradually began to return by the end of October, but the road to recovery was slow. While his frail body never fully recovered, Wilson's intellect was relatively unimpaired.

Wilson's illness certainly prevented him from exercising active Presidential leadership during this crucial time when the fate of the League hung in the balance. Although he did recover to some extent, there can be little doubt that for at least a few weeks after his stroke the President was incapacitated and disabled. The Constitution of the United States does mention Presidential inability but this provision had never been implemented when previous Presidents were disabled; there was uncertainty over the declaration and the procedures for Presidential inability.

Since the Vice-President, Thomas Marshall, was not inclined to take any action on his own, no serious attempts were made to bring about Wilson's resignation. Secretary of State Robert Lansing did, however, call Cabinet meetings during Wilson's convalescence, and when the President later was informed of these meetings and displayed his displeasure, Lansing submitted his resignation. The ailing President did not call a Cabinet meeting himself until April 1920, six months after his collapse. While the President was recovering, twenty-eight bills went unsigned. Affairs of the nation, both foreign and domestic, could not be dealt with by a part-time President. His leadership was impaired by his illness and emotional strain made him more stubborn and sensitive to criticism.

Meanwhile, the Senate was debating the Treaty of Versailles. While friends, advisers, and even his wife wanted Wilson to compromise, the President stood firm. He sent a letter to Democratic Senators urging them to reject the Lodge reservations, which Wilson felt would nullify the treaty. The Senate voted on the treaty with and without reservations on November 19, 1919. Neither side compromised or had enough votes to assure passage of the treaty, either with or without the Lodge reservations. Each side blamed the other for the defeat of the treaty.

The physically weakened Wilson remained unswervingly committed to the League. He even considered seeking the Democratic nomination and running for a third term. If he won he hoped to obtain ratification of the treaty and then resign. He thought of the third term as a means to fulfill his life's work—the United States's entrance in the League of Nations.

With the nation calling for a compromise, Wilson and Lodge each waited for the other to compromise. Wilson indicated that if the Senate passed the treaty with the Lodge reservations he would not ratify the treaty. Still, a number of Democratic Senators felt that the treaty with reservations, even Lodge's, was better than no treaty at all. However, President Wilson in early March 1920 sealed the fate of the treaty, in rejecting even a mild version of the Lodge reservations. The final Senate vote came on March 19, 1920. The treaty with the Lodge reservations failed to get the necessary two-thirds' majority by seven votes. The League had been rejected and Wilson had been defeated.

Wilson's righteous adherence to principle, his personal antagonism to Lodge, his illness, and his temperament further complicated a basically difficult situation. The times demanded a wise and vigorous President with an extraordinary temperament. Wilson, who had written so much about responsible Presidential leadership and who had fulfilled that role so well during his first six years in the White House, was by 1919–20 no longer in control of the nation's destiny. Tragically, he left the Presidency in 1921 a broken man, hoping that history would vindicate him.

Wilsonian leadership did leave an indelible mark on the shaping of the modern Presidency. In displaying the techniques of a prime minister, Wilson demonstrated quite skillfully that the President could lead his party and the Congress. His moral leadership made him an eloquent spokesman for the people and guardian of their welfare. In foreign affairs especially, Wilson played a number of roles: protector of the peace in his neutrality stance from 1914 to 1917; wartime leader during World War I; and chief diplomat and peacemaker after the war. Further, he showed that the American President had become a world leader as well as a national leader.

Wilson expanded and strengthened the powers of the Presidency. In the first decade of the twentieth century, Theodore Roosevelt had revitalized the American Presidency; he demonstrated through his stewardship theory that the President could assume leadership in the American governmental system. It was Wilson who further developed many of the roles of the twentieth-century American Presidency. A lifelong proponent of responsible leadership, he rejected the Whiggish ideas which emphasized the balancing of powers and embraced the notion of an active and energetic executive who would take the reins of leadership in the American constitutional system.

Wilson's successes and his failures have served as examples and lessons to his successors in the White House. Many of his successors have endeavored to learn from the Wilsonian experience. Most noticeably, Wilson's Assistant Secretary of the Navy, Franklin D. Roosevelt, recognized the influence of his former chief. Roosevelt, while certainly more pragmatic than Wilson, recognized the Presidency as a place of moral leadership. The ghost of Wilson haunted Roosevelt when he dealt with the dilemma of neutrality and wartime policies; in his guidance of the United States to membership in the United Nations, Roosevelt, unlike Wilson, successfully sought bipartisan Senatorial support. FDR and all of his successors have, like Wilson, undertaken summit diplomacy with varying results.

The influence and roles of the Congress and the President have been modified since the days when Woodrow Wilson wrote *Congressional Government*; Wilson not only took notice of that change in *Constitutional Government in the United States* but played an important role in revealing the possibilities and dangers of vigorous Presidential leadership.

One can contend that he did fulfill his own theory of the American Presidency. His successful leadership in domestic affairs was unprecedented in American history; his course of action in foreign affairs worked successfully until 1918, when he lost his greatest challenge. The Wilson experience demonstrated the need for resourceful Presidential leadership in the future. Richard Neustadt has put it well. In commenting on Wilson's words on the necessity of selecting the Chief Executive from a small group of "wise and prudent athletes," Neustadt concludes, "Regardless of the dangers, presidential power . . . still has to be sought and used. . . . We are now even more dependent than before upon the mind and temperament of the man in the White House."

9

HERBERT HOOVER

and the

GREAT DEPRESSION

by Robert F. Himmelberg

Few Presidents stood so high in public admiration and expectation when they began their terms as did Herbert Hoover when he entered the White House in March 1929. Fewer still had fallen so low in their countrymen's esteem as Hoover had by the time he left it four years later. The Great Depression, which began in the fall of 1929 and worsened steadily for the next four years, accounts for Hoover's fall from grace. Public scorn reached such remarkable proportions by the end of his Presidency, however, precisely because it had begun with such high expectations. As he approached his Presidency in 1929, scores of friendly journalists portrayed him as a problem solver, a masterful "social engineer" whose inspired planning would rout the nation's economic and social problems. When Hoover's policies failed to stimulate recovery, there was a natural reaction against the oversold image. Many Americans bitterly resented his refusal to adopt certain types of antidepression policies. Had these critics paid greater heed to the political philosophy he had expressed during the 1920s, they would have been less surprised, for although he was indeed a social planner committed to an active leadership role for the federal government in overcoming the nation's ills, he felt there were strict limits to the government's direct role in the economy.

In almost fifteen years of service in the Wilson, Harding, and Coolidge administrations, Hoover opposed in most circumstances the extension of federal economic regulation, the provision of subsidies or other supports for particular economic interests. His conception was that most economic problems could be solved through "associational activities," that is, through cooperative activities of the members of a group which was experiencing a problem. The federal government's role was to stimulate associationism, provide ideas and leadership and perhaps initial financial

"Of Course We Are All Keeping Our Heads and Doing All We Can to Help," December 18, 1931. *J. N. ("Ding") Darling Foundation, Courtesy Herbert Hoover Presidential Library*

support, but not to manage directly the different segments of the economy. If government regulation were required, this should be provided at the state and local level if possible.

The sources of this philosophy lay in Hoover's devotion to the principle of equal opportunity. In *American Individualism*, a slender volume published in 1922, he had summarized the substance of his belief that equal opportunity for every citizen had made America unique. Unlike Europe, in Hoover's view, America was free of class divisions and conflicts because of its system of open opportunity and social mobility. To keep this system functioning under modern industrial conditions required much more than reliance upon laissez faire or even upon the antimonopoly policies the nation had inherited from progressive Presidents such as Wilson. To maintain equality of opportunity required stabilizing the business cycle to prevent widespread periodic unemployment,

"The New Antitoxin," January 18, 1932. *J. N. ("Ding") Darling Foundation, Courtesy Herbert Hoover Presidential Library*

eliminating poverty by improving performance of "sick" industries, upgrading farm income, and solving many other problems. These objectives, Hoover believed, could be achieved through associationism. Associational activities could of course go too far and Hoover acknowledged this. Cooperation among businessmen in trade associations to increase productivity was good, but cooperation which reduced the stimulus of market competition would be wrong.

Hoover insisted upon avoiding extremes in the application of the association method for much the same reason he insisted upon avoiding direct government regulation and management of the different segments of the economy. Too much power in the hands of the groups within the economy—the farmers, workers, and businessmen—would turn them into power blocs and transform politics into a scramble for federal largesse. Too much government intervention would make the bureaucracy an overweaning influence. Either eventuality meant the end of the American system as Hoover saw it, a system of competitive enterprise in which talent and work were transformed into personal mobility and in which the expectation of economic progress benefiting everyone was continuously fulfilled.

There was much in Hoover's private career which enhanced his image as the self-reliant and resourceful social engineer. Born in the tiny village of West Branch, Iowa, orphaned at nine, raised in the households of relatives in Iowa and on the West Coast, he had managed to enter the first class at Stanford. Graduating in 1895, he soon won recognition as a mining engineer in Australia, China, and elsewhere in the Orient. By 1908 he was an established consulting engineer with worldwide responsibilities. With headquarters in London, he was fast becoming independently wealthy, when in 1914 the British government asked him to administer the Allied relief program in war-torn Belgium. During the next two years the skill and ingenuity he exerted there brought him international acclaim and launched his career in public service. In 1917, as America entered the war, President Wilson called him home to head the Food Administration, the war-mobilization agency charged with boosting agricultural production and securing proper allocation of food supplies.

Shortly after the Armistice, Wilson and the other Allied leaders appointed Hoover director general of European relief, food administrator for millions in Eastern Europe, where the breakup of the Hapsburg empire and other old political relationships had disrupted production and starvation threatened millions of people. In Hoover's view his task had political as well as humanitarian implications. The survival of parliamentary government in the newly created states of Eastern Europe depended upon stemming both monarchical reaction and Bolshevist revolution, and he felt the relief of distress was the key to political stability. Most Americans concurred with this judgment and applauded Hoover's energetic efforts to preserve free government and national self-determination, ideals for which they had fought the war.

Hoover returned to America in September 1919, a hero. Probably no other American was more frequently praised in magazines and newspaper editorials, no one's views given greater weight and currency than Hoover's during that troubled reconstruction winter of 1919–20. A Presidential boom for Hoover enjoyed substantial support from the voters but not from the politicians.

After the election of 1920, Harding asked Hoover to join his Cabinet. Hoover chose the Commerce Department, believing this would offer the most scope for his interests and abilities. He soon earned the reputation of being "Secretary of Commerce and Assistant Secretary of everything else," for he projected solutions for all the major ills of American society. Hoover was a vigorous empire builder, continuously pushing to annex bureaus and functions from other departments and make Commerce the central government agency for economic planning and development. His influence emanated throughout the whole array of government departments.

He influenced the Republican labor policy of the 1920s more than the Secretary of Labor, helping develop a policy which avoided antiunion rhetoric and activities and, though hardly supportive of the advance of unionism on a broad scale, was regarded by the AFL as relatively friendly. After Secretary of Agriculture Henry C. Wallace died in 1924, Hoover was able to influence the selection of the new Secretary and to bring the policies of that department into accord with his own ideas. Hoover advocated government assistance in setting up stronger farmer-operated marketing cooperatives and opposed what he called "socialistic" proposals for government regulation of farm prices, and he had his way. One of his most visible and popular roles came in 1927 when Coolidge asked him to direct the distribution of federal relief after a disastrous flood in the lower Mississippi Valley.

By 1928 Hoover's public image, his political philosophy, and his methods for achieving reform and development were firmly fixed. He secured the Republican Presidential nomination in 1928 precisely because his friends could tap a vast reservoir of public respect and admiration for him, not because he had cultivated close relations with Republican-party chieftains. When he entered the White House, Hoover expected to continue and expand the economic programs he had projected as Secretary of Commerce by exercising strong executive leadership. He apparently had little concern for Congress. Much of his associationist program could be carried through without reference to new legislation. Where Congressional action would be required Hoover evidently expected to secure it, but his experience in manipulating the lawmakers through persuasion and pressure was slight and his taste for it even slighter. Hoover had shown great ingenuity as Secretary of Commerce and in his previous administrative posts in developing public support for his projects through an adroit management of the press. He had numerous sympathizers among the journalists and his public-relations techniques had served him well during the 1920s.

The record of the first part of Hoover's Presidency, before the intrusion of the depression, casts a somewhat ambivalent light on the question of how well he would have succeeded with his program and his methods had the economic decline not intervened. The successes of this segment of his Presidency were notable. He moved quickly to call Congress into special session and soon extracted from it the Agricultural Marketing Act. Though the act was too weak for the taste of many farm-bloc leaders, Hoover seemed to have the weight of public opinion on his side and Republican leaders were constrained to respect the impressive mandate he had secured with his fifty-seven percent plurality of the popular vote in the previous fall. Hoover immediately implemented the new farm legislation by appointing the Federal Farm Board, which was to carry out the program he had presented years before.

With equal energy and considerable public fanfare, Hoover called a meeting of oil-state governors in June 1929 to propose his solution for one of the most notorious economic problems of the late twenties, wasteful extraction of petroleum and the concomitant problem of overproduction and low prices. The President proposed enactment by the states of uniform conservation measures and enforcement of them through an interstate compact, but the politics of the oil industry were too complex to direct by a simple appeal to reason. The oil operators wanted a more direct method for raising petroleum prices and neglected Hoover's plan in which efficient extraction methods, not production limitation, were the primary considerations. An interstate compact encompassing much of Hoover's proposal was not consummated for two more years.

Congress now proved as difficult to manage as the oil industry. Without Presidential invitation and against his wishes, Congress began a long-drawn-out debate over tariff revisions which dragged through the summer and fall of 1929 and was renewed in the regular session in the winter of 1929–30. The ultimate product, the Smoot-Hawley Tariff, drew much criticism for its increased rates. Hoover had done little to control his own party in Congress during the debate and failed to secure the only provision he had fought for, Presidential power to raise or lower rates as much as fifty percent according to economic circumstances.

Given his ideology and methods, his inexperience with Congressional politics and his distrust of many of the most influential Representatives and Senators of his own party, it was predictable that Hoover would try to fight the depression, when it was heralded by the stock-market crash of October 1929, without new legislative programs. At the time few suspected the awesome downward swing of the economy, which worsened continuously for the next four years. The gross national product was over 25 percent lower in 1932 than in 1929. Unemployment rose from 1,500,000 in 1929 (3.2 percent of the work force) to 12,000,000 in 1932 (a staggering 24 percent of the work force); and these percentages reflect, in 1932, only those completely unemployed; many millions more were on short hours.

Hoover's efforts to deal with this calamity were limited by his commitment to voluntary associationism and his conviction that recovery could come only from a return of business confidence and from consequent loosening up of investment funds and expansion of industrial facilities. Businessmen were almost universally leery of inflation and higher taxes. Federal expenditures in excess of income were thought to lead to these outcomes and a balanced budget was therefore a major objective for Hoover, as it was, for that matter, for nearly every political leader. Not until 1931, however, did balancing the budget become a paramount aim for Hoover.

Hoover acted within the limits of these conceptual constraints. During the 1920s he had become convinced that large-scale industrial depressions were not inevitable natural occurrences. An economic downturn could be limited in extent, he thought, if consumers' buying power and business investment in repairs and new equipment could be sustained. Government could help directly by expanding public-works spending. These policies were now promptly executed. During November and December of 1929, at a long series of White House conferences, the President called together leaders from all the major industries and received pledges that wage rates and employment levels would be maintained despite the threatened downturn. Participants also promised to sustain planned investment in industrial plant and equipment. When Congress met in December, Hoover obtained a modest tax cut, intended to release private purchasing power. In December, at Hoover's behest, Julius Barnes, chairman of the Board of the Chamber of Commerce of the United States, called business leaders together for a meeting known as the National Business Survey Conference, an attempt to boost the morale of the business community. Aside from optimistic talk, the conference actually did not accomplish anything, and optimism decreased and finally faded away quietly. By the latter months of 1930, the business news was uniformly bad. Hoover's program of voluntary cooperation to sustain wages and investment was not working.

As unemployment mounted during 1930 the need for leadership in providing relief became pressing. Federal spending for construction mounted by some $55,000,000 during 1930 over 1929, and spending by state and local governments grew, partly as a result of Hoover's exhortations, by a substantially larger amount—approximately $335,000,000. Hoover set up the President's Emergency Committee for Employment, a national committee with branches in thousands of communities, in the fall of 1930. It was, in effect, a giant propaganda machine urging cities and states to expand unemployment relief and those workers who still had jobs and incomes to contribute to local relief funds. No doubt it helped stimulate the major increase in public and private relief expenditures which was forthcoming during 1930, 1931, and 1932. But even by mid-1931 it was becoming clear that local government and private agencies could not carry the relief burden much longer without federal assistance.

By early 1931 the economic picture was grim. Farm prices had plummeted despite the Federal Farm Board's massive purchases of staples under its emergency powers. Unemployment had reached catastrophic proportions and business was in full retreat from its pledges of 1929, entirely unable to sustain them. Astounding weaknesses in the banking system had been uncovered late in 1930 when a series of bank failures swept the Middle West and spread throughout the nation during 1931. Bankers became preoccupied with maintaining a strong liquidity position, unwilling to risk making loans for business purposes except in the safest circumstances. The economic system seemed to have entered a deflationary spiral, which the usual self-corrective mechanisms could not halt. Hoover spent 1931 in a search for a way to arrest this unrelentmg downward trend of prices, production, and employment. He became convinced that the banking system's weakness was the major factor which prevented recovery and acted accordingly.

His first step was a proposal for a one-year postponement of all intergovernmental debt payments. The purpose of this moratorium, agreed to in June and July 1931, was to give the major European nations an opportunity to strengthen their banking and monetary systems. Their weakness, Hoover believed, aggravated the American banking system's problems and also was a factor in the loss of American markets abroad. Though a bold and significant step, the moratorium failed to stem the American banking crisis. In October Hoover called the leading bankers together, asking them to create a credit pool to prop up failing banks.

When this last effort to stop the downward trend through voluntary methods failed, he changed course. In December 1931, he announced a new program to Congress, the cornerstone of which was the Reconstruction Finance Corporation. Promptly approved by a Congress now controlled in the House by the Democrats, the RFC was an agency empowered to lend vast sums to banks and other financial institutions.

There were several additional measures in the new Hoover program, all having the same aim as the RFC, to prop up the nation's financial structure, loosen up credit, and make a revival possible. Congress quickly accepted a bill providing additional capital for the Federal Land Banks, banks established years before to provide credit to farmers but now reluctant to lend because of frozen assets. The legislators later in the session adopted a proposal similar in purpose for a Home Loan Bank system. Another measure, launched by the administration though sponsored by Democratic legislators, the Glass-Steagall Act, revised the rules governing the amount of gold the Federal Reserve banks were required to hold to back up their currency. The effect of the bill was to end the threat that speculators might force the nation off the gold standard, a threat which had been an unsettling influence in the calculations of bankers and businessmen. Collectively these measures stemmed the banking crisis. By midsummer 1932, the bank-failure rate was reduced nearly to its predepression level and bank deposits were on the rise.

Hoover secured this recovery program from a willing Seventy-second Congress during its opening months, between December and March 1931–32. This was despite the Democratic victory in the House in the 1930 elections and despite the fact that the administration's hold over the Senate, evenly balanced between Democrats and Republicans, was very tenuous. Hoover's legislative success owed little to his political skill, much to the bankruptcy of independent ideas among the Democratic leaders and their eagerness to cooperate with the President lest they be branded as obstructionists at a time of national crisis. This political situation changed abruptly in March, first when a majority of Democratic Representatives rebelled against their own leaders and refused to endorse the sales tax which the Ways and Means Committee had reported out to meet Hoover's repeated and strenuous demands for a balanced budget. The upshot was tax revision which steeply raised surtaxes on high incomes, a tax increase for the rich rather than the average consumer.

Even more significant was the struggle the Democrats mounted between April and July 1932 for a federal unemployment-relief measure. Hoover's recovery strategy was to restore confidence and stimulate private borrowing and spending. He felt that increases in federally financed public works and appropriation of direct relief funds for the unemployed would both be counterproductive to the goal of recovery, since both threatened to create a budget deficit and raise fears among businessmen of higher taxes. Hoover's veto prevented passage of initial Democratic-sponsored public-works and relief bills, but the President finally had to compromise and assent, in July 1932, to the Emergency Relief and Construction Act, which appropriated moderate sums for both these purposes.

The Democrats had sensed that the mood of a majority of voters was moving toward support for direct, even if unorthodox and experimental, action to relieve unemployment and end the depression. Public opinion no longer accepted as the last word Hoover's insistence that the stability of financial institutions, balancing the budget, and shoring up business confidence was the only effective and legitimate road to recovery.

At the end of July 1932, with Congress safely adjourned, the banking situation much improved, and some economic indices (especially the index of industrial production) turning up, Hoover believed conditions had been created in which an effort to mobilize businessmen for recovery might have a chance for success. He called together a Conference of Banking and Industrial Committees, which met late in August 1932. Hoover would not expand the direct governmental economic intervention the RFC had represented. The August conference accordingly proposed a new batch of committees to advise and exhort businessmen to borrow and spend. Its answer to the desperate unemployment situation also was voluntaristic, a "Share-the-Work" movement, under which a national committee would urge employers to divide up the available jobs by shortening the work week for workers already employed.

The August business conference proved futile, in both the economic and political sense. Hoover had intended the meeting as the beginning of his drive for reelection but it seems doubtful anything short of a miraculously steep upturn of the economy could have won him another term in the White House. Hoover's public image had been deteriorating since 1930. The image of the extraordinarily gifted administrator and social engineer which the press had built up during the 1920s served him ill when the depression proved intractable. Hoover's public image suffered during the depression because his contacts with reporters were infrequent and handled clumsily. He seemed to become withdrawn and dour, failing to project to the people that he sympathized with their problems or cared deeply about the suffering the depression had brought.

Hoover's handling of the problem posed by the Bonus Expeditionary Force in July 1932 is the most cogently cited example of actions which made him appear callous and unfeeling toward the unemployed. The BEF, or Bonus Army, was a motley collection of World War I veterans, numbering approximately twenty thousand by July 1932. They had been encamped on Anacostia Flats in Washington for months, trying to bring pressure upon Congress to grant an immediate cash bonus for all veterans. The Senate defeated the measure in June and several weeks later Hoover, apparently convinced the Bonus Army was becoming a mob subject to influence by the Communists, who had been seeking unsuccessfully to control it, ordered General Douglas MacArthur to move against it in force.

There were many experiments and demands Hoover set his mind against in the summer and fall of 1932 in addition to those of the Bonus Army. Farm organizations were pressing various schemes for federal price fixing; business organizations alternately begged and demanded protection from competitive pressures, for the right to fix prices by agreement and force all businessmen to adhere to them. Pressure mounted for extensive, direct federal-relief expenditures. Hoover stood firm because he believed such actions would actually retard, not hasten, recovery and, more importantly, because he thought they would destroy the American system of individualism and enterprise and create a rigidly bureaucratized social order.

In the campaign duel between Hoover and Franklin Roosevelt during September and October 1932, Roosevelt showed himself much more open to experimentation, to accepting the programs the economic groups were demanding. Hoover denounced Roosevelt's attitude, claimed that "grass would grow in the streets of a hundred cities" if his opponent were elected. He always believed that recovery had been within his grasp during the summer of 1932 but that Roosevelt's campaign oratory had caused a lapse of business confidence and crushed the economy's momentum.

In believing recovery was imminent in the summer of 1932, Hoover was probably wrong, for despite all the activism of the New Deal, the depression continued for several more years. The depression defeated Hoover's voluntaristic methods, and hindsight indicates that he ought to have experimented with a more direct role for the federal government. That his policies failed to bring recovery, however, should not blind the recognition that they constituted a complete rejection of the old fatalistic, do-nothing attitude toward depression, that they were consistent with much of the most intelligent economic thought of his era, and that they were an assertion that American democracy could surmount problems of the utmost difficulty through planning and yet retain its traditional characteristics of enterprise and fluidity.

10

FRANKLIN D. ROOSEVELT: CRISIS LEADER

by James MacGregor Burns

Franklin D. Roosevelt was an extraordinary man who emerged from comfortable patrician surroundings to compete with and combat some of the most formidable men in this nation and in the world. His life began January 30, 1882, in Hyde Park, New York, in a loving family with a doting mother and a proud father. He was an only child and had no siblings to fight or compete with. There was a powerful bond between young Franklin and his mother, especially after his father's death. Roosevelt went on to Groton School in Massachusetts, where his life was very much like the life he had in Hyde Park. It was very secure; it was very serene. He lived among boys his own age and background—all Easterners, perhaps effete Easterners, they might be called today. Then on to Harvard where he lived in what was called the "Gold Coast" of Harvard, the housing section for affluent undergraduates. There again he was cut off from the turbulent world around him and this intensifies the great mystery about Roosevelt—how he came out of that serene background to be the formidable politician that he was.

At Harvard he was not a brilliant student but he was keen and eager, very social, and editor of the Harvard *Crimson*, an important post at school. He did not achieve any great records in the way of grades at Columbia Law School either. He dutifully went through his years there in order to be a lawyer, but still not really knowing quite what he wanted to do in life. What young Franklin would do in life was something of a problem in the Roosevelt family, particularly for his mother, Sara Roosevelt. She did not want him to go into the turbulent world of politics. She did not want him to associate with some of the rough-and-tumble types in Tammany Hall and in the Democratic party. She much preferred that he remain an "aristocrat," that he lead a genteel life protected from the brutalities of the real world. While Roosevelt's future was still unclear, he did do one very wise thing during this period of uncertainty. On March 17, 1905, he married a young woman named Eleanor Roosevelt. This was wise, not just because she was well connected with the other great Roosevelt family—the Theodore Roosevelts—but also because she had the potential to become one of the most committed and compassionate and indeed also politically minded people of her generation.

In 1910 a great opportunity opened up for young Franklin to run for state senator as a Democrat. Without much else to do he jumped at the opportunity, and 1910 was a good year for Democrats. He won, and all of a sudden he was in the New York State Senate as a young reform-minded Democrat. After two rather successful years in the New York State Senate, Roosevelt was swept up in the reform movement led by Woodrow Wilson. It is not surprising that Wilson saw Roosevelt as an impressive young man, the kind of man he wanted in his administration. He appointed him Assistant Secretary of the Navy.

This was a job Roosevelt just loved. One might say Roosevelt was almost born to be Assistant Secretary of the Navy. He loved ships, he loved sailing, he loved being involved in military things. Of course, this was also the post that his distant cousin, Theodore Roosevelt, had occupied and used to gain a career in national politics. When America entered World War I in 1917, Roosevelt was all for it. He assumed a martial pose while exhibiting an ability to administer a huge establishment, which the Navy came to be by 1918. He established a good reputation for himself and showed such vigor, dash, and esprit that in 1920 the Democrats, conscious also of his last name, turned to the young Roosevelt and nominated him as their Vice-Presidential candidate. At the behest of President Wilson, who was broken in body and spirit over the issue, the Democrats championed America's entry into the League of Nations during the campaign. Roosevelt did not play it safe in this early period of his career. He believed in the League; he believed in Wilson. Roosevelt was sick at heart over what had happened to Wilson and his broken hopes. With James Cox at the head of the ticket, Roosevelt campaigned for the League in the election of 1920 and he and Cox were completely defeated, probably as much as anything, on that issue.

Roosevelt's future was again unclear. He was without any immediate prospects in politics. The question again came up as to whether he would return to the leisurely life of Hyde Park. That had not been decided when catastrophe—personal catastrophe— struck. Polio, then called infantile paralysis, afflicted Roosevelt in August 1921 while he was vacationing off the coast of Maine. Once again and more insistently than ever his mother urged and beguiled her crippled son to return permanently to Hyde Park. He obviously would never walk again and she felt more than ever that he should lead a sheltered existence. Certainly he had a right, after this terrible illness and after his early contributions to public service, to go back to Hyde Park for the rest of his life. But he did not want to do it and Eleanor Roosevelt did not want him to do it. After several years of fighting courageously to restore himself physically, at least to some degree, by crawling on the beach, inching his way forward, he slowly regained the use of much of his body but never finally of his legs. He came out of that kind of crisis in the early 1920s with a new vigor for life. By 1928, with the help of Al Smith, he was elected governor of New York and two years later was reelected to a second term.

By 1930 the national scene was quite different from what Roosevelt had known most of his life. The Great Depression was tightening its grip on America, and Herbert Hoover was in the White House. When it became more and more evident during 1931 that Hoover and the Republican party would be a "great act to follow" in 1932, there was an intense contest for the Democratic Presidential nomination. Roosevelt played it very skillfully. He showed a remarkable political ability to form a coalition within the Democratic party, which was as divided in that day as it is today. He got the nomination with the help of people like Jim Farley, Louis Howe, and other very helpful associates in his entourage.

Then began a very curious campaign. It could have been a period of powerful passions in this country—millions of people could have revolted against the depression and the Republican party or Roosevelt could have gained power on a great wave of protest. But it did not happen this way. People were not passionately aroused during the early phases of the depression. They seemed to be asleep or "hunkering" in their homes. Most Americans seemed inert and unable to move, not knowing what to do. Roosevelt, in the face of that national mood, did not run a tumultuous, left-wing campaign rallying the forces of the poor and

FDR campaigning. *Franklin D. Roosevelt Library*

the homeless. Instead, he ran a very cautious campaign. He campaigned sometimes to the right of Hoover, sometimes to the left of him, sometimes above and around him. Poor Hoover could not deal with this illusive figure feigning and darting and manipulating. The 1932 Presidential election was not really a great confrontation, but Roosevelt did win. Perhaps his tactics were the most effective possible for a time when the American people were more bemused and paralyzed than really aware of what they wanted to do next.

In contrast to the election campaign, Roosevelt's inauguration and the weeks that followed were one of the most electrifying periods in American history. In his first inaugural address Roosevelt boldly asserted, "The only thing we have to fear is fear itself." He set such a standard of courage and optimism that people seemed to regain hope just from his strong personality. It was Roosevelt's personality, perhaps as much as any other factor, that determined his view and use of the Presidential office.

Roosevelt seemed to know exactly what he wanted to do. He was going to get the nation moving again. There were the "hundred days of action" where farmers got very quick relief, as did homeowners who were in danger of having their mortgages foreclosed by banks. Emergency railroad legislation and all kinds of shot-in-the-arm remedial recovery-type legislation went through in a great rush. The most important of these, and again the most unforgettable for those who lived during the period, was the NRA (the National Recovery Administration), which tried to get people to work together instead of competing with one another. Perhaps these New Deal programs did not turn the economic tide but they did have a tremendous psychological effect. People felt they were working together. The new solidarity was marked by demonstrations—happy, peaceful demonstrations. In response to FDR's efforts, organized labor and business leaders cooperated in the effort to end the depression. To a large extent, he restored the hope and faith of the American people in their economic and governmental institutions.

All through this period, Roosevelt maintained contact with the people. Roosevelt knew he could not get these bills through Congress unless it felt a great surge or pressure from the people. To achieve that effect, he used the new communications media—radio. For the first time in Presidential history, the White House was in direct and instantaneous contact with the American people. In a series of fireside chats Roosevelt with his velvet voice conveyed a sense of calmness and strength which reassured the people during those dark days. I still remember sitting in a dormitory room with other students, when I was in college—and students do not ordinarily bother to listen to Presidents except perhaps during times of great crisis—I remember even to quite skeptical college students like us, that voice came as a great message of hope. With his skillful use of the radio he cemented a strong bond between himself and the American people.

Then a very interesting thing happened in the United States. Although the depression did not seem to arouse people, the first couple of years of the New Deal period did arouse them. Once they

President and Mrs.
Roosevelt on the porch of
the executive office.
*Franklin D. Roosevelt
Library*

began to have hope, once some of their needs began to be realized, they wanted more—much more. Labor wanted more, business wanted more, the farmers wanted more, and the people who were particularly suffering—the old people and those living in impoverished rural areas—wanted more. A group of leaders began to rise in the nation, in response to this call for greater action, the most prominent of whom was Huey Long. "Kingfish," as Long liked to call himself, preached "Share the Wealth," and argued that the

New Deal should be much more egalitarian than it was. He said that Roosevelt was just an instrument of the rich, and that it was only people like himself who really knew the needs of the poor. His movement became a powerful force on the American landscape. At the same time, Father Charles Coughlin of Detroit was stirring the industrial masses in the East with his denunciations of Wall Street, of stockbrokers, and, one must say, of Jewish influence in the United States. Francis Townsend was leading a remarkably active group of elderly people, particularly out in California, who were insisting that something be done for the elderly because they did not have adequate economic protection.

Roosevelt responded to that tumult, to that upheaval, with what I like to call "the second hundred days" of 1935. This period was perhaps not quite so exciting or electrifying as 1933, but it was more historic because it was a period when the enduring reform legislation of the New Deal was written: the National Labor Relations Act, which has meant so much to organized labor, and the Social Security Act, which has meant so much to older people and the unemployed. A host of other important measures also was passed during these years. In a sense, it was a very radical period in American history. Of course, Roosevelt had men in his administration who very quickly became identified in the public mind with radical causes—men such as Henry A. Wallace, who was Secretary of Agriculture and very concerned about the plight of the farmer.

It was also during this period when the conservatives of the country commenced to break with Roosevelt. They had stood on the sidelines during the early period because they desperately wanted Presidential leadership—anything to get the nation out of that terrible morass of the depression. By 1935, when this radical legislation went through, they were becoming very disaffected. Even Al Smith, Roosevelt's former friend and sponsor, had become increasingly unhappy with the new trends. The leadership of the Republican party and most of the business leadership of the nation felt Roosevelt had gone too far. There was a bitter reaction. The hatred of Roosevelt became very strong, and among some people it never disappeared. In retrospect Franklin Roosevelt followed a middle-of-the road course. His New Deal policies did not satisfy the radicals of the left such as Huey Long and they alarmed the business interests on the right.

The second hundred days set the stage for Roosevelt's campaign for reelection in 1936. In that year, unlike in 1932, he did run a liberal, or as some would say, a left-wing campaign. He did appeal directly to the poor, and to the homeless. He did promise more New Deal legislation. It was a good year for Roosevelt, as recovery seemed to be on the way and he had shown his ability to govern while maintaining that marvelous direct contact with the people.

He carried that fight against Alf Landon, the Republican nominee, right up to the ultimate moment when the President appeared in Madison Square Garden in New York City on October 31, 1936. The speech he delivered that day not only highlighted his campaign but gives one a sense of how polarized the nation had become in 1936 and how desperate a fight this seemed to be to both parties. Amid the raucous tumult in Madison Square Garden, where (if you listen to the recording) you can still hear the anger in people's voices coming out of that crowd, Roosevelt said—and remember this is the genteel Roosevelt who came out of that peaceful background of Hyde Park—"I should like to have it said of my first Administration that in it the forces of selfishness and lust for power met their match." The crowd broke in with a tremendous response to that first sentence, but Roosevelt didn't want to spoil his point, so he waited for silence. Then speaking more stridently and lifting his voice, he said, "I should like to have it said of my second Administration that in it these forces met their master!" The crowd erupted in a tremendous roar and Roosevelt pledged to continue his program of domestic reform. Well, the election results of 1936 were a tremendous vindication of Roosevelt, a colossal lopsided victory— the Democrats winning all but two states.

The Roosevelt coalition that was created as a result of the election of 1936 was helpful to Democratic candidates for decades to come. It was mainly composed of the Democratic South, organized labor, intellectuals, blacks, and other ethnic groups. With very large Democratic majorities, Congress seemed secure under the President's control. Everything looked rosier than ever for Roosevelt in January 1937. He had won this magnificent victory; he had a solid record of achievement. But there were clouds on the horizon. One cloud was the Supreme Court, which he felt was simply anti-Roosevelt and anti–New Deal. Its members were for the most part conservatives appointed by Republican Presidents. The

Court seemed determined to block reform and had ruled that many of the most important New Deal laws passed in FDR's first term were unconstitutional.

Roosevelt was worried that the Court would continue to hamper him at every turn. So he decided that he would pack the Court, not abolish or reform it. He tried to get legislation through Congress that would give him the power to appoint more justices under certain conditions. This was not a very well considered move, at least not the way Roosevelt did it. I like to refer to Roosevelt as both lion and fox; certainly he had been the lion in 1936, but now he was more the fox, for instead of meeting the Supreme Court issue head on, he thought perhaps he could manipulate the Court by adding judges who were more sympathetic to his New Deal program. Thus he would avoid the necessity of frontally attacking the Court, which of course held a high position in the regard of the American people. He tried to get this legislation through Congress but Congress just would not go along with him and he was defeated. It was the first severe—some would say the *only* severe—Congressional defeat that Roosevelt ever encountered.

His attempt to bring the Supreme Court into the Presidential orbit was unsuccessful. There was an outcry of public opinion, and Democrats in Congress took the initiative against their own leader. The restraints within the American constitutional system had been tested and Presidential power had been checked. Later, it is true, the Supreme Court acted more favorably on New Deal legislation, but the Court-packing episode was costly for Franklin Roosevelt. He had lost the backing of some conservative Democrats and some of the American people. The opposition that rose from his proposed reorganization of the Court would reappear when Roosevelt was dealing with American foreign-policy issues in the late 1930s.

Another cloud on the horizon which got bigger and bigger during the period 1937–38 was a growing recession. It was a major one. This seemed impossible, because everybody felt that Roosevelt was overcoming the depression. But in the latter half of 1937, industrial production fell off and by 1938 the United States was deep in a recession that brought it back practically to the low point of 1931–32. This was particularly difficult for Roosevelt, because he had prided himself on his ability not only to get the country out of the depression but also to sustain a high degree of recovery. Now he was not sure whether he should try to go back to some of the more conservative remedies or whether he should try to go further to the left and adapt the type of radical programs that some of the so-called left-wing elements of the Democratic party were calling for at that time.

Another problem for Roosevelt during this period was the defection on the part of conservatives in the Democratic party who combined with the Republicans in Congress to defeat any further extension of the New Deal. There were many people still jobless in the late 1930s but the period of domestic reform was essentially over. Nevertheless, Roosevelt's bold initiatives in addressing the severe problems of the depression had been unprecedented in American history. Franklin Roosevelt, unlike his predecessor Herbert Hoover, was an astute politician who did not hesitate to use Presidential power during the time of a grave national crisis.

By far the worst cloud on the horizon was the one that was forming over Europe. The Nazi regime and its leader, Adolf Hitler, after some uncertainty in the middle 1930s were now in complete control of the German government. No real opposition was left to Hitler within Germany by the late 1930s. It was rather ironic that Hitler came to power in 1933, the same year that Roosevelt entered the Presidency; at least they had a good chance to measure each other's progress by 1938 and 1939. Roosevelt hated Hitler. He hated everything that Nazism stood for and so did most Americans, but there was an even stronger element at that point who felt that the great mistake of involvement in world war should never be repeated. By this time the isolationists had organized themselves very effectively; they had great heroes among their leaders, such as Charles Lindbergh of early Atlantic-crossing fame. It was a formidable movement and how to deal with it was a difficult problem for Roosevelt because, here again, there were many Democrats who were leaders of the isolationist movement.

In September of 1939 war did, once again, come to Europe. The United States was pretty much paralyzed by the isolationists and by Roosevelt's own indecisiveness in foreign policy in that strange interlude which occurred between the fall of 1939 and spring of 1940. It was clear by the spring of 1940 that Franklin D. Roosevelt faced one of the most difficult problems of his career, but he was a master at dealing with political problems. The so-called Phony War had been going on in Europe since September 1939 and isolationists in the United States were contending that there was really no threat of war in Europe, that the Phony War was just a kind of manufactured thing. Then Hitler's armies began to roll in the spring of 1940, and they roared through the whole northern part of France and threatened to keep on moving across the English Channel to Britain. This turn of events made isolationists more concerned than ever that Roosevelt might use the Nazi onslaught as the way finally to bring the United States into war.

At this crucial time, Roosevelt was nearing the end of his second term. American tradition had always been that a President should serve only two terms in office; no man had ever succeeded in breaking that tradition, though some had tried. Many Democrats as well as Republicans and independents felt that even at this moment of crisis the two-term tradition should not be violated and that Roosevelt had been President long enough. They believed it was time for new and fresh blood in the White House.

After evading the third-term issue in early 1940 and suggesting to other Democrats that they would make fine Presidential candidates, Roosevelt finally decided to seek his party's nomination for a third term. He declared that in ordinary times he would have retired to his beloved Hyde Park, but in view of the world crisis he would be available for another term as President.

Roosevelt had no trouble being renominated; incumbent Presidents usually dominate the convention and certainly he did in 1940. His troubles were not over, for the Republicans nominated their strongest candidate since 1928, Wendell Willkie. Willkie was not a politician; he was a very successful utility executive, but more than that he was a man of parts, a man of great political ability. Willkie had started an intensive and dramatic campaign for the Republican Presidential nomination only a few months before the party's convention. With some help from *Time* magazine and, to some extent, the *New York Times*, *Washington Post*, *New York Herald Tribune*, and other liberally oriented Eastern newspapers (whether Democratic or Republican), he dramatically obtained it. His personal charm, seeming political innocence, and whirlwind campaign attracted considerable attention from press and public alike. This fresh, energetic opponent must have caused some worry for Roosevelt, particularly in light of the fact that he was also fighting lingering animosity over the two-term tradition.

The most difficult thing about 1940 was that the Nazi success in France and its threat to England forced FDR to confront the whole question of American strategy that he had previously been able to evade. In the face of these intractable and unpredictable situations Roosevelt once again did what he found had been the most effective thing in his career. He went to the people. He waited for Willkie to denounce and drub him week after week, while he occupied himself with handling foreign affairs. He waited quite long, until many people in his entourage were very worried that the election might be lost. With about three or four weeks left before the election, Roosevelt suddenly unleashed a stunning full-blown campaign. Those who had forgotten what a master politician he was were quickly reminded. He brought off one more clear victory over the Republicans, though compared to his previous ones this was relatively close.

Here he was beginning his third term in January 1941 and also inheriting all the problems of his second term, particularly those in foreign relations. His strategy at this point—the period before the United States was in the war but after it had made a commitment to help out the European democracies and particularly Britain—was one that we have become quite familiar with in the years since—all aid to the democracies short of war. This sounds simple but in fact was very complicated; aid meant giving billions of dollars in credit and supplies to Britain. In order to accomplish this, Roosevelt had to calm the taxpayers and somehow circumvent the neutrality laws.

He faced a number of difficult problems in other parts of the world, too. For instance, China by this time was deeply invaded by Japan and was calling for help. Roosevelt was very sympathetic toward the plight of the Chinese as were many Americans. Yet here again the isolationists were adamant that we should not take any step that could lead to a full-fledged war against Japan.

Then in June 1941, in a series of fast-unfolding events, Hitler, through some genius of his, or more likely through some madness, sent German troops to invade Russia. He committed several million men to what would be the most colossal military combat the world had ever known and perhaps ever will know. This dramatic turn of events in some ways helped the situation, but it also complicated it. The danger of a Nazi invasion of Britain was relieved, but now Russia immediately and desperately needed help from the United States in the way of munitions, tanks, artillery, and the rest. In spite of some opposition in Congress and among the American people, Roosevelt did not hesitate to give ample lend-lease assistance to the Russians in the fight against Nazi Germany.

With a heavy commitment in Europe, Roosevelt's policy in 1941 was to be fairly cautious in the Pacific. As commander in chief, his basic strategy in the period before our entry into the war was to try not to provoke Japan unduly but to do all we could to help Great Britain and also Russia. It was a "Europe-first" or "Atlantic-first" policy. This meant, of course, protecting the sea lanes.

Roosevelt, I believe, by mid-1941 felt that war between the United States and Germany was all but inevitable. The question was, how would it come and when would it come? Some people believed he deliberately forced our entry into the war. This is not quite true, for Roosevelt did not think in such broad and gross terms. However, it is certainly true that he considered Nazism to be the most monstrous evil ever inflicted on human kind and he felt the United States had an enormous stake in stopping it. Roosevelt wanted somehow to mobilize our strength but he was not sure how to do it. The upshot was that he tended to be somewhat provocative in the Atlantic. Those encounters between American naval units and German submarines in the shroudy mists of the Atlantic were as often the result of our efforts to aid the Allies as the fault of the Nazis. It is very hard to find the truth but certainly we were not innocent bystanders, though we remained technically neutral.

While Roosevelt was willing to take certain risks in the Atlantic, he was relatively conciliatory in the Pacific, because he did not want war with Germany and Japan at the same time. The problem in the Pacific was that Japan might conquer China and would then be able to pull its troops out of the mainland and concentrate them against us in the Southwest Pacific. Roosevelt's strategy of anti-Fascist "neutrality" failed on December 7, 1941, when the bombs fell on Pearl Harbor. Those bombs not only destroyed much of our fleet and killed thousands of people, they also destroyed Roosevelt's strategy along with the isolationists' appeal in the United States. In other words, those bombs cleared the deck. There was a whole new ball game, in effect, within a few hours after Pearl Harbor. Roosevelt could now rally a united people in a common effort. We had had the attack that I think he knew ahead of time would rally the people, even though I do not believe by any means that he plotted—or knew in advance about—Pearl Harbor. But one can say he helped bring about a situation where some kind of attack was very probable. After Pearl Harbor, he finally had to work out a strategy; he could no longer be the indecisive Roosevelt of 1939, 1940, and 1941. He had to work out a strategy in coalition with the British and with the Russians to face the united ranks of the Axis.

The Russians desperately wanted the Americans and the British to open a vast second front in Western Europe as quickly as possible. By 1942, the Russians were bleeding in a way that has no precedent in world history. Their forces were being lacerated; the losses on the Russian front were unbelievable. The only hope the Russians saw at the moment was to get the Americans and the British to invade Europe from the west and thus take pressure off the Russian front.

Winston Churchill, the gallant prime minister of England, did not want an early second front. He remembered what had happened in World War I when the flower of the British Army died in the Battle of the Marne and in other great battles. He felt that England had suffered terribly from the decimation of its finest manhood in World War I. Above all, he was determined that never again would Englishmen be slaughtered in the kind of strategy that had been used in World War I. He wanted to delay. Churchill was not unduly bothered that the Russians would take the brunt of the Nazi onslaught. In effect, he was willing to let them take it until the British and the Americans were perfectly ready to make their own attack. He realized there would have to be a second front from the west but he was in no hurry to bring it about. Roosevelt was caught in a dilemma because on the one hand he was desperately anxious to help the Russians. He was afraid, for example, that the Russians might collapse, in which case there would be a terrible situation facing the British and the Americans. But at the same time he had to work in close union with Churchill, for the Anglo-American alliance was at the heart of our strategy.

He had another problem in the United States—many people

did not want a European strategy at all. They wanted a "Pacific-first" strategy. They wanted us to conduct a huge naval and amphibious advance across the Pacific against Japan and let the British and the Russians deal with Germany. Our main interests lay in the Orient, they believed, and besides Japan, not Germany, had attacked us. Out of these raucous voices and different plans, Roosevelt built a strategy. He built it, of course, with the indispensable assistance of men like Dwight Eisenhower, not very well known in 1942, but a very important man in the war planning of this country, and of course Ike's chief, General George Marshall. The military in this country, under the direction of Roosevelt, agreed that there would have to be a second front as soon as possible. Roosevelt, in fact, promised the Russians a second front. He did this partly because he meant it, but he also did it to keep the Russians fighting. There was always a little uneasiness that maybe the Russians would suddenly drop out and make another alliance with the Germans, the way they had done so unexpectedly in 1939. We were very suspicious of the Russians and they were suspicious of us. The Russians misinterpreted Roosevelt's pledge; they thought he meant a very early second front of massive proportions.

Instead Roosevelt decided on a more cautious policy. What he did was to open a second front, but not the enormous second front that the Russians wanted. Following Churchill's lead, Roosevelt decided to go first into northern Africa, then across the Mediterranean into Italy, and only after that to make the kind of effort that the Russians were waiting for. This plan worked out quite well from our standpoint. The attack in North Africa in November 1942 was a very precarious one, but it came off quite successfully. During 1943 the British and Americans invaded Sicily and southern Italy and meanwhile the Russians were getting more and more impatient. Angry words were exchanged between Joseph Stalin, the Russian premier, and Churchill and to some degree between Stalin and Roosevelt. Stalin accused the Allies of welshing on their promises. "Where is the second front?" he kept asking. "Where is the second front?" But the English and the Americans were not to be hurried. Very deliberately, while they were slowly building up their enormous military power back home, they made their cautious advance up through Italy toward France.

During the war years, Roosevelt, as chief diplomat, met on

many occasions with Churchill and on two occasions with Stalin. The Big Three, as they were known, exercised an enormous amount of authority in their personal diplomacy. Roosevelt's personality and diplomatic skill at these meetings played a vital part in keeping the Big Three alliance viable.

Another critical year in the life of this nation and certainly in Roosevelt's career was 1944. It was somewhat strange the way an election year coincided so often with great crises or great decisions during Roosevelt's life. Here we were coming into 1944 with the second front not yet launched and with the fear that if it was launched prematurely it would fail and cause a shattering blow to the war effort and of course to Roosevelt's personal fortunes. But Roosevelt had to gamble; militarily he could not wait any longer on the second front. Finally, in the spring of 1944 the English and the Americans and all their allies felt ready and they did launch the biggest seaborne, cross-water invasion in the history of the world on June 6, 1944.

At the same time, under Roosevelt's direction and with the help of some exceptionally able people in his administration, the United States had been effective in mobilizing its economic and industrial power so that we were able not only to conduct a kind of "Europe-first" policy but also to wage a tremendous campaign in the Pacific. This was possible above all with the help of the American people, who made their sacrifices, who were willing to take price rationing and all those other inconveniences, who did their job, and worked long hours overtime. During the war years, the arms of the federal government, particularly the executive branch, played an enormous role in controlling the economy. World War II was probably the last time Americans were united as a people in such a common effort. By 1944 we were in the position of waging a war almost as effectively against Japan as we were against Germany.

This was all accomplished in time for the 1944 Presidential election, which was very fortunate for Roosevelt. Maybe in a way he helped out on the timing. In any event, he was able to conduct his campaign for reelection after the Normandy invasion had taken place, and after we had won some notable victories in the Pacific. Still the Republicans were determined, as any opposition party should be, to beat him whether there was a war on or not. Again, they nominated a very impressive candidate in Thomas Dewey, who had been exceptionally successful as governor of New York. Dewey, besides being youthful, was a man of energy and determination. He carried the battle directly to Roosevelt in 1944, charging him with incompetent management of the war, excessive interference with the people's liberties, fostering an enormous bureaucracy, wasting billions of dollars, and being unduly influenced by left-wing forces. Once again, Roosevelt played the part of the man above the battle and he did not campaign until the last few weeks.

The old master was holding his hand until the last minute. About three weeks before election day in 1944, Roosevelt once again opened up with that enormous political effort that had always proved effective. This was the year, of course, of the famous speech about his dog, Fala, in which he said that the Republicans had accused him of sending a destroyer back to pick up Fala when the dog had been left in Alaska. He said that he did not mind an attack on him or his family, but when they attacked his dog, that is about as low as people can get! He received a tremendous response to this slightly demagogic speech, and then he stepped up his campaign.

He could not go very far from the capital but he did speak in the major cities, and the highlight of this campaign was a tour of New York City in the rain. It happened to be a very rainy day but the champion campaigner toured around fifty miles in New York City in an open car. Why? Because one of Dewey's major charges was that Roosevelt was too feeble to govern. Many Republicans and Roosevelt haters were saying that he was really a sick man and indeed was practically bedridden. Roosevelt campaigned for long hours, being seen by millions and millions of people; he showed that he could take it when that rain just poured down, and of course Fala was in the front seat just having a good time. The final climax of the campaign came at Soldier's Field in Chicago when over one hundred thousand people gathered to hear Roosevelt speak about his vision of the new day that would come after all the heroism and sacrifice of World War II.

He won a fourth term in a close election, but by November and December 1944 Franklin Roosevelt was tired. He was a sick man. Unknown to the public, Roosevelt had a very serious heart condition that had been diagnosed earlier in the year and he was taking digitalis in order to keep going. But there was a tiredness, I

think, of the spirit as well as the body. He was inaugurated for the
fourth time, not at the Capitol the way Presidents are usually
inaugurated, but at the White House before a small crowd. Others
tried to assume some of his burden. His indefatigable wife, Eleanor
Roosevelt, continued to help by performing many of his duties for
him, visiting the sick in the hospitals, and making long trips out to
the battlefields to represent him.

The Big Three at Yalta—Winston Churchill, Franklin Roosevelt, and Joseph Stalin. *U.S. Army Photograph*

Despite his weariness, there were two great tasks still remaining: to end the war and to try to establish a postwar peace
through the United Nations. In order to achieve these goals
Roosevelt felt he had to gain Russian cooperation. He had always
recognized Russia's importance both to the war effort and to hopes
for a peaceful world afterward. He had tried to get a second front

despite Churchill's opposition. He had sent great quantities of material to Russia not only to keep her in the war but also to gain Stalin's confidence in the four years that Roosevelt assumed were left to him in the fourth term of his Presidency. This set the stage for the final summit meeting of Churchill, Stalin, and Roosevelt at Yalta.

Yalta is a very complicated story, and justice cannot be done to it in limited space. The basic problem was how to get Russia to help us in the Pacific when she felt we had not been very helpful in Europe. Stalin felt our aid, while useful, had really come too late to prevent the Russians from taking a severe blood bath in Europe. The American military estimated that we would lose up to a million men if we had to invade Japan. If Russia could be persuaded to enter the war in the Pacific and launch a massive offensive against Japanese territory on the Asian mainland, then it would be much easier and cheaper—in human lives—for us to invade Japan itself. Stalin was shrewd and he was in an excellent bargaining position at Yalta. In exchange for Russian help, he exacted from Roosevelt concessions in Asia and in Europe concerning boundaries and future Soviet power that helped lay the seeds for postwar discord between the United States and Russia.

Roosevelt, however, knew exactly what he was doing. He was trying to save American lives. America was still left with a war in the Pacific to fight and at that point Russian assistance seemed essential. The Russians were not willing to give that help for nothing. Roosevelt came back from Yalta feeling that he had established such a basis of confidence with Stalin that Russia would come in and play a full part in the United Nations. Roosevelt firmly believed he had laid the foundation for a durable post–World War II peace. These dreams would never reach fruition, but he was spared from that knowledge.

His last days were, I think, happy days. Roosevelt spent most of them at Warm Springs, Georgia. He knew that the war was almost over and he spent his time there with good friends, trying to build up his strength for the great effort that lay ahead. He was not to have that opportunity. He died in Warm Springs on April 12, 1945.

As America's wartime leader, Franklin Roosevelt amply expanded the President's power as commander in chief and chief diplomat as he dealt with the most devastating war in modern history. How his successors used this power under other circumstances is another story.

11

HARRY S. TRUMAN
and the
POSTWAR WORLD
by Philip C. Dolce

Harry S. Truman's administration marks an important transitional stage in American history. It began with a triumphant victory in World War II, which was achieved by the absolute power of the atomic bomb and the unconditional surrender of our enemies. Truman's Presidency ended in a protracted limited war in which he refused to light the world again in the deadly glow of an atomic explosion. His administration was a period in which the United States moved from absolute goals to limited objectives without forsaking its international obligations. While helping to define America's role in the postwar world, Truman also institutionalized and extended many of the powers of the executive office.

Harry Truman's early life in Missouri is an important element in understanding his Presidency. He was a nearsighted boy who at an early age was forced to wear thick eyeglasses and this prevented him from participating in rough games with other boys. Young Harry turned to quieter things. He read a great deal, played the piano, helped his mother around the kitchen, and tended his younger sister. The glorious deeds he read about in countless history books intensified a desire for a more active manhood, which was probably why he joined the National Guard and later volunteered for service in World War I. Truman's ability to lead other men was demonstrated during the war when he was known as "Captain

Harry" and won the respect of his rough, unruly soldiers by keeping his promises and "giving 'em hell" when necessary.

While army service compensated for a missing part of Truman's childhood, there were other failures that had to be rectified. His father, John Truman, had many jobs and managed to fail at most of them as he pursued the American dream of sudden fortune. Truman seemed destined to repeat his father's record of failure as he moved through a series of occupations ranging from farming to clothing retailing. His problems were compounded when he married Bess Wallace, a member of an upper-class Independence, Missouri, family. Truman and his bride moved into his mother-in-law's house and lived with her for the rest of her life. Madge Gates Wallace was certain her daughter had married beneath her station and did not bother to hide her contempt for Truman.

These early years gave Truman a sense of his own limitations and certainly left him with no illusion of infallibility. They toughened his spirit of adversity and humbled him, thus freeing Truman of the greatest vice in a leader—excessive ego. Above all, Truman's early life left him with an urge to succeed, to become somebody. The Army had provided a temporary success but now he needed more permanent evidence. Success would prove his own manhood, compensate for his early failures as well as for his father's, and show people like his mother-in-law that they had been completely wrong about him.

In politics, Truman finally found a profession that combined his need for masculine friendship, status, and success. He became part of the Pendergast machine in Kansas City and established a good record in local politics, both of which helped him to win election to the United States Senate. In the Senate, Truman developed a sound record and managed to maintain contact with all major elements of the Democratic party. Thus he was the ideal choice for Vice-President on the Roosevelt ticket of 1944. As Vice-President, Truman had relatively few duties and was not briefed on national policy. When Roosevelt died, the unprepared Truman was suddenly thrust into the Presidency.

Initially, Truman's attention was focused on World War II. For most Americans, the military problems confronting the nation were only technically difficult and centered on the best strategy for ending the war. Morally there was no difficulty, for it was generally

believed that World War II was a crusade against an evil that had
to be completely crushed and exorcised from the land. Truman's
decision to drop the atomic bomb on Japan culminated this brief
age of absolutism. There were alternatives available, but unfortunately he felt that the bomb was the only course that would
guarantee the end of the most costly international war in history.
Though the absolutist mentality fostered by the war would linger
on, Truman never again succumbed to it. Instead, his course as
President would be marked mainly by limited goals and aspirations.

Truman inherited a Presidency which already was the focal
point of national and international policy. His contribution would
be to institutionalize and increase the power of the executive office.
However, this was not apparent when he first assumed the
Presidency. All Vice-Presidents who succeed to the highest office by
accident or appointment face the problem of asserting their
leadership, because they lack a public mandate. Truman's problems
were compounded by the fact that he was succeeding a legend as
well as a man, for Roosevelt had personally embodied the cause of
domestic reform as well as hopes for world peace. In addition, the
postwar Congress was openly hostile toward domestic reform
proposals and determined to curb the extended powers of the
Presidency.

Ironically, it was only after the disastrous 1946 midterm
election, when the Republicans gained control of Congress for the
first time in sixteen years, that Truman came into his own. He
blunted Congress's attempt to roll back domestic reform by making
maximum demands for new legislation and letting the onus fall on
Congress for failing to pass them. Truman proposed a whole series
of domestic programs including a more progressive tax structure,
expansion of Social Security, federal aid to education, extensive
housing programs, and a national medical-insurance program. As he
must have expected, most of these programs were sharply curtailed
or not adopted at all, but by speaking out for them he prevented
Congress from repealing the progressive legacy of his predecessor
and pointed the way for future reform. Truman's election victory in
1948 institutionalized the New Deal and ensured that it would
never be challenged as a totality again.

While Congress at first was able to prevent the extension of
most domestic reforms, it was forced to cede more power to the

Presidency because of the emerging Cold War. The World War II anti-Fascist alliance with Russia was premised on opposition to Nazi Germany. Once the major reason for the alliance ended, relations between the two superpowers were bound to change as new problems emerged. In 1947, when Great Britain was no longer able to support the existing regimes in Greece and Turkey against what

Republican Efforts to Control Truman Were Ineffective. *Library of Congress*

seemed to be Russian expansion, the President proposed the Truman Doctrine, which not only made the United States the dominant power in the Mediterranean but also verbally committed the nation's strength to stop Communism around the globe.

The Truman Doctrine reversed America's traditional peace-time isolationism and led to Truman's policy of containment, which proposed to prevent the expansion of Communism beyond the areas where it already existed. Under this policy the Marshall Plan was instituted, in part to strengthen the economic and political structures of Western European nations in order to prevent their collapse into the Soviet sphere of influence. This was quickly followed by the North Atlantic Treaty Organization, which was not only an extension and militarization of Truman's containment policy but also America's first peacetime military alliance.

While Truman had departed from traditional American foreign policy, he still maintained his lifelong attitude that accomplishment rested on accommodation and compromise. The confrontations with Russia in Greece, Turkey, and Berlin showed Truman's restraint and were peacefully resolved at a time when the United States enjoyed a monopoly in nuclear weapons. During the Berlin blockade, Truman chose not to consult Congress or ask it for authority to take action. He easily could have started an undeclared war over the issue but instead showed his determination by airlifting supplies to the beleaguered city.

Truman's moderation was masked by outrageous rhetoric that enabled him to mobilize the American people behind his new foreign policy. More importantly, the rhetoric temporarily satisfied those elements in society which considered compromise with Communism immoral and demanded the kind of absolute solutions that characterized World War II. This tactic, first learned in the Army, suited Truman, who believed that unequivocal language preserved the principle involved and made it possible to compromise from a position of strength. Hence, when Republicans tried to force the administration to extend massive aid to China to prevent a Communist victory, Truman refused despite the global rhetoric of the Truman Doctrine. "Giving 'em hell" really described the form but not the substance of Truman's Presidency in both domestic and foreign policy.

Aside from the sweeping power he exercised in foreign policy, Truman extended Presidential authority in other ways. During his administration a number of executive agencies were created and institutionalized, such as the Council of Economic Advisers, the Atomic Energy Commission, the National Security Council, the Central Intelligence Agency, and the National Science Foundation. These agencies not only strengthened the President's control over policy decisions but also gave him access to expertise and information with which he could overcome legislative objections to his proposals. Lacking these resources, Congress found it difficult to resist administration recommendations, especially in the area of national security.

Another area of executive concern was American scientific development. Truman strengthened and institutionalized the ad hoc relationship which had previously existed between science and government. In 1947 he vetoed the first National Science Foundation (NSF) bill because it placed the agency almost completely outside Presidential control. The administration intended that science be fostered through executive agencies responsible to the President. Undoubtedly scientific progress since World War II has been in large measure due to the encouragement and funding received from such agencies as NSF and the Atomic Energy Commission (AEC). Yet it also was true that the administration could now set scientific priorities for the nation. This sometimes led to controversial decisions such as Truman's order that the AEC institute a crash program for the development of the hydrogen bomb despite strong objections from the scientific community.

Truman's policies had a major impact on the American military establishment. In his proposal for the creation of the Atomic Energy Commission, Truman insisted on excluding the military and putting the commission under civilian control. His decision meant that nuclear weapons would be under the supervision of civilians who would report directly to him. The nation's military leaders were determined to control atomic energy and an intense conflict developed. Yet Truman refused to change his position and thus vindicated the principle of civilian supremacy over the military. The AEC also added a new dimension to Presidential power which it never before had in peacetime. As the first President to be responsible for nuclear weapons, Truman established policies which are still followed.

The Chief Executive's control over the armed forces was strengthened by the National Security Act of 1947, which reorganized the military under the control of the Secretary of Defense. This legislation also made provision for the creation of the National Security Council and the Central Intelligence Agency. The latter organization centralized the gathering of intelligence information under Presidential control, while the NSC was to advise the Chief

Executive on the integration of domestic, foreign, and military policies relating to national security. The mandate of the NSC recognized a crucial point—that the neat division between foreign and domestic policy had all but vanished after World War II, and this fact alone would separate Truman's administration from all previous ones including Roosevelt's.

Truman's most important impact on the home front was in those areas where foreign policy overlapped what were once considered exclusively domestic concerns. He was the first President in this century to advocate a full-scale civil-rights program. Truman created the President's Committee on Civil Rights and asked Congress to enact legislation based on its report. Although Congress refused to act, Truman, after some hesitation, took steps which needed no legislative approval. He created a civil-rights division in the Department of Justice, ordered the Secretary of Defense to eliminate racial discrimination in the armed services, and established fair-employment policies in all agencies of the executive branch of the federal government.

Aside from Truman's conservative but nevertheless genuine concern for civil rights, Communists were exploiting the issue of racial discrimination and this was a distinct liability in dealing with the emerging nonwhite nations of the Third World. The Cold War was forcing the United States to prove that its democratic heritage extended to black Americans. Moreover, Truman's actions increased the scope of the Chief Executive's power by permanently placing civil rights on the Presidential agenda no matter how hard some of his successors tried to avoid the issue.

Foreign-policy considerations also allowed Truman to exert leadership in the field of immigration, which had long been considered a domestic issue controlled by Congress. The national-origins quota system enacted into law in the 1920s was designed to establish the basic immigration policy of the nation as one of limited entry and favored treatment toward the countries of northwestern Europe. After World War II European refugees became a major concern for the Truman administration not only for humane reasons but also to enhance America's image in the Cold War struggle for supporters. Truman was able to force Congress to pass special legislation which allowed approximately four hundred thousand refugees to enter the country, many of whom would have been ineligible under standards established in the 1920s. Moreover, despite strong Congressional attempts to regain control of immigration policy, Presidential influence continued to erode the national-origins quota system until it was finally abandoned in 1965.

Foreign-policy considerations had made it possible for Truman to act in certain domestic areas which desperately needed reform, but increased Presidential power was not an unmixed blessing to the nation. Truman's domestic-loyalty program had an adverse effect on the guarantees provided by the Bill of Rights despite some attempts by the administration to safeguard individual rights. The program did not go far enough to satisfy right-wing critics of the administration and only served to reinforce popular fears of a serious internal threat to national security by native Communists.

The most dubious action Truman took in domestic affairs was in 1952 when he ordered the Secretary of Commerce to seize and operate the steel mills to prevent a nationwide strike during the Korean War. Although industrial seizure was customarily reserved for Congress, Truman claimed that in a national emergency the President could act on his own discretion. It was not clear what he thought the limits of Presidential emergency powers were and fortunately the Supreme Court ruled this precedent unconstitutional.

The Korean War highlighted both the breadth of Presidential power and its limitations. Truman alone made the decision to intervene in Korea and throughout the war he never sought approval from Congress or the American people. This precedent dangerously enlarged the power of future Presidents to take the nation into other major undeclared wars. Nevertheless, by the fall of 1950, the North Korean invaders had been repelled and thus the major objective of U.S. intervention achieved. Truman now enlarged his objective from the preservation of South Korea to the conquest and unification of the entire Korean peninsula. The President's decision to invade North Korea was a serious deviation from his containment policy because it meant the military destruction of an existing Communist nation. However, once the Red Chinese entered the war, Truman realized he had blundered and he was willing to settle the war by diplomatic means.

Even before the Korean War became stalemated, the President was experiencing difficulty with General Douglas MacArthur. The brilliant but egotistical general disagreed with the concepts of limited war and began to issue public statements which contradicted U.S. foreign policy. MacArthur's public disagreement with Truman's policy was in reality a direct challenge to his commander in chief. Despite the tremendous risk of relieving a popular general who promised victory in a stalemated war, Truman fired MacArthur and thereby reaffirmed the President's power as commander in

General of the Army
Douglas MacArthur and
President Harry Truman.
*U.S. Army Photograph,
Courtesy Harry S. Truman
Library*

chief as well as civilian supremacy over the military. More importantly, Truman refused to extend the Korean conflict into a world war or use the awesome weapons at his disposal to end it.

The stalemated war in Korea and MacArthur's dismissal only heightened the problems of the Truman administration, which was being undermined by other powerful forces at home. A series of scandals, collectively known as "The Mess in Washington," were fully revealed during the early 1950s. Though no hint of corruption ever touched him personally, Truman's predictable loyalty to friends and subordinates prevented him from dealing with the issue firmly. During the same period the administration was crippled by charges of Communist subversion, which at times reached hysterical proportions. To Truman's credit, he tried to stem the flood of reaction and preserve civil liberties while opposing Communism at home and abroad.

This moderate position became untenable in an atmosphere that demanded absolute solutions to the problems of corruption, Korea, and Communism. Ironically, Truman was being condemned for lack of vigorous leadership despite the fact that he had institutionalized and extended the powers of the Presidential office. Yet he refused to succumb to the power at his disposal or yield to the demands of his critics. By 1952 Truman was thoroughly discredited and even the Democratic Presidential candidate, Adlai Stevenson, refused to campaign on his record.

After Eisenhower's inauguration Truman left Washington for his home in Independence, Missouri. He went by train, unescorted and suddenly, without all the pomp and ceremony that surrounds a President. Yet the transition was not a difficult one, for he had never really left Independence. Humble by nature, he never denied his origins. Some years after leaving office, Truman said this about the Presidency:

> I was there more or less by accident you might say, and I just never got to thinking that I was anything *special*. It's very easy to do that in Washington. . . . But I did my best not to let it happen to me. I tried never to forget who I was and where I'd come from and where I was going back to. And if you can do that, things usually work out all right in the end.

12

DWIGHT D. EISENHOWER'S PRESIDENCY: A GENERAL'S FINAL MISSION

by Herbert S. Parmet

After eight years in the White House, Dwight D. Eisenhower left the Presidency with a fairly unique accomplishment: the preservation of his personal popularity. Over two-thirds of American voters had retained their high opinion of his administration. Many observers were quick to agree that, if constitutionally possible, Ike could have had a third term. His departure from Washington caused no changes in his standing. It was not even hurt by the turbulence of the 1960s, although considerable blame for the social explosions was often attributed to his negligence. At a time when the leading candidates for the 1968 election dominated the news—George Wallace, Richard Nixon, Eugene McCarthy, and Hubert Humphrey—sixty-six percent of the respondents to a Harris poll still approved of the general's Presidency. Seventy-five percent gave him top grades for having unified rather than divided the country. Soon afterward, the Gallup Poll provided additional confirmation. Ike, even on the eve of Richard Nixon's first inauguration, was still the most widely admired American.

Specialists, however, had not revised their interpretation. From the days of the Stevenson nomination by the Democrats in 1952 and Eisenhower's midcampaign concessions to the likes of Joe McCarthy and Senator William Jenner of Indiana, journalists, historians, political scientists, and an overwhelming array of intellectuals took a dim view of the general who had allowed himself to become enticed into running for the Presidency.

Confidently, the specialists anticipated the verdict of history. Eisenhower's Presidency would be regarded more or less as William V. Shannon had described it, a "time of postponement," a charade that camouflaged all imperfections. It would also be memorable for dangerous Cold War truculence that antagonized rather than healed, that substituted slogans for statesmanship and left the globe tottering on a precipice created by Eisenhower's Rasputin for foreign affairs, John Foster Dulles.

Nevertheless, as the Eisenhower administration is viewed from a greater distance some of the things that seemed so obvious become less clear. Reassessment may not necessarily bring historical rehabilitation. It may, instead, recognize that the Eisenhower period was dominated by a Presidency that operated neither from atop Olympus nor out of ignorance or indifference. It may also question the conventional portrait of Dwight Eisenhower. To see him as merely a country bumpkin who could not get his sentences straight may ignore the qualities that had enabled Eisenhower to cement an alliance of obstreperous, ambitious, scheming, and suspicious powers during World War II and later to take command of North Atlantic Treaty Organization forces at their most critical phase.

His basic political strength came from the absence of partisan affiliations. As early as 1949, Columbia University sociologist Robert Merton analyzed the sources of the general's popular appeal and found thorough substantiation for believing that it was not confined to partisans of either major party. His popularity was not centered in any particular region; it did not divide the electorate along such lines as geography, religion, or sex. At the same time thousands of ordinary citizens were appealing to the general to declare his candidacy, a large number of Democrats, and they included President Truman, pressed him to become their candidate. Few were even aware that he had any ideological convictions, or even seemed to care.

Yet, to those who knew him well, his Republicanism was no surprise. The family that had been raised in Abilene, Kansas, had never regarded Democrats as particularly legitimate. Moreover, the traditional rural American values, including the virtues of balanced

budgets, dominated his thinking. He echoed Republican denunciations of big government and seconded Herbert Hoover's arguments
in behalf of local control. Such tenets, which were to him positive
virtues of the American way of life, permitted little sympathy for
either a welfare state or the interests of big labor. Indeed, some of
his limited public comments about such matters, uttered long

President Eisenhower playing golf. *Dwight D. Eisenhower Library.*

before his candidacy, were vehement endorsements of laissez faire
capitalism. His conservative convictions were probably deeper than
most people ever realized.

Only when it came to foreign policy were his views close to the
ruling Democrats. A patriot but not a chauvinist, he had strong
convictions about the importance of internationalism. His greatest
impatience was toward those who, like Senator Robert A. Taft,

believed that America could be secure behind an insular fortress. As on a battlefield, buffer zones were essential. But military strategy alone did not dictate his concern for a strong alliance with Western Europe. Economic viability was crucial to the entire non-Communist world. West Germany, he pointed out, had been deprived of vital markets by the Sovietization of Eastern Europe. Any power vacuums that might result had to be plugged. Therefore, it was natural for General Eisenhower to become a strong advocate of the Truman administration's efforts to achieve Western unity. As President, he continued to press for mutual-assistance programs consistent with his predecessor's objectives. Further, the Eisenhower administration utilized businessmen such as Clarence Randall of the Inland Steel Corporation to support widening trade relations with the Soviet bloc.

Indeed, that segment of the Republican party most interested in global business and most passionately devoted to a Wilsonian view of the world became the main sponsors of the Eisenhower candidacy. Financiers and industrialists teamed up with "Eastern-establishment" politicians. Numerically, they represented a minority in a party that, during the 1950 Congressional elections, had taken a pronounced rightward step. By 1951, New York governor Thomas E. Dewey, who had twice been the Republican Presidential candidate, became Eisenhower's chief advocate. Along with such other promoters as Senator Henry Cabot Lodge of Massachusetts and General Lucius Clay, they convinced Eisenhower that his leadership was essential to save the party from isolationism and a hopeless drift to the far right.

Their efforts were complemented by hard work in the primaries. Remarkable showings in several contests, particularly impressive for a noncandidate with no political record, demonstrated the breadth of his support. Finally, in the spring of 1952, just in time to mount a late but effective personal campaign before the Republican convention, the general agreed to run and quit the Army. Having joined partisan political competition, Ike promptly applied his skills as a tactician to a new field.

The Presidency was another mission, although in unfamiliar territory. Fully appreciative of the eminence of his office, he harbored contempt for Harry Truman not only for what he had considered Truman's misuse of the Presidency but also for his having effaced its dignity. He was no longer merely "Ike" to close friends but "Mr. President," and only after January 20, 1961, did his old nickname return. Despite all the fame his career had already brought, he was in awe of the office he occupied. Like a good soldier, he tried to guard its interests, its prestige, and its dignity. Most of all, there was a job to be done. He liked to remind associates about the importance of taking their jobs rather than themselves seriously.

From his administration, subsequently, came the charge that he did not care about party politics, that the apolitical general was bored with the details of government. While it is true that he had little patience with ward-level chicanery and often expressed suspicion and even contempt for self-seeking politicians, he never lost sight of the vital ingredients of his own objectives. Shortly after he had taken office, for example—at the very time critics were saying that the political novice was indifferent to his task—he worked to shore up the party's patronage plums. Desperate Republicans, out of control of the White House for so long, were eager for their share of jobs. To Commerce Secretary Sinclair Weeks, who was a thoroughly partisan politician, Eisenhower directed a personal memo of complaint. Holdover Democrats he pointed out, were not being purged rapidly enough. They represented somewhat of a Fifth Column within the administration. Their positions, he wrote, were in the hands of individuals who believe "in the philosophy of the preceding administration."

A study of the man's entire career, of his personal makeup, points to an alteration of his very way of life, even of his manner of speech, to meet the requirements of popular leadership in a democracy. Old associates found themselves perplexed at the tone of public statements that came from politician Eisenhower. They contrasted sharply with the eloquence of his widely celebrated 1945 speech in London's Guild Hall, a speech that he both wrote and delivered. Former aides were also puzzled by his mangled sentences that were filled with platitudes but left journalists wondering what he had really said. The Ike they had known could dictate papers flawlessly, paragraph after paragraph, with a perfect flow of well-constructed sentences. There is no reason to believe that his literary gifts had suddenly vanished. As President, he was the most scrupulous editor in the White House. At one point, Australian ambassador Howard Beale joined with an Assistant Secretary of State to write a document that Eisenhower was to send to the Prime Minister in Canberra. When the President was shown the paper, he read it carefully and then asked the man from the State Department, "Did that Australian write this?" "We wrote it together," the man replied. "He must have," said the President, who then explained that the word "chances" had not been used as an American expression and replaced it with "happens." Additionally, the two best books that were published under his byline were the ones written largely by himself, without the benefit of committee authorship. *Crusade in Europe* came out in 1948 and *At Ease,* which has been recognized as one of the most remarkable books ever written by an American President, appeared following his term in office.

As a politician, Eisenhower assumed a different role. Throughout his post–World War II career, he had been surrounded by a bevy of businessmen, financiers, and other manipulators of investment capital. Yet, on the campaign stump, he could tell rural audiences that he shared their suspicion of any man who would describe himself with such an affectation as the word "economist." He could stand before the White House press corps and field questions about the banning of suspected works in American overseas libraries, civil rights, and Joe McCarthy in a manner that left journalists at a loss to construct a lead story. As one astute observer has noted, if the reporters did not know what he was saying, that mattered little, because the public was getting the message it wanted to hear. There is no better example of his technique than the time his press secretary, Jim Hagerty, worried that an indiscreet response to questions about the Chinese Communist pressures against the offshore islands of Quemoy and Matsu could lead to diplomatic embarrassment. "Don't worry, Jim," Eisenhower replied. "If that question comes up, I'll just confuse them."

Did he, for example, support the Supreme Court's integration decision in the case of *Brown* v. *The Board of Education of Topeka?* The verdict was not only unanimous, but it had been written by a Court under a recent Eisenhower appointee, Chief Justice Earl Warren. Since the President's news conferences lacked any hint of direct approval, however, he could be pictured as a Chief Executive forced into a distasteful position. But, on the other hand, nothing that he ever said indicated his position; possibly he was just being consistent in his convictions about the separation of powers. About all that was clear was the sensitivity of the issue for the Republican party; the GOP had just begun to make significant inroads into the traditionally Democratic Solid South. Yet, when he ran for a second term, little more than two years after the Court had spoken, he received an increased vote from all sectors of the electorate, even among blacks, who for the first and only time since the New Deal reversed their anti-Republican trend. Even when he later responded to the challenge implicit in Arkansas Governor Orval Faubus's denial of Little Rock's Central High School to black children, the President insulated his political position by emphasizing that his act was necessary for constitutional reasons. Only in private did he express his real attitude toward desegregation of public schools, which was one of regret that the Court had chosen to mandate a move that the American people were not prepared to digest and that innocent schoolchildren would, thereby, be made the pawns of a social experiment.

Eisenhower knew, further, the political art of detaching himself from difficulties created by subordinates, of above all, preserving the Presidency from unnecessary controversies. At one meeting of the Cabinet, he recalled that President Truman had had a disastrous encounter with Henry Wallace. Wallace, while serving as Commerce Secretary in 1946, had won the President's approval for a speech on the Cold War, only to face vehement opposition from Secretary of State Byrnes because it included a contradiction of the administration's foreign policy. In his own administration, Eisenhower made clear to his Cabinet, each man would have to take care of himself. He did not want speeches submitted for advance clearance. He would thereby maintain his complete freedom to react according to the best interests of the office. He added the warning that anyone placing himself in an untenable public position should not assume the President's support. Thus, when Harold Stassen accused Senator McCarthy of interference with diplomatic matters, he had to digest what amounted to a Presidential rebuke in a subsequent White House news conference.

If the prestige of the Presidency had to be preserved, that meant it must remain "above the battle." The Presidency must not become crippled by petty interests. Decisions were to be made by the team, which meant the administration, and the President must remain a symbol of national unity rather than of partisanship. Thus, Eisenhower conducted his Cabinet sessions as virtual seminars in which each member could participate in discussions regardless of their personal areas of specialization. And the meetings were held with faithful regularity. Moreover, a similar purpose was served by the National Security Council. Established by the Defense Act of 1947, Truman had given it only perfunctory recognition. Not only did Eisenhower preside over its sessions personally whenever possible, but during his administration's first 115 weeks the NSC held 115 meetings, compared to an average of once every two weeks during Truman's five years. It fulfilled a vital function during one of the most sensitive moments of the Eisenhower years, the rejection of American money for Egypt's hope to construct the High Dam at Aswan. While the response was conveyed by Secretary of State Dulles, and critics jumped on the Secretary for supposedly brutal treatment of the Egyptian ambassador and for having provoked the subsequent seizure of the Suez Canal, the decision to reverse the offer of assistance had been made with the advice of the NSC. In this case, the NSC had carefully examined and ratified the President's recommendation, a position that had been suggested by the British. But domestic political blame for adversities in the Middle East were nevertheless borne by Dulles.

However much the 1950s may have come to be viewed as "placid" in contrast with the storms of the next dozen years, the Eisenhower Presidency cannot be understood, nor his own accomplishments fully appreciated, without understanding the very serious contentions that he faced. Far from a period of harmony, it was a time when approval of the Eisenhower brand of leadership was about the only thing that resembled a national consensus.

Both the country and his party had been enduring heated debates. Truman's popularity had fallen to a disastrously low level. The Korean War was becoming drawn out and also politically divisive. Within his own party, Eisenhower had to contend with a considerable faction that had favored either abandoning the effort or striking at the enemy for a rapid military victory. Even with the Eisenhower landslide in 1952, Republicans had managed only slender majorities in each house of Congress; after the midterm elections of 1954 and for the rest of the administration, they did not enjoy even that much. So for most of his eight years, Eisenhower had to contend with latent hostility within his own party and a Democratic Congress.

Eisenhower's view of his legislative relationship was expedient as well as consistent with the interests of constitutional government. Drawing back from the Presidential domination that had become so marked since the New Deal, he emphasized that the Presidency and the Congress were coordinate branches of the government. From the man in the Oval Office to the Secretary of State and lower echelons of the White House staff every effort was made to maintain close and trustworthy connections with Capitol Hill. His relations with the Democratic majority leader, Lyndon B. Johnson, were, in fact, so harmonious that they became an important source of liberal criticism of the Texan. During the Indochina crisis of early 1954, when he was determined to avoid any overt American involvement to extricate the French as imminent disaster neared at Dien Bien Phu, he quietly arranged for the leadership of both parties that virtually guaranteed the veto of hawkish plans being proposed by Admiral Arthur Radford; meanwhile, the President carefully absented himself and left the Secretary of State with the dirty work. Regardless of how intemperate and reckless Joe McCarthy became, Eisenhower shied away from a Presidential attack on the Senator that would risk having fellow legislators rally to the defense of a colleague who had been victimized by a violation of the principle of separation of powers. When Senator Ralph Flanders took the floor for a bitter denunciation of McCarthy, the President discreetly sent a confidential personal note of appreciation to the Vermont Republican. And the administration worked behind the scenes to push the Senate condemnation of the demagogue that finally came in 1954. Constantly concerned with the sense of Congress, he warned his Cabinet that they had better adjust to the economic and social programs that had been devised for the federal government during the past twenty years; regardless of how obnoxious they were to conservative Republicans, he warned, they were there to stay. The annual shaping of the administration's legislative program inevitably bore a typical Eisenhower stamp: an admonition about adjusting the list to reflect only those items that stood a reasonable chance with the Congress.

Nowhere was the administration's style, which combined caution with considerations of Republican unity and Democratic sensitivities, better demonstrated than in the area of foreign policy. To please the hawks on the Republican right, there was condemnation of Truman's containment policy. That was "immoral." It left millions of people destined to remain "enslaved" under Communism. So hope was offered for the liberation of the "captive peoples" of Eastern Europe. Even Chiang Kai-shek, relegated to his last redoubt on Formosa and hardly secure on that island, would be "unleashed" and permitted to invade the Chinese mainland. There was talk, too, of massive retaliation, of getting the free world's muscles strengthened to combat the immoral, atheistic, international Communist menace—while the President was pushing his New Look military program so he could reduce military spending by pruning the size of the armed forces.

Despite the militant noises, it was the Eisenhower administration that brought the first significant moments of thaw to the ordeal of Soviet-American relations. Experts scoffed at the meager results of the Geneva summit conference of 1955, but that became the necessary prelude, the conditioning for more significant contacts. In opposition to the Cold War ideologues, Eisenhower and the many businessmen close to the administration were eager for a rapprochement—but it had to be one that avoided both political and military hazards. After the Korean War, the administration was forever conscious that the achievement of a solution had come close to disrupting party harmony. With the fighting resolved virtually along the old thirty-eighth parallel division of the country, the administration had been forced to avoid any ostentatious display of triumph. Several prominent Republicans had come close to open rebellion over the armistice; had it been done by a Democrat and not by an Eisenhower, the domestic as well as the Korean complications would have been enormous.

It was not easy for Eisenhower to accomplish one of his major objectives, that of keeping the party in the hands of its internationalist and moderate wing, or of reshaping it to suit what he called "modern Republicanism." The White House staff worked hard in 1955, during the President's crisis that followed his heart attack, to prevent leadership from passing to Vice-President Nixon, who was much more congenial to the rightists and anathema to the "Eastern establishment." The following year, Eisenhower himself tried to keep Nixon off the ticket for a second term; he hoped to replace him with Robert B. Anderson. But all his efforts at reshaping the party, including moderating the membership of the Republican National Committee, resulted in frustration. While the Vice-President moved adroitly to make himself more acceptable to the center,

President Eisenhower in Korea. *Dwight D. Eisenhower Library*

as he also established his strength with the party's professionals, he came to be agreeable to Eisenhower, albeit reluctantly, as the GOP's Presidential candidate in 1960.

It can be argued that the President had managed to restrain the Republican right, to hold them in check while domestic and international policies were safeguarded. It is less convincing, however, to claim that the party had been remolded along more moderate lines. The pressures from the right could not be constrained much longer.

If Eisenhower is also charged with depending upon prosperity to veil difficult problems, of subordinating public spending to faith in private enterprise, the alternatives offered by the Democrats must be considered. For most of the eight years, the combined opposition of Lyndon B. Johnson and House Speaker Sam Rayburn offered few challenges. Frustrated liberal Democrats virtually exiled themselves to an apartment on Washington's Connecticut Avenue from which they could propose programs that their Congressional wing seemed to be ignoring. Thus, the Democratic Advisory Council printed reams of position papers; but they were addressing themselves, as it turned out, more to the future than to the Johnson-Rayburn leadership. Had Eisenhower, during the existing climate, completely disregarded his own conservatism and capitulated to the demands of the limited number of progressive liberals, he would have found himself with even more trouble from his own right wing. At the same time, it should be remembered that he did manage to overcome conservative resistance to make some limited but important gains, particularly in the areas of the extension of social security and aid to education. But what really mattered during the 1950s, what was recalled more frequently by those who remembered the circumstances of his election in 1952, was that he had managed to end the Korean War with relative speed and had gone on to keep Americans from fighting elsewhere.

Eisenhower, then, offers a fine illustration of the inadequacy of ranking Presidents by playing rating games. His attributes were of distinct value to both his party and the nation during the 1950s. To wish more had been possible is to wish that the times had been different. While he fell short of some of his major goals, he filled a vital function, possibly better than any President since World War II. The country considered him necessary, and so he was.

13

JOHN F. KENNEDY:
YEARS of LIGHTNING,
DAYS of THUNDER

by Roger Hilsman

John Fitzgerald Kennedy was the first President born in this century. He began his term on January 20, 1961, and was killed by an assassin one thousand and sixty-six days later, on November 22, 1963. Over a decade has now passed, and at least the outlines of John Kennedy's role in American history are becoming clear.

Interestingly enough, Kennedy changed history before he ever became President. He was not a traditional politician. Clean-cut, highly intelligent, well-educated, sophisticated, he was something new to American politics. Perhaps the greatest political contribution Kennedy made was that he excited the interest of young people and got them to work actively in politics. Eugene McCarthy, Robert Kennedy, and George McGovern relied even more on young people, but Jack Kennedy was the first. Kennedy was also the first Catholic to be elected President. The consequences are profound. If a Catholic can be elected President, so can a Jew, a black, a woman, or a member of any other minority group.

When Kennedy actually moved into the White House, he was faced with an assortment of problems that were urgent and immediate, but none that were of lasting importance. In the first six months of his administration, he proposed and Congress passed a housing bill, an area-redevelopment bill, a farm bill, the liberalization of Social Security, an increase in the minimum wage, new unemployment benefits, and benefits for the children of the unemployed.

Some of the other problems facing him on the domestic scene seemed routine and ephemeral, but they were in fact the beginnings of difficulties with which the nation would wrestle for many years. One was the question of ecology. He called the first White House Conference on Conservation in fifty-four years and gave Stewart Udall, the Secretary of the Interior, strong support as he took steps toward meeting the ecological crisis that was only beginning to be recognized. Among the bills passed was one on water pollution.

Another seemingly familiar problem, but one that was actually the vague beginnings of something quite new, was the state of the economy. In the early 1960s the United States was beginning to transform itself into something entirely novel in the world's history—a superindustrial or postindustrial society. Kennedy did not foresee all of the implications but he did see some, and in these respects the proposals he came up with were more far-reaching than most people realized at the time. He understood that unemployment had become a more persistent, chronic problem than ever before and that poverty would not necessarily disappear just because the economy had become affluent. He understood that the unemployed were not always poverty-stricken and the poverty-stricken were not always unemployed. From this understanding he came forward with a program for a "war on poverty."

His other economic proposal for meeting the problems of the new society seemed to be concerned with technical economics. But it was in fact revolutionary, the first practical proposal for dealing with these new problems. Orthodox economists called for balanced budgets. Even orthodox Keynesian economists called for deficits only in depression years to be balanced off by surpluses in years of prosperity. What Kennedy proposed was a deficit, to be accomplished by a tax cut, even though the country was at the peak of an economic cycle rather than at the trough. A tax cut would stimulate the economy and increase jobs even though it ran the risk of further inflation. By no means was the proposal the final answer to the problems of the coming superindustrial society, but it was a step in the right direction.

Also on the domestic scene, Kennedy boldly turned to the field of health. His goal was complete medical and hospital care for everyone beginning with Medicare for the elderly. Even this modest step, he knew, would have a hard time in Congress and would probably not pass right away. But the Congress would have to debate it; the press would have to report about it; and sooner or later people would get used to the idea, see its merits, and push Congress for its passage. Medicare finally did become law after Kennedy's death. His goal of health care for everyone is still not realized, but it is interesting that it is his younger brother, Edward, who is leading that struggle.

Another fateful Kennedy move was in the field of civil rights and equality for blacks. The first significant legislation on civil rights since the Civil War had come in 1957. The landmark Supreme Court decision on school desegregation had come even earlier, in 1954. But little progress had been made in carrying out either the legislation or the Supreme Court decision. The blacks themselves moved toward a different strategy, symbolized by the bus boycott in Montgomery, Alabama, led by Martin Luther King, Jr., and by the sit-in movement. Kennedy, as he told King and Roy Wilkins, was convinced that gradualism would mean nothing but drift. Contemplating his narrow margin of victory in the election and the domination of the Congress by the old coalition of Southern Democrats and conservative Republicans, Kennedy recognized that he had no hope of obtaining further legislation any time soon. So he adopted a strategy of executive action—such moves as ending discrimination in federal housing by Presidential order and vigorously recruiting blacks for posts in the administration, in the civil service, and in various departments and agencies. The Justice Department under Robert Kennedy pushed local authorities to carry out the laws and Supreme Court decisions already on the books. The crisis precipitated by James Meredith's attempt to enroll at the University of Mississippi and the similar crisis at the University of Alabama, when Governor George Wallace stood in the door, were battles in which executive action could and did accomplish a great deal.

By June of 1963, Kennedy decided that the time had come for new civil-rights legislation. Much of this legislation was not passed until after his death. Historians will give a substantial share of the credit to the manipulative skills of his successor, Lyndon Johnson. But the initiative was Kennedy's, and the bills would have eventually passed in any case.

In the field of foreign affairs, the Cold War was at its height when Kennedy took office. Just two weeks before his inauguration, Khrushchev had made one of the most belligerent speeches ever given by a Soviet leader. The world situation, Khrushchev said, was more favorable to the Communist side than the "boldest and most optimistic predictions and expectations" had foreseen. He put the new President on notice that the Soviet Union intended to evict the Allies from Berlin. For the rest of the world, he foresaw a wave of so-called "wars of national liberation," and he promised Soviet support to rebellions in Latin America, Africa, and Southeast Asia.

The eagle in the Presidential seal grasps arrows in one claw and an olive branch in the other. Kennedy used both. Under the Eisenhower administration, defense policy was based on the strategy of "massive retaliation." The idea seemed to be that the United States would meet the threat of nuclear war as well as limited wars with nuclear weapons. Defense policy, accordingly, emphasized bombers and missiles at the expense of ground and naval forces. Even so, many observers were convinced that as an economy measure the nation's missile forces had also been allowed to slip. Kennedy instituted the strategy of "flexible response"— meeting the threat of nuclear war with a nuclear deterrent and the threat of limited war with a limited ground and naval deterrent. Accordingly, he increased ground and naval forces, and he also made sure the nuclear deterrent was adequate by increasing missile forces as well. At the same time, he showed his willingness to negotiate—by meeting Khrushchev in Vienna, by the Geneva Agreement of 1962, which neutralized Laos, by his resolution of the Cuban missile crisis, and by negotiating the Limited Nuclear Test Ban Agreement.

Kennedy's thinking on Southeast Asia went through three phases. When he first came to office the issue was not Vietnam but Laos, and he was rather hawkish. At his news conference of March 23, 1961, he stood before three maps showing progressive Communist incursions, and after repeating that the United States goal was a neutral Laos, he said that if Communist attacks did not cease the United States would have to "consider its response." Such words are the classic language of diplomacy for conveying a threat to intervene.

Then came the fiasco of the Bay of Pigs invasion of Cuba by Cuban refugees trained by the CIA. From this disaster, Kennedy drew two lessons. The first was that a President should never let himself be captured by experts—especially intelligence and military experts. The second was that since the American people did not

President Kennedy signs the proclamation quarantining offensive missiles from Cuba. *John F. Kennedy Library*

want to use American troops to remove a Communist regime in a small country only ninety miles away, how could he ask them to use troops nine thousand miles from their shores?

This marked the beginning of Phase II of Kennedy's policy toward Southeast Asia. He telephoned Averell Harriman and told him that he had concluded that a military solution to Laos was neither possible nor desirable and that what he wanted was a political solution. He then appointed Harriman chief negotiator in

Geneva, and in due time Harriman came back with the Geneva
Agreements of 1962 that neutralized Laos. Harriman is fond of
saying that he got all the instructions he needed for six months of
negotiations in a five-minute telephone call.

Kennedy's Phase II policy for Vietnam was to continue to give
aid to the South Vietnamese and actually to increase the number of
American advisers there. The strategy, however, was against using
American combat forces. When Kennedy was killed there were only
16,500 Americans in Vietnam. His strategy, in fact, was against
relying on military measures at all, whether American or Vietnamese. It was a three-pronged strategy. The first prong was to protect
the people—avoid bombing and shelling, avoid chasing enemy
guerrillas through jungles, and use military force only to protect
villages from attack. Second, win the people—through land reform,
education, health care, and other social measures. Third, arm the
people. Once the loyalty of the people was assured the guerrillas
could not survive.

For the next two years it was this strategy that the administration urged on the South Vietnamese. Unfortunately, President Diem
of South Vietnam never gave it anything more than lip service. The
American high command in Saigon, too, was never more than
lukewarm. As a consequence, the strategy was never implemented.

Phase III of Kennedy's policy toward Vietnam began in the
spring of 1963 with the Buddhist crisis. The Buddhists felt that
President Diem, who was a Catholic, discriminated against them,
and they opposed him by demonstrations and by Buddhist priests
burning themselves.

Kennedy had always believed that the use of Americans in
Vietnam would be self-defeating. In the final analysis, he said, "it is
their war. They are the ones who have to win it or lose it. We can
help them, we can give them equipment, we can send our men out
there as advisers, but they have to win it, the people of South
Vietnam." Then as the Buddhist crisis developed, he became
increasingly skeptical of the capacity of the South Vietnamese and
their government. Since he was determined never to make Vietnam
an American war, he began to position himself for negotiations that
would neutralize Vietnam as the Geneva negotiations of 1962 had
neutralized Laos. (I personally had particular reason to know what
was in his mind. Early in 1963, I had replaced Averell Harriman as

Assistant Secretary of State for Far Eastern Affairs, and as the spring and summer of 1963 wore on, Kennedy telephoned me more and more frequently to express his concern. "Remember Laos," he would say, and go on to explain that we must not become so involved in Vietnam that we could not negotiate its neutralization, as we had done in Laos.)

With the exception of the Bay of Pigs, Kennedy's foreign policy was good and often wise and farsighted. The Alliance for Progress program in Latin America and his policy of friendship and help for the emerging states of Africa showed his understanding of the developing world. So did his conviction that the driving force behind the guerrilla struggle in Vietnam, Laos, Indonesia, and elsewhere was not Communism but nationalism.

On China policy, Kennedy took the first initiative. He tried to recognize Mongolia at the very beginning of his administration, and was acutely disappointed when the Congress blocked his efforts by threatening the Alliance for Progress and his aid program for Africa. Later in 1963, in accordance with his wishes I arranged, as Assistant Secretary for Far Eastern Affairs, to make what became known as the "open-door" speech calling for a normalization of relations with Communist China. Again, the policy was blocked—this time, ironically, by Communist China itself, which was not ready for such a step until almost ten years later, in 1972.

The Cuban missile crisis, finally, was a dazzling success in which Kennedy brilliantly combined firmness with understanding and a willingness to negotiate that permitted a peaceful resolution of the crisis without humiliating either side. But much more important were the measures he took afterward. When the dust of the crisis had settled, on June 10, 1963, Kennedy delivered at the American University what historians will undoubtedly regard as one of his greatest speeches. He sought to assure the Communist world that the United States rejected any idea of a "Pax Americana." He appealed to the American people to reexamine their attitudes toward peace, toward the Soviet Union, and toward the Cold War—asking Americans "not to see only a distorted and desperate view of the other side, not to see conflict as inevitable, accommodation as impossible and communication as nothing more than an exchange of threats." He called for a nuclear test-ban treaty and measures to halt the arms race, and he appealed to both sides to take concrete and realistic steps toward peace. "So," he said, "let us not be blind to our differences—but let us also direct attention to our common interests and the means by which those differences can be resolved. And if we cannot end now our differences, at least we can help make the world safe for diversity."

All this illustrates that Kennedy understood that the true art of

President Kennedy answers questions about his Indochina policy. *John F. Kennedy Library*

statecraft is not always to adjust to events or always to attempt to dictate them, but to distinguish between those to which we must adjust and those which we may influence.

Beyond this, he had the prime ingredient of wisdom—a doubt that anyone, including himself, could be infallible, and a respect for human weakness. He had a large perspective, a sense of the ebb and flow of events, that permitted him to look beyond the immediate crisis—as he looked beyond the Soviet affront in putting missiles in Cuba to the opportunity that the resolution of the crisis gave for alleviating the dangers of nuclear war. Both of these qualities helped him in dealing with the untidiness, the inconsistencies and internal contradictions of foreign affairs. He had an inner calmness, a slightly detached, cool, and objective view of himself and those around him that freed him from compulsiveness. There was in his makeup a high idealism, but this 'was coupled with a wry capacity for laughing at himself that made him impervious to flattery and contemptuous of any form of sycophancy, and these are great assets in judging between competing views.

In spite of his coolness and clean intelligence—and partly because of them—President Kennedy had a capacity to attract able men and women to work with him and to excite their loyalties, to win their personal commitment to strive in a great cause. Men and women who were part of those gallant Kennedy years will call it their great adventure, to be recounted in their old age.

Kennedy's capacity to elicit personal commitment naturally had its obverse, and he had his enemies. No one moves a nation without opposition—a public figure without enemies is a political eunuch. But if Kennedy had his enemies, they were good and passionate enemies and by and large the right ones, in that they stood for an outmoded status quo.

All these qualities ensured the loyalties of his own people. But statesmanship is a higher art than partisan leadership, and Kennedy could also reach across and establish a relationship with adversaries. It was based not only on an instinct that one ought to avoid cornering an enemy but on a reasonableness, and openness, a largeness of spirit that permitted him to understand how the other fellow might see things differently. "I suppose," he said once in the days immediately following the Cuban missile crisis, "that we ought never to forget the possibility that the Soviets really believe what their propagandists write." He was tough and determined, but he also had magnanimity.

But above all else, President Kennedy had a vision of the future and a capacity for communicating it to the world's peoples. He was an idealist, but not an ideologue; the old icons were being broken on all sides, and Kennedy's gift was to approach the world in new words and new sincerity. As he said over and over again in the election campaign of 1960, he wanted to get America moving not only for its own sake but so that it could provide the inspiration and leadership to get the world moving, too. He saw not only a world of peace and mutual respect, with a "world economy in which no nation lacks the ability to provide a decent standard of living for all its people," but also a world meeting new demands, overcoming new crises, realizing a new fulfillment for humankind.

The agony of grief that swept the emerging countries of Asia, Africa, and Latin America upon news of his tragic death testifies that he had touched the peoples there as no other American since Franklin D. Roosevelt. But their grief was more than sorrow at the loss of a man who had understood them and their aspirations. It was the promise they sensed in the combination of his understanding, his abilities, and his vision for the world. More was killed in Dallas than just the man.

There remains a poignancy about the administration of John F. Kennedy that will never be dispersed. His time was too short. He never had time to achieve the goals he envisioned or to complete the enterprises, both domestic and foreign, that he set in motion. Future historians will list some Presidents as great, some as mediocre, and some as bad. But they will always reserve a special place for John F. Kennedy—the President of great promise whose life was cut short before it could be fulfilled.

14

LYNDON B. JOHNSON:
FRUSTRATED ACHIEVER

by Henry F. Graff

Presidential reputations are not fixed forever and their rise and fall is often determined by events and personalities entering the scene long after the Presidential terms in question. Ulysses S. Grant, who for a hundred years had been denounced for the corruption in his administration, is now recovering his reputation as awareness dawns that under him black people enjoyed more civil rights than they would have again for generations. Harry Truman, who was hailed for presiding over the stirring efforts to resuscitate Europe after World War II, at present is under heavy criticism for also being the founder of the American part of the Cold War.

It is never too early to estimate a President and no one can say that a later estimate is better than an earlier one. The perspective of history is changing constantly and the judgment is never final. It takes no particular courage, then, for a historian to try to assess a President as recent as Lyndon Baines Johnson.

Lyndon Johnson was the second President born in this century; the first had been John Kennedy. Both men grew up after the Progressive Era; neither of them, therefore, had had instilled in them as schoolboys that keen commitment to a homogenized America without ethnic differences and without foreign accents that the Progressives envisioned as the nation's ideal. But where Kennedy was reared amid affluence and access to high culture, Johnson's origins were modest and Texas-rural. Both men's Presidencies—like all men's Presidencies—were stamped by the peculiarities of the America of their boyhoods—and by the character of their place on the social and economic ladder.

Lyndon Johnson was born near Stonewall, Texas in 1908. His father Sam had been a member of the Texas House—broke but honest—who had recently lost several thousand dollars as a speculator in cotton. Lyndon Johnson's mother, Rebekah, who had lived in Fredericksburg, fifteen miles away, was the daughter of Joseph Baines, who had previously occupied the seat that Sam Johnson held in the House. Baines had sent Rebekah to Baylor College at Belton, for she had a rare love of learning that her father aimed to encourage.

When Lyndon was five years old, the family moved to Johnson City. Sam Johnson was struggling to make a living by selling real estate. The family lived in a comfortable little clapboard house and Rebekah Johnson worked earnestly at making a home and guiding the children. But there was never enough money, and Lyndon would never forget the steady diet of grits, greens, cornbread, and fatback. Nor did he ever forget the fact that he had to wear homemade clothing. Old-timers in Johnson City recall that at one point, to his dismay, he had to wear a Buster Brown suit.

Johnson was deeply attached to his mother. He later would say that until her death he never made a major decision without consulting her first. When—as frequently appears to have been the case—he was unprepared for school and his mother found out, she would seize his textbook and commence to drill him on the lesson for the day, even accompanying him to the front gate still stuffing him with what he had to know.

Mrs. Johnson, who had been an elocution teacher, did some private tutoring in elocution in order to afford dancing lessons and then violin lessons for Lyndon. He detested the instruction in both subjects, and after a short time at each, refused to take any more such lessons. He was not going to be marked a "sissy"—an old word not used much any longer—as Harry Truman had been a few years earlier in Missouri. The intensity of Rebekah Johnson's eagerness to make something of the boy became a spur to his entire life. Who can say that the desire he often expressed in the White House to be remembered as the "Education President" was not generated as he sat on his mother's lap learning to read?

In Johnson's family lore was a deep respect for forebears and friends of forebears—for Texas history. Mrs. Johnson owned a letter she prized dearly that Sam Houston had written her grandfather. Johnson learned to love the history of his family too. He also felt keenly and insistently that the future beckoned as well as the past. Johnson early decided that he wanted to be a rich man like some of the ranchers he saw profiting from the beef boom that was rising in

Lyndon B. Johnson. *Lyndon B. Johnson Library*

the country during the years he was growing up. But how could a young man acquire the capital to get started?

Johnson put in time working for farmers in and around Johnson City; he worked as a printer's devil for a local paper; he shined shoes in a local barber shop. He seemed to those who knew him to be both aimless and ambitious.

If Lyndon was determined to be a millionaire, he was also determined to be a politician. In 1919 Sam Johnson went back into politics, winning back his old seat and Lyndon now had a good opportunity to learn the craft. He quickly saw the intimacy that his father enjoyed with constituents, the detail with which he cared for their interest, the way in which to please an audience. In Austin, Johnson was often at his father's side on the floor of the Texas House.

In the summer of 1924 Lyndon Johnson just out of high school joined some other boys on a trip to California. When they ran out of money, the boys separated in order to seek jobs—dishwashing, fruit picking, waiting on tables. The experience of being broke and practically alone remained a powerful ingredient in Johnson's social outlook. Two years later he came back to Texas, glad to see home again, but still resisting his mother's efforts to get him to go to college. Again he found only menial work, including a stint on a road gang that he never ceased recalling to friends in later conversations. In 1927 he finally concluded that doing manual work was not the quickest pathway to the goal of being a millionaire. His mother enrolled him in Southwest Texas State Teachers College— south of Johnson City at San Marcos, a distance of about forty miles.

In late 1928 things turned increasingly sour for Sam Johnson once again, and Lyndon through the efforts of the president of his college obtained a teaching job at Cotulla, Texas, that paid the handsome sum of $125 a month. The day Johnson arrived the principal's position opened and he accepted an offer to fill it too. The school had a large Chicano population, and while the aim seems chiefly to have been to teach the children English—they could be spanked for speaking Spanish—Johnson at the same time became acquainted with the grinding poverty in which Mexican-Americans had to live. The following year he returned to college.

The Great Depression hit Texas just as he was getting his diploma. To find work was now harder than ever, and he took another schoolteaching position, this time in Houston. But the wider world of politics had set its lures. He seized an opportunity to campaign for Dick Kleberg—the son of the owner of the King Ranch, the largest ranch in the world—a task to his liking and an opportunity with immense personal possibilities.

Johnson's workaday world, henceforth, would be Washington, D.C., as much as southern Texas. From the start, he took worshipful counsel from Speaker of the House Sam Rayburn, a fellow Texan.

No one guessed, though, that what was being launched would turn out to be one of the most luminous Senatorial careers in the modern history of Capitol Hill.

Johnson served in turn as secretary to Kleberg, and then as state director of the National Youth Administration. In 1937 he was elected to Congress to fill the unexpired term of Representative James P. Buchanan in the Tenth District. Johnson was reelected five consecutive times, serving until 1948. In 1949 he was elected to a seat in the United States Senate which he would occupy until he was elected Vice-President of the United States in 1961. He served two years as minority leader and from 1956 to 1960 he was the majority leader. His elevation to the Vice-Presidency was the outcome of a disappointing effort to obtain the nomination for President.

It is easy to guess that Johnson's personality was fully formed by the time he first came to Washington. He was a man of powerful determination who counted on the people loving him. The eager heartiness with which he embraced others by taking them into his confidence (he was much given to secret conferral) may have been an indicator of his concern that he was not really loved in return. The scatological language that has been a characteristic of many politicians, and that he turned into a personal hallmark, suggests the possibility also of a deep feeling of inferiority that his huge size—he stood six feet three inches—could not overcome. His response to the fact that there were people luckier and richer in early life than he had been seemed to show in his keen attention to creature comforts and in the meticulous intensity with which he assembled the parcels of land for his ranch on the Pedernales River. It showed also in his frequent comment that he came from "the wrong part of the country"—a resentful reference to the patina of elegance in language and personal style that the Kennedys displayed, which Johnson envied and admired on the one hand and detested and rejected on the other.

But history will judge that Johnson's positive qualities also grew out of his beginnings: his commitment to self-improvement— for all people; his keen self-consciousness of the American past as providing clues and inspiration for future action; his capacity to understand not only intellectually but viscerally as well what it means to start life disadvantaged or handicapped. In the White

House, visiting politicians were sometimes brought up short by nose-to-nose encounters with the President during which he might demand angrily, "Do you realize what it means to be black?"

While growing up in Texas, Johnson appears also to have come to know and respect the richness of American resources and the effectiveness with which they could serve Americans if high human intelligence was applied imaginatively and public projects were administered judiciously. Above all, Lyndon Johnson, as he had from the time he was a little boy, learned from his experiences and grew steadily—in comprehension, in compassion, and in his belief that politics is an instrument of government, not an end in itself, and that government can be the great servant of the people and must never be its master.

When Johnson was Vice-President he suffered under the neglect and what he felt was the contempt, too, that is reserved for the holder of that office as its occupant waits in the wings of history. When he suddenly became President in the wake of President Kennedy's assassination in 1963, he was veritably Energy Unleashed. But, in addition, by the serendipity of history he became free to be an achiever. A coalition of Republicans and of conservative Democrats had been resisting Kennedy—as it had resisted Truman earlier—in efforts to produce significant federal aid to education, fresh civil-rights legislation, long overdue medical care for the aged, and even a tax cut to stimulate economic growth.

Johnson, the first President from the South since Woodrow Wilson, was determined above all else to see the desired legislation through the Congress. He had, to be sure, the sympathy of many of his old colleagues on the Hill—and also the attention of millions of people somehow seeking a memorial-in-deeds to balm their anguish over the loss so early of handsome young Kennedy. But Johnson was also the last of the New Dealers. He had gone to school to the words and actions of Franklin Roosevelt. Bill Moyers, Johnson's close aide, once said that to LBJ Franklin Roosevelt was a book to be read and reread. In private conversation Johnson overestimated how close he had been to Roosevelt; the evidence in the Roosevelt Library files at Hyde Park is that the relationship was more like that of schoolmaster and young pupil. Nevertheless, the influence was enormous. In Johnson's private quarters in the White House hung a photograph of Roosevelt and a youthful Lyndon Johnson, bearing on its mat the crisp words—Johnson's own—"I listen."

Secondly, Johnson the acknowledged master of Congressional politics was bent on achieving consensus—finding that common ground on which most Americans could agree—as he had so often on the Hill found the common ground on which his colleagues could

Lyndon Johnson sworn in as President. *Lyndon B. Johnson Library*

agree and take a stand. One of his favorite sayings—"Come, let us reason together"—became a kind of clarion call to Congressional leaders and to the people alike. Though Lyndon Johnson was at first an uncertain performer before the television camera and lacked the spontaneous wit and personal magic that John Kennedy could offer, he nevertheless conveyed an image of strength. He projected the idea that with his bare hands he could seize the country's great problems and make them cease to exist as if by legerdemain. At the least he would destroy them with an injection of the right legislation. And in the years of his Presidency, his record in producing new social legislation surpassed even that of FDR, whom he had made his model.

Johnson, who had suffered a severe heart attack in 1954 and carried with him a clear remembrance of how the nation had languished in the period of Wilson's incapacity in 1919 to 1921, had a personal fear he never articulated in public until late in life that he had no time to lose, that perhaps the clock was running hard against him. In consequence, he drove Congress, he drove his staff, he drove himself to achieve much and to achieve greatly. I think he may not have imagined himself perched on Mount Rushmore with Washington, Lincoln, and Theodore Roosevelt—although like most Presidents he was probably reaching for immortality—but in his best moments he wanted to be remembered by the American people as one who came out of the heartland of America unsophisticated but eager and slew Goliaths and dragons in behalf of the people. He wanted to do on a national scale perhaps something like what he had done for Johnson City, where he had once felt ashamed and inadequate. There, by pressing the levers of power he had built one of the most splendid post offices in the United States and a facility for senior citizens that it never could have built on its own. In a way, Johnson was bent on making his own monument—a glorious mountain of social legislation; in a way he was bent on outdoing his greatest teacher, on out-Rooselvelting Roosevelt.

As Johnson was warming up for a massive assault on his laundry list of national problems, the White House staff always knew that one of his expressed concerns was that he would run out of problems to solve—never out of solutions. In 1964 he sought election to the Presidency in his own right. Still in the honeymoon period of his administration he was returned in a lopsided victory over Barry Goldwater, Senator from Arizona. Now the White House was *all* his. Thoughtful men had once written about their hope to create a good society; Johnson's legacy as President was going to be Texas-size: the *Great* Society.

Johnson was aware, as he pressed for the social and economic programs that would usher in the Great Society, that the world itself was being remodeled. His Texas accent and manner were not to be construed as a sign that he was provincial; he well knew that there was a world "out there" with which the United States would have to come to terms. He spoke telling, some people must have thought chilling, words in his inaugural. "We have become a nation," he said, "prosperous, great and mighty." But, he added thoughtfully, "We have no promise from God that our greatness will endure." He spoke of the world "out there" as a place "where change and growth seem to tower beyond the control, and even the judgment of men."

As a spate of Johnson's proposals was turned into law—a new immigration bill signed in the shadow of the Statue of Liberty; a Medicare bill signed in the presence of one of its fathers, Harry Truman; the great voting-rights bill signed as many heroes of the civil-rights struggle looked on; an education bill signed in the little schoolhouse in Texas that Johnson himself had attended—the Great Society full of people with optimism and high spirit somehow failed to emerge. Johnson's "war on poverty," which became the linchpin of the Great Society, aroused brave hopes that quickly turned into disappointment and despair.

And the old response to leadership from the White House seemed to be missing. Perhaps the dynamism of the Roosevelt-Truman era followed by the calm loftiness of the Eisenhower era had made it impossible for the public to rearouse enthusiasm for a reforming President. Perhaps the medium of television had made Americans too familiar with their leaders and White House calls to action too ordinary. The mystery that had traditionally served to create a bond between the people and their leaders as well as a basis for governmental authority was now vanishing.

Hand in hand with this undraping of the Presidency on television was the most painful and tragic trauma of the decade, the Vietnam War. Practically without plan the United States had been slipping ever more deeply into involvement in what many people all over the world understood as a civil war in Vietnam.

Beginning in 1954 under Eisenhower, and continuing through the Kennedy years, the United States had gradually been increasing its commitment of men and treasure to the cause of stopping Communist aggression in Vietnam. Once again Johnson was trapped by his sense of history and the Rooseveltian experience he had had growing up in politics. Like others of his generation he had not responded foreseeingly to the rise of Hitler. He understood the large price that had been paid by the free people of the United States and the Western World to bring down the totalitarian dictators. The free world had been brought to the brink; such a threat must never be allowed to flourish again. And the brilliant Cabinet and advisory staff that Johnson had inherited from Kennedy largely agreed with him.

In the North Vietnamese move against South Vietnam, Johnson, who tended like most Presidents up to now to see the world

President Johnson confers with his military advisers. *Lyndon B. Johnson Library*

through red, white, and blue eyeglasses, saw a Communist advance he could liken to the advances that Hitler and his fellow dictators had made in the 1930s. Not to act—it appeared—was to lay open to destruction a freedom-loving people—although Johnson never explained how he knew this fact. At any rate, Johnson in his mind's eye was pursuing the same kind of vigilance he was now sure Roosevelt should have exercised in the 1930s when Hitler first began his rise to power. And in sending American bombers north into Communist Vietnam, LBJ was continuing the foreign policy of his great mentors—Roosevelt, Truman, Eisenhower: use the might of the United States directly or indirectly to prevent aggression. Even the destruction that American armed strength might produce was in the interest of a greater good—the triumph of freedom and a peaceful world living under the rule of law.

But the Vietnam debacle would not yield to the methods of World War II—bomb and bomb, strafe and strafe, burn and burn, and then send in the infantry. By 1968 the joyful mood of inauguration day 1965 had given way to a much grayer mood. The war that Johnson could neither win nor extricate himself from had become the albatross around his throat.

As his administration drew to a close, Johnson must have felt betrayed by history and by his closest advisers—and by old friends like Senator J. William Fulbright, the carping chairman of the Senate's Foreign Relations Committee. Johnson's wondrous dreams for America were not going to come alive. The civil-rights struggle had not yet completely moved from the streets into the courts, although, despite the burning cities in the late sixties, that process was clearly underway. Johnson knew he was at the wrong point in history. Much that he wished America could bring to pass immediately would have to await for another day.

Meanwhile, Americans will continue to ponder the incomplete triumph of its first cowboy President who came out of the hill country of Texas full of a sense of what was right and what was wrong—and of how wrongs could be put right. He proved to be too quick on the draw, and as he left office to return to the ranch and to the other substantial interests that his political successes had given him the opportunity to acquire, he could contemplate with considerable satisfaction what he had accomplished on the domestic scene—and hope that one day Americans with a longer perspective on the Vietnam War would judge more favorably than contemporaries the central role he played in it.

15

RICHARD M. NIXON:
A TENTATIVE EVALUATION

by Robert B. Semple, Jr.

PHILIP C. DOLCE: Mr. Semple, prior to becoming Deputy National Editor of the *New York Times*, you were that newspaper's White House correspondent for four years. During that time you covered part of President Johnson's administration and President Nixon's first term. One point that has always amazed me about Richard Nixon is that even before Watergate his political career constantly was surrounded by controversy. How can a man who is so controversial survive politically for so long?

ROBERT B. SEMPLE, JR.: I think there are probably a couple of reasons for that. First of all, despite the fact that there are a couple of hundred million people in this country, our political system does not routinely yield up many individuals who want to run for President. Some men do not have the ambition. Others, like former Governor William Scranton of Pennsylvania, try once and find they do not have the stomach for it. But if Richard Nixon had any prominent characteristic, it was ambition coupled with the durability of a long-distance runner; every four years, when the Republicans convened to nominate a man for the Presidency, Richard Nixon was there. Secondly, he understood his party, and prior to Watergate the very crises and controversies that angered the liberals and Democrats did not upset the rank and file of his own party. To them, he was the supreme loyalist and hard worker. They appreciated his efforts in behalf of their party, particularly during the eight years of the Eisenhower administration. Ike was almost "above party." The only fellow who was prepared to go out and do tough partisan work during those eight years was Richard Nixon. When 1960 rolled around, he was practically a "shoo-in" despite the fact that he was not a popular figure or a winning or engaging personality. He stayed out of it in 1964 because the party wanted Barry Goldwater, but when 1968 rolled around, he had done enough work in the vineyard, despite all his crises and controversies, to win once again the almost automatic affection of the rank and file of the Republican party.

PCD: Every President reconstructs the Presidency to meet his own psychological needs. What was the impact of Nixon's personality on the Presidency?

RBS: Well, that is worth a book, but to oversimplify somewhat, I think Nixon reinforced some trends that had already begun. Ever since Roosevelt the Presidency has been growing ever more powerful. There are many reasons for this. The dawn of the nuclear age gave credence to the proposition that only a President unencumbered by a laborious decision-making process could respond quickly enough to avert threats from abroad. Secondly, Congress, rather than representing the nation as a whole, tends to represent diverse and often contradictory interests. One result has been that whoever sits in the Oval Office in the White House is called on more and more to reconcile local and state differences, especially as domestic problems grow in size and complexity. Thus, for both foreign and domestic reasons, the Presidency has acquired increasing strength.

Nixon imposed on that situation, which he had little or nothing to do with, some peculiar traits of personality, peculiar not in the sense of bizarre or weird. Nixon was a loner. He was not instinctively happy, as Lyndon Johnson was, going out and campaigning among the people. He was never really comfortable in the job and with his own power, and, therefore, he tended to withdraw—whether to his Oval Office, to San Clemente, to Key Biscayne, or Camp David in the mountains of Maryland—to become progressively more isolated and detached. In addition to having a powerful Presidency, we had an increasingly out-of-touch and remote President. This combination of office and man did very little to lessen and may even have increased an ominous drift toward Presidential rule in this country at the expense of Congressional power and the power of ordinary people. Because of Nixon, we will keep a much closer watch on the occupant of the Oval Office and not allow him the latitude that we have permitted not only him but his predecessors over the last two or three decades.

Richard Nixon inaugurated President of the United States—January 20, 1969. *National Archives*

PCD: Were Nixon's attitudes toward the Presidency apparent when he assumed office in 1968?

RBS: Actually Nixon surprised me. I thought he was going to run the Presidency in the Eisenhower mold—that he would give his Cabinet members real influence, that he would try to return power that had flowed to Washington back to states and cities, that he would concentrate principally on foreign affairs and let the

Congress and agencies of government run the country at home. In 1968, for example, he made a speech that sounded remarkably like the things Senator Eugene McCarthy was saying during the early primaries of 1968, namely, that we have exaggerated the capacities of the President.

When he got to Washington, however, he became quickly and increasingly disenchanted with Congress. He discovered that the people he appointed to bureaucratic jobs were not as responsive and loyal as he thought they were going to be; Walter J. Hickel, to give you a classic illustration, George Romney, to give you another. His own personality, his natural reclusiveness, also helped persuade him to impose a kind of radicalism on the conduct of the Presidency, radical in the sense that never before had there been such centralization of power inside the White House.

PCD: Despite Nixon's wide political experience, could it be that he really did not understand the nature of the Presidential office?

RBS: I think he did sense what the job was all about. I do not think he was proceeding out of total ignorance when he started to revolutionize the distribution of power in Washington.

Looking back in time, President Kennedy grew increasingly disenchanted, for example, with the ability of the State Department to carry out foreign policy in the way that he wanted it. Therefore, Kennedy ceded more and more power to the people in the White House basement like McGeorge Bundy, the National Security Council, and so on and became increasingly impatient, as Arthur Schlesinger says, with Dean Rusk, who was his Secretary of State.

Similarly, Lyndon Johnson and the people around him became dismayed with the ability of the domestic agencies of government to carry out their proposals; in time Johnson ceded more and more power to Joseph Califano, his most powerful domestic aide. This process was already well underway when Richard Nixon came to office. Add that to the other forces at work for years, acting to endow the Presidency with more and more power, and it is understandable how Nixon after the first few months could in effect say, "I was wrong—cabinet government did not work under Ike, did not work under Kennedy, did not work under Johnson, so I am going to accept the obvious and the inevitable and proceed along this path of transferring ultimate authority to my most intimate aides." But the key thing was his personality, and how it interacted with the job. Richard Nixon's world was populated with enemies. He was a suspicious man, a loner. For that reason, he may in the end have concentrated real influence among far fewer people than his predecessors did.

PCD: Nixon has always prided himself on his expertise in the area of foreign affairs. His transition from cold warrior to advocate of détente is simply amazing. How do you explain this?

RBS: A couple of articles Nixon wrote before and during the 1968 campaign suggest that even then, long before he knew Henry Kissinger well, he was thinking seriously about opening new avenues to the Soviet Union and to the Chinese Communists. Whether this was a matter of personal conviction or whether it was a matter of political ambition, I simply do not know. Whatever his motivations, he did much to diminish the nationalistic and rather messianic impulses that had led the United States into an unwise war, exaggerated commitments, and an outdated hostility toward the Communist nations.

I think he perceived early on, as Johnson had, that the only way that he was really going to end the Vietnam War short of just atomizing the whole country, demolishing it entirely, was somehow to enlist the People's Republic of China and the Soviet Union, the principal suppliers of North Vietnam, on his side.

He had to persuade them by artful negotiation that it was in their interest as well as ours to end the war in Vietnam. This was important to him because I am sure he sensed that he could never survive beyond a first term unless he ended that war. He had promised to do so in the campaign and that is the one promise everybody would have tried to hold him to. The new avenues to China and Russia may have been part of the larger strategy of ending the war in Vietnam, in which case they were the results of pragmatism rather than philosophy. But, you know, I have never held any politician to the test of consistency and Richard Nixon least of all. He was a man of considerable antennae, so sensitive and large that they often dwarfed the body in the middle, and I think he sensed that if he was going to achieve any place in history, it would have to be in terms of ending that war; and, by definition, if he was going to end that war, he would first have to improve relationships with Russia and China. Nixon was not naive about Moscow and Peking; they have been and remain aggressive and, in the case of Moscow, cruelly expansionist systems. But Nixon showed that hard work can produce temporary accommodations without major loss of national self-esteem. Given his early career, one would not have expected this result.

PCD: In the domestic area the cornerstone of Nixon's policy would be titled "The New Federalism," that is, returning power to state and local governments. Did that work?

RBS: There were two basic elements to this. One was called General Revenue Sharing, under which the federal government would send billions of dollars in revenue collected from people like you and me back to states and cities and they could do with it whatever they wanted. The second program was called Special Revenue Sharing, under which federal programs would sort of collapse into six big areas: education, welfare, so on and so forth, thus making it easier to administer them and giving more flexibility to state and local managers. General Revenue Sharing is now part of the law, but it is really too early to tell whether the states and cities are going to get enough money to make a difference, and we still do not know enough to tell what states and cities are doing with it, which is the test of the program, it seems to me. Meanwhile, only a small part of the original scheme for "special" revenue sharing has been enacted into law.

Whether it will work in time, I do not know. Philosophically, I think the country as well as the government in Washington was ready then for that kind of redistribution of power. These programs point out one of the ironies which characterize Nixon's Presidency. Here was a man who, philosophically, wanted to send money back to states and cities but who, politically, not to mention emotionally, found himself hoarding more and more influence at the center. I continue to be impressed by the irony of this. Nixon was not a Hamiltonian by nature or training. Abstractly, he cared little for federal solutions. That, after all, is at the heart of Republican philosophy. We could argue all day as to whether or not Nixon is a true blue Republican but I do not think he was a centralist by instinct and it is one of the oddities that we discovered during the whole Watergate business that he was a decentralist in one sense but a rabid centralizer in another.

PCD: Nixon and his supporters have always claimed that the so-called Eastern media establishment, including the *New York Times*, the *Washington Post*, and the major television networks were hostile to his administration. Is this true?

RBS: Well, if you add up all the newspapers in this country, Nixon received a pretty fair shake over the years. It is also true that the so-called Eastern establishment press is probably more disposed to support liberal rather than conservative candidates. I think it is also fair to say that the majority of working reporters are Democrats rather than Republicans, but none of this adds up to the kind of bias that was attributed to us by Mr. Haldeman, Mr. Agnew, and Mr. Nixon. They saw it as a conspiracy, a vendetta. If anything, the so-called Eastern establishment press is perhaps far too tolerant of people in power, whether Democrat or Republican, particularly during the beginning of their terms in office. Mr. Nixon was an intended beneficiary of this. He was given many opportunities to talk to us, to see us, to explain his programs to us. If a real hostility developed, I would argue that they brought much of it on themselves. They came into office determined to wage war with the press, in part because it was politically advantageous to do so. There are many votes to be gained if you can prove that the so-called Eastern press is against you. And, thus, whatever overtures the Eastern press made were spurned.

During the Nixon Presidency, the White House spent far less time trying to persuade us of the virtues of their programs than they did advertising our vices. Furthermore, I never thought they fully understood what we were in business to do anyway, which was to convey information to people. I am not holding Nixon entirely to blame for this, but he has had a long history of antagonism toward the press. It goes all the way back to the late 1940s and 1950s but primarily to his belief that the press was heavily pro-Kennedy in 1960. I think Theodore White in his book *The Making of the President 1960* says it was, and maybe Nixon had a legitimate argument. Kennedy quarreled with the press when he was in office. Johnson also got very angry at the press, so it was hardly a problem unique to Richard Nixon. But when Nixon and his people politicized the media issue for their own purposes, they did themselves, the press, and the people a great disservice. It is in the nature of the Presidency and the press to be combative. They are destined, properly so, to be adversaries. Nixon just took it much further than anyone else. He suspended ordinary modes of discourse.

PCD: The term Watergate involves many complex but related acts dealing with the Nixon White House. There have been many scandals in the White House such as the ones in the Grant administration, the Harding administration, and the Truman administration. Was Watergate just another example of misconduct blown out of all proportion?

RBS: No, I think it was something bigger and something special. I think it is fair to say that scandals of the past were best defined by isolated acts of venality, usually involving individual larceny, Teapot Dome in the Harding administration being a classic case. The Watergate scandal, however, had its roots in a much broader and more dangerous thrust for political power. Money was no object in this scandal, except to the extent that the Committee for the Reelection of the President engaged in illegal activities to raise money for the Nixon campaign. At issue here was a series of related acts whose primary objective was to increase Nixon's power in office and to increase his political power in the country at large. That is why they broke into the Democratic headquarters in Watergate; that is why they bugged Daniel Ellsberg's psychiatrist's office; that is why they engaged in a so-called campaign of dirty tricks. The ambitions were not monetary but political.

PCD: What does Watergate tell us about the operation of the Nixon White House?

RBS: We have learned a great deal about the operation of the Nixon White House as a result of Watergate. One's first impression is that Nixon's White House was a closed shop. Only a few men—John Ehrlichman, H. R. Haldeman, Charles Colson—enjoyed access and influence. Second, in a strategic sense, it tells us that this was a very defensive operation. Remember what Herbert Porter, a Presidential assistant, said. He said that when he arrived on the scene, one of the younger men at the White House told him, "One thing you should realize early on, we are practically an island here." It was a staff that was at once very tightly knit with only a few men who could make decisions of any consequence. Defensive by nature, the staff seemed to live in fear that if it reached out to the rest of the country, something terrible would happen.

In fact, it was a passion for privacy and secrecy combined with a sense of political vulnerability that led to Watergate. Fear, plain and simple, led to the creation of the Plumbers unit, to which I trace a great deal of the things that happened after that. They

President Nixon and the Watergate tapes. *United Press International Photo*

sensed a need for an extralegal apparatus to guarantee their continuation in power. It was not enough for Nixon and for his people to say, "Look, I think we can beat Dan Ellsberg in court." No, they had to do something else. I do not want to play the psychologist, but I think much of this can be traced to the White House's sense of insecurity.

Much of what happened could not have occurred in a different kind of philosophical and psychological climate. I am a firm believer in the notion that it is the President of the United States who establishes that climate. Even if Nixon was not fully aware of all events, his senior assistants would not have acted this way if they had feared his anger. He may have expressed anger at certain specific things he heard about, but he did much to create the atmosphere in which they could occur.

Nixon was a politician, but he seems never to have learned that the essence of successful politics is consultation and compromise. Therein lies one of the many puzzles about the man: confident abroad, fearful at home, successful abroad, a failure at home. He worked always in an atmosphere of suspicion and mistrust. His senior assistants did nothing to dispel this atmosphere. Thus, his characteristic response to perceived threats was to exaggerate the threat and counterattack accordingly. Hence, overkill; hence, Watergate. The results were ruinous to him and deeply damaging to the opportunities he had seemed to give his party.

PCD: While Nixon was still in office he made the claim over and over again that Watergate was in part an attack on the Presidency. Will Watergate weaken the Presidential office?

RBS: I think there will be some temporary but overdue slippage for the institution. We went through those Camelot days of Kennedy, where people turned out by the millions to yell and cheer. I rather think that that was an unfortunate period because during that time we continued to cede more power to the Presidency. The office diminished somewhat under Johnson because of criticism of the war, but it reached a low point under Nixon, for the obvious reasons we have been talking about here. I worry more about diminishing respect for the institution of government as a whole, for the processes of democracy, for the processes of justice. I worry about the weakening effect of the whole thing much more than I do about the specific institution of the Presidency. On the contrary, I think that one of the hopeful things that might come out of this—one of the good things that might come out of it—is the restoration of some of the balance between the component parts of government. I think it is about time that the Presidency was taken down a notch; it may do people some good in this country. But I hope that while we are taking the Presidency down a notch, people do not give up or become excessively cynical about the processes of democracy in government. I know that sounds like a locker-room pep talk, but you see more and more people being turned off and it is sad. I think if we come out of this with a renewed respect for decency in government, for guys who tell the truth, for people who deal openly, we will have gained in the long run.

16

WAITING in the WINGS:
THE VICE-PRESIDENCY
by Irving G. Williams

By the grace of Richard Nixon and a majority vote of both houses of Congress, Gerald Ford became fortieth Vice-President of the United States on December 6, 1973. Eight months later he was President. In an unprecedented move, Mr. Nixon resigned the Presidency on August 9, 1974 to avoid impeachment.

President Ford nominated Nelson Rockefeller, former governor of New York, to fill the vacancy created by his own succession. He had to undergo the same confirmation process that Ford had so recently completed. Twice within a year, Vice-Presidential vacancies had to be filled. Heretofore, whenever a vacancy in the office arose, it remained until a new election and administration took over.

Gerald Ford as Vice-President was the product of the first implementation of Section 2 of the Twenty-fifth Amendment (1967): "Whenever there is a vacancy in the office of the Vice President, the President shall nominate a Vice President who shall take office upon confirmation by a majority vote of both Houses of Congress."

The President's sole power of nomination conforms to the usual pattern that, in all other instances, requires confirmation only by the Senate. Including here the House of Representatives acknowledges the distinct significance of the Vice-Presidency as an office of greater magnitude than other appointive posts.

Prophetically, some members of Congress felt that they were

involved in selecting a potential Chief Executive when they questioned Ford during the confirmation hearings. Indeed, this was one of the possibilities available under Section 1 of the Twenty-fifth Amendment: "In case of removal of the President from office or his death or resignation, the Vice President shall become President."

Throughout its history, the Vice-Presidency has been inextricably linked to the first office in the land. The office was established in order to solve the problem of an emergency succession to the

Gerald Ford sworn in as Vice President. *Wide World Photos*

Presidency. Dissatisfaction with having Congress elect the President led, late in the Constitutional Convention, to the proposal of a special electoral college that should vote for two men for President, one of whom had to come from outside the elector's home state, with the majority-vote winner becoming President of the United States, and the one who came in second becoming the Vice-President.

The office of Vice-President was itself agreed to on September 7, 1787. Some members objected to it, chiefly because they felt it would violate the separation-of-powers principle. Elbridge Gerry of Massachusetts said, "We might as well put the President himself at the head of the Legislature. The close intimacy that must subsist between the President and Vice-President makes it absolutely improper." Gouverneur Morris rejected Gerry's reasoning: "The Vice-President then will be the first heir apparent that ever loved his father." It was ironic that Gerry should fear the Vice-President as a sort of spy in the Senate for the White House. Only one of the fifty-five delegates to Philadelphia in 1787 ever became Vice-President, and that was Elbridge Gerry himself. Elected in the twilight of his years for James Madison's second term, he died in office before his tenure was half over. There was no "close intimacy" between them.

The constitutional components of the office of Vice-President are few. Originally, he was the second choice of the Presidential electors. Therefore, he was in fact and in theory a man deemed worthy of the Presidency. The incumbencies of John Adams and Thomas Jefferson and their subsequent elevation to the Presidency by election seemed early indications that the expectations of the Founding Fathers were being realized. But the system faltered with the tie vote for President between Jefferson and Aaron Burr in 1800. This brought on the prospect of high constitutional crisis before Jefferson's ultimate selection by the House after thirty-six ballots. The way was cleared for the change in the election system that still remains. Electors were thereafter to vote in separate ballots for the two offices. Overall, the effect on the caliber of men nominated to run for Vice-President would be devastating.

The Twelfth Amendment now required that the Vice-President be a majority choice of the total number of electors. If no such majority existed, then the Senate would choose a Vice-President "from the two highest numbers on the list." The Senate has only once been called upon to exercise this power of choice. Richard Mentor Johnson, Martin Van Buren's running mate in the election of 1836, fell one vote short of election in the electoral count. The Senate chose him, thirty-three to sixteen, over his Whig opponent, Francis Granger.

Though the framers of the text of Section 2 of the Twenty-fifth Amendment had in mind occasions arising from the death of a Vice-President, the first application resulted from the resignation of

Vice-President Spiro T. Agnew on October 10, 1973. Of the preceding sixteen vacancies, only one had been due to resignation. In 1832, John C. Calhoun voluntarily resigned, writing a one-sentence letter addressed to the Secretary of State. This procedure still existed when Mr. Agnew was induced to resign in the first year of his second term as part of a plea-bargaining arrangement. If Section 2 of the Twenty-fifth Amendment had not existed, under the terms of the Presidential Succession Act of 1947 the Speaker of the House stood in direct line of succession after the Vice-President. Since the Speaker, Carl Albert of Oklahoma, was a Democrat, this would have complicated a near-disastrous situation arising out of the House impeachment inquiry of President Nixon and his subsequent resignation.

The relatively rapid implementation of Section 2 in 1973 by all concerned restored a measure of confidence and credence that the system was still capable of managing sudden high crisis in an orderly, brisk fashion.

Named by the President on October 12, Mr. Ford was confirmed by the Senate, 92 to 3, on November 27 and by the House of Representatives on December 6, by 387 to 35. Later that same day, he was sworn into office before the President, a joint session of Congress, and the nation via television.

Martin Van Buren was the last Vice-President to make the jump directly from the Vice-Presidency by normal nomination of his party and election by the nation. All other successions have been accidental. Indeed, since Van Buren in 1836, it was not until 1960 that an incumbent Vice-President was even nominated for the Presidency by a major party. And then Vice-President Richard Nixon lost out in a close race to John F. Kennedy. Eight years later, Vice-President Hubert Humphrey repeated the experience, losing out to Nixon.

A Vice-President, like the President and all civil officials in the national government, is liable to impeachment for "treason, bribery, or other high crimes and misdemeanors." No Vice-President, however, has ever been impeached. Though Vice-President Aaron Burr was indicted in two states for the murder by dueling of Alexander Hamilton in 1804, no question of his having committed a possible impeachable offense was ever raised. Indeed, the Vice-President returned to the dais of the Senate and himself presided at the impeachment trial of Associate Justice Samuel Chase (who was acquitted of "misbehavior" charges). In 1826, Vice-President Calhoun insisted on and got a House inquiry into some rumors accusing him of malfeasance when he had been Secretary of War. A House committee looked into the matter, found the charges groundless, and completely vindicated Calhoun.

Vice-President Agnew, shortly before his resignation, appealed to the Calhoun precedent for similar action by the House with regard to his troubles stemming from his state offices. The House refused to move.

The main reason, of course, for establishing the Vice-Presidency was to have a ready-made stand-in available if accident befell the Chief Executive. Before the Nixon resignation, this had occurred eight times, four each in the nineteenth and twentieth centuries. In addition, seven Vice-Presidents died in office, two others resigned, but the country was never without both officers at the same time. If it should have happened (at least before 1967), statute law provided for an acting succession.

The first emergency succession in 1841 actualized the basic problem that lay dormant in the text of the succession clause of the Constitution (Article 2, Section 1, paragraph 6). Did a Vice-President on the death of a President succeed to the "office" or merely to the "powers and duties" of the office? In other words, did he become President or was he only acting President? Despite evidence that the framers of the Constitution intended the latter, John Tyler assumed the title and office of President. Through every succeeding emergency succession, this Tyler precedent was followed. He also began the practice of taking the Presidential oath of office as soon as possible after the vacancy arose as a sign of the transfer of the power and the office. This practice was sanctified by the phraseology of Section 1 of the 1967 amendment to the Constitution.

But if Tyler had solved his problem to his and other accidental successors' satisfaction, he had left another problem. Suppose a President became "unable to discharge the power and duties" of the office? By that same succession clause the Vice-President was also charged to take over in such a case. But was he now simply an acting President, replaceable when the President's disability ended, if it ended, or was he also President, as in the case of a removal,

death, or resignation? The Constitution did not say; no law of
Congress clarified the subject. This is why when Presidents have
become ill, even sometimes disabled, the nation has muddled
through until the President either recovered or expired. In 1787,
John Dickinson had queried, "What is the extent of the term
'disability' and who is to be the judge of it?" No one answered him
then, and it is not even certain that the Twenty-fifth Amendment
has given a complete answer.

John Tyler. *Library of
Congress*

The applicability of the inability clause was not raised until the
shooting of James A. Garfield in 1881. Unlike Lincoln, who had
been shot on an April evening in 1865 and died the following
morning, Garfield lingered between life and death for an eighty-day
period during which he was usually unconscious. The Vice-President, Chester A. Arthur, never saw Garfield during this time but did
receive periodic reports from Secretary of State James G. Blaine.

Government appears to have carried on under Blaine's regency. Arthur, deeply troubled, made no moves to upset this system. He could not know whether the President might or might not recover, and, without guidance from any law of Congress, no one knew whether an Arthur "takeover" would displace Garfield permanently or not. The one certainty was that there could not be two Presidents of the United States at the same time. This confusion, compounded by the Tyler precedent, probably accounts for Garfield's Cabinet making no effort to bring Arthur into its councils.

When Garfield ultimately died, the crisis did, too, for now Arthur was President. He himself vainly tried to have Congress establish procedures for the future. Congress only begged the question after Arthur left office by altering the succession after the Vice-President, transferring the officials who would be "acting President" from the leaders of Congress to Cabinet members in order of seniority of the departments.

The shooting of McKinley in 1901 raised no questions of disability; he died within a week. A much more complicated situation arose when President Woodrow Wilson suffered a stroke in October 1919. He nearly died, was left partially paralyzed for the rest of his life, and for a considerable period in 1919–20 he was unquestionably disabled in both the constitutional and physical sense. A White House coterie carried on as best it could under an indomitable First Lady.

The Vice-President throughout Wilson's two terms was Thomas Riley Marshall of Indiana, who found himself in Arthur's dilemma. He had a responsibility under the succession clause but no means to discharge it. He never saw the ailing President—Mrs. Edith Wilson turned him back when he once tried—and he did not receive any official reports of the actual status of Wilson's condition. When Secretary of State Robert Lansing tried to determine whether a disability succession should be set in train, he only started a process that led to his own forced resignation from office. Wilson's old political mentor, Colonel Edward M. House, urged the President to resign for the good of the country and the Treaty of Versailles. To House, Wilson's ill health was a perfect justification and it might even rescue his pet project, American acceptance of the League of Nations Covenant. There is no record that House's appeal was ever answered. Perhaps the League and the treaty could not have been saved under any circumstances, but it is well to remember that they were lost during a period of Presidential inability.

Sporadically, thereafter, when Presidents fell ill the matter of doing something about the inability clause arose. President Dwight Eisenhower's heart attack in 1955 was one such occasion. Vice-President Nixon and the nation were kept fully informed of conditions, and governance continued seemingly unimpaired. Thereafter an informal arrangement was worked out by the President and Vice-President, and this was renewed by subsequent Kennedy-Johnson and Johnson-Humphrey administrations. The essence of the arrangement in all cases was that if he was able, the President would inform the Vice-President of his temporary incapacity. The latter would then be an acting President until the President recovered. If the President for any reason was unable to declare his inability, the Vice-President, after such consultation as seemed appropriate, would step in as caretaker. In any event, he would step aside when the President declared his fitness to resume the office.

Though some constitutional purists complained that this procedure was not legal, it had a common-sense practicability that led to its general acceptance. It has since been formalized and further explicated in Sections 3 and 4 of the Twenty-fifth Amendment. The major difference between the prior informal arrangements and the amended Constitution is in a Section 4 disability. A non-Presidentially-declared inability will not necessarily terminate by a President's declaration of resumed fitness. The Vice-President and the consultative body he used to declare the President's inability may disagree with the President. Congress would then have to decide the issue within a prescribed time period, during which the Vice-President would continue to be an acting President. Only time will tell whether these procedures are the answer; at any rate, some parameters for the perplexing problem have been established.

Historically, the American Vice-Presidency has been little affected by legislation. An exception is the 1949 amendment to the National Security Act of 1947. This made the Vice-President a member of the National Security Council, established by the basic law as the highest advisory body to the President in matters relating to the defense and security policies of the nation. Commencing with Vice-President Alben W. Barkley, all Vice-Presidents have sat on this body and have necessarily been privy to affairs of state as these have come before it. At least in theory, the Vice-President has the opportunity to be educated in issues of high policy that he might be called upon to administer if succession takes place. Membership here also provides him with an opportunity to measure the men whom he would inherit if an emergency succession occurred.

Basically, the value of the Vice-Presidency for its occupants is a matter of the President's regard for the office and its occupant. If the President likes and trusts his Vice-President he will be made use of in a variety of ways: as another set of eyes and ears both domestically and abroad; as one who lightens the President's load by taking on ceremonial assignments; as an effective liaison with Congress—especially the Senate; or even as one who may have administrative work assigned to him.

Since the first administration of Franklin D. Roosevelt, all Vice-Presidents have also sat in the Cabinet and, since Eisenhower's time, have been the acting chairman if the Chief Executive is absent.

These memberships on the National Security Council and the Cabinet can be educational and political experiences for the incumbent both in the normal course of events and in case of emergency. Whether these agencies will themselves be the core of decision making is largely up to the President.

If the President distrusts his Vice-President, the latter's capacity for growth and prospects for the future will necessarily suffer. Visits to the White House will drop off, Cabinet sessions will become less frequent or purely formal, the National Security Council may be sidetracked in favor of other ad hoc advisory groups. In general, a Vice-President who is out of favor may be largely reduced to his purely constitutional role of Senate president while waiting in the wings for an accident to befall the President of the United States.

The essential problem of the Vice-Presidency remains what it has always been: the proper selection of men to run for the office. No better short-term description has ever been given than the original one, "the second-best man." But how often has this really been honored? It is difficult enough to remember the names of many who became Vice-President; who could compile offhand a list of those who ran for the office on the losing ticket? Too many times since the rise of the two-party system and the adoption of the Twelfth Amendment the second position on the ticket has been, as Gouverneur Morris predicted in 1802, "bait" to catch small fish in a crucial state.

The disgraceful circumstances of Vice-President Agnew's resignation in 1973 dealt a blow to the prestige of the second office of the land. It undercut a Vice-Presidency that included such major luminaries in the early period as John Adams, Thomas Jefferson, John C. Calhoun, and Martin Van Buren and in the twentieth century incumbents like Theodore Roosevelt, Thomas R. Marshall, Calvin Coolidge, Charles G. Dawes, John Nance Garner, Henry A. Wallace, and Harry S. Truman. Franklin D. Roosevelt ran for the Vice-Presidency in 1920 and found the losing experience useful for his long-term goal. John F. Kennedy made his bid for the Democratic Vice-Presidential nomination in 1956 and, although he did not get it, was sufficiently encouraged to organize his run for the top position four years later.

There is nothing wrong with the Vice-Presidency that honorable, talented men cannot overcome. More and more, the people will demand that the parties nominate only people who are capable of growing in the office and able, if necessary, to step from the wings to the center of the stage as President or acting President.

PART III

KEY ISSUES

17

THE AWESOME POWER:
THE PRESIDENT as
COMMANDER in CHIEF

by Louis W. Koenig

The President's awesome military power refers in part to his power over the nuclear weapons in his custody. Under law, the President alone can order the use of nuclear weapons. Thus far, this has occurred only once, and the sufficiency of justification on even that occasion is still being debated. Near the close of World War II, in 1945, President Truman approved the employment of the atomic bomb against Japan; within days, bombs fell upon heavily populated Hiroshima and Nagasaki. Truman asserted that the bomb was necessary to avoid an invasion of the Japanese mainland, where, it was predicted, American casualties would be very high. To Truman, that factor was paramount, and he never acknowledged any doubt or remorse about his decision.

Since Truman's time, the use of nuclear weapons has sometimes been threatened or implied. President Eisenhower, faced with the protracted Korean War, and pledged in his 1952 campaign to terminate it, encountered resistance in the negotiations from Communist China, a belligerent. Eisenhower threatened to use the atomic bomb against China if it did not negotiate seriously, and a truce was successfully and promptly concluded. In his 1962 confrontation with the Soviet Union over missile sites and emplacement of missiles in Cuba, President Kennedy ordered the armed forces on maximum alert, including units with nuclear arms. For days, the United States and the Soviet Union teetered on the brink of nuclear conflict, but fortunately, the crisis was resolved.

Again, in the 1973 Middle East War, on an occasion when Soviet forces seemed poised to relieve an Egyptian army under siege by the Israelis, President Nixon ordered a standby alert, which applied to the Strategic Air Command and other commands equipped with nuclear weapons. Fortunately, that situation too was resolved and the holocaust averted.

Not surprisingly, contemporary Presidents have endeavored to avoid incidents that lead to nuclear confrontation, to reduce the likelihood of international misunderstandings or lapses of weapons management that could produce catastrophe, and, most of all, to slow, if not halt, the nuclear arms race. Following the Cuban missile confrontation, Kennedy established the "hotline" between Moscow and Washington, to provide immediate communication that would forestall the escalation of incidents and misunderstandings into crises. After Eisenhower did considerable groundwork, Kennedy consummated the Test Ban Treaty of 1963 with the Soviet Union, a landmark in diminishing the nuclear arms race. Similarly, Presidents Johnson and Nixon have entered agreements to limit the use of nuclear weapons. However, these treaties are usually limited in scope and characterized by loopholes that are promptly exploited. Nevertheless, the habit of discussion and agreement may still lead to fruitful results. The arms race is far from the point when mankind can breathe a confident sigh of relief that it is now safe, but the habit of discussion and agreement is important.

The awesome power of the commander in chief has another dimension, however, the phenomenon of Presidential war—war originated or enlarged wholly by the President's own initiative, without a declaration of war by Congress. The Korean War and the Indochina War were such wars. Unlike the two world wars, neither evoked a Congressional declaration of war and both, particularly the Indochina War, rank among the longest and most costly in American history. Few aspects of the contemporary Presidency have evoked greater criticism than Presidential war, for the President appears to have more personal discretion in disposing of questions of war and peace than the prime ministers of countries with parliamentary systems, where power is shared in a cabinet. Even in the Soviet Union, the solitary leader or principal power figure is normally expected to consult with the Politburo, a committee of leaders, if he considers embarking on war, or if, like Brezhnev, he wishes to institute an era of détente, or more peaceful relations with the United States.

Did the Founding Fathers intend that the President possess so much power? Certainly, debates during the Constitutional Convention and the spare language that designates the President as commander in chief, without appending qualifications or limitations, suggests an intention to vest strong military power in the President.

On the other hand, the Constitution reposes substantial military powers in Congress, unmatched by any legislature of a major nation. Congress is empowered to raise and support armies and to declare war. Its appropriations for the executive branch are indispensable for maintaining or enlarging the armed forces. Its power to legislate enables Congress to create and revise the military's administrative structures, such as the Defense Department and the Joint Chiefs of Staff. These and other powers are substantial, and if actively asserted, could make Congress a reckonable force in questions of war and peace at any time it chose to be. In effect, in dealing with military affairs, the Founding Fathers applied two structural principles often utilized in other sectors of the Constitution. First, they meant to create a strong President and a strong Congress and allotted substantial military power—as well as other powers—to each. Second, the framers applied the principle of checks and balances. They envisaged a continual struggle between the branches over military affairs, with the outcome favoring one branch in a given historic era, and the other branch at another time.

In the nation's early experience, several minor actions, or limited wars, were initiated by Presidents, as commander in chief, to protect the lives, safety, or property of American citizens. Thomas Jefferson, by reputation a strict constructionist of the Constitution, dispatched, solely by his own decision, naval frigates to engage the Tripolitan pirates who were marauding American commerce in North African waters. The Mexican War was a declared war, although it was virtually prearranged by President James K. Polk, with Congress a mere ratifier.

The first major use of the commander-in-chief power occurred in the Civil War. When it broke out, Congress was not in session, and Abraham Lincoln feared that if he summoned it, the government would be paralyzed by divisions of opinion in Congress over the appropriate response to the crisis. Consequently, he delayed calling Congress into session for nearly two months and meanwhile invoked what he termed the "war power," which rested on the President's power as commander in chief, his duty to see that the laws were faithfully executed, and his oath of office, in which he swore to defend and protect the Constitution.

On his own authority, Lincoln expanded the armed forces and appropriated funds, without Congressional sanction, from the Treasury to pay the fast-rising costs of the war. He suspended the writ of habeas corpus, a basic civil liberty, and imposed a system of censorship on the postal system. In time, the Lincoln government shut down some newspapers critical of the war, and leading agitators for peace—the Copperheads—were summarily arrested and imprisoned by the military under Presidentially imposed martial law. Eventually, when Congress convened, Lincoln reported many of his initiatives and urged that they be "ratified" in legislation, which, for the most part, was done. Typically, Congress expressed its approval retroactively to the time when Lincoln took his initiatives. In effect, faced with a threat to the nation's survival, Lincoln claimed an indefinite power to legislate for the needs of the war. He visualized the legislature as, at most, a belated participant whose chief function was to acquiesce to his initiatives.

In the other major wars of the nineteenth century, the War of 1812 and the Spanish-American War, the pendulum swung back to Congress. The War of 1812 emanated from a declaration of war by Congress, with the President, James Madison, a reluctant participant in that difficult struggle. In the Spanish-American conflict, the chief impetus for war again emanated from Congress; President William McKinley was reluctant to undertake the venture. Procrastinating as best he could, he was finally overwhelmed by events, Congressional insistence, and public opinion aroused by a jingoist press. Thus, an ascendant Congress is by no means a constant force for peace, nor is the President always found on the side of war.

In the nineteenth and early twentieth centuries, Presidents occasionally ordered American armed forces into small-scale military actions, chiefly against Central American countries. That military intervention might occur far from the American mainland was demonstrated when William McKinley dispatched a modest force to China to join other nations in quelling the Boxer Rebellion. Probably the most serious initiative of the earlier twentieth century was Woodrow Wilson's dispatch of forces into Mexico, during the civil war in that country, but formal war did not ensue.

The two world wars adhered to prescribed constitutional procedure. In both, the President urged Congress to declare war, and in both Congress did. In these wars, the declaration was the first step of an extended pattern of joint action by the President and Congress, particularly concerning the domestic aspects of war. A draft army was raised by Selective Service legislation. Price and rent controls and the rationing of scarce commodities were based on legislation, such as the Lever acts in World War I and the war-powers acts of World War II. In accord with guidelines and standards set out in acts of Congress, the Presidents in both wars delegated to subordinate administrators powers for regulating the economy, initially delegated by Congress to the Chief Executive. The awesome power of major nations to make war rests on an economic and industrial base, over which Congress has authority through its enumerated powers, but in the two great wars it freely delegated authority to the President.

World War II illuminates another side of the Chief Executive's power that especially concerns contemporary critics who view the Presidency as an office of excessive power. Franklin Roosevelt is really the innovator of modern Presidential war making, on whose precedents his successors have built. World War II had raged for two years before Japan's attack on Pearl Harbor resulted in a Congressional declaration of war. During this time, Roosevelt launched many initiatives, although the United States was technically not a belligerent.

A neutrality act, for example, barred the use of the Navy to convoy arms to a foreign power; nevertheless, Roosevelt dispatched quantities of aid, protected by American naval vessels, to Britain. When reminded that he was violating the Neutrality Act, Roosevelt answered that the Navy was not convoying, adding that military convoying was out-of-date. Instead, he said, the Navy was engaging in "neutrality patrols," by which it watched for hostile submarines and reported their presence to the arms-laden ships. Later, when this modest and seemingly improbable definition of task proved insufficient, Roosevelt ordered the Navy to "shoot at sight" any Axis naval craft it encountered, and several violent engagements ensued. Again, when Germany invaded and overran Denmark, Roosevelt moved American forces into the Danish possessions of Greenland and Iceland, steps that were close to, if not technically, acts of war.

But the swiftest enlargement of Presidential power occurred after World War II, particularly in the lengthy era of the Cold War, denoted by deteriorating relations with the Soviet Union. Among other things, the Soviet supported Communist forces in the civil war in Greece, and a succession of "wars of liberation," or proxy wars, in which others did the fighting supported by Soviet arms. The Presidency responded in ways that were extraordinarily expansive of its powers. Acting autonomously, Presidents announced America's assumption of military obligations of unprecedented magnitude. The Truman Doctrine (1947), for example, undertook a commitment of global policing to check Communist assertion wherever it might appear. Presidents established a series of military alliances around the globe, such as NATO (North Atlantic Treaty Organization) and SEATO (Southeast Asia Treaty Organization). They also instituted numerous military-assistance programs for individual nations, with the heaviest outlays of arms and funds to nations on the Soviet periphery, undertakings which Congress supported freely with appropriations. For the first time in its history the United States maintained its armed forces on a continuous wartime scale, with military expenditure the largest component of the national budget. Above all, Presidents developed an ever-expanding concept of "Presidential war," or the commitment of forces to combat solely by order of the Chief Executive, notwithstanding the absence of the constitutionally prescribed declaration of war by Congress. Presidential wars in Vietnam and Korea rank among the longest and costliest of America's wars.

One of the leading Presidential wars was Harry Truman's commitment of American forces to the aid of South Korea, invaded by Communist North Korea in 1950. Truman acted independently, without a declaration of war by Congress, although his action was acclaimed by the legislators and widely supported by public opinion. But the war dragged on inconclusively in a land far distant from and little known to the American public. Soon the nation wearied so of the war that Truman decided against running for reelection in 1952. The awesome power carries awesome political risks. A major factor in Dwight Eisenhower's electoral victory that year was his pledge to "go to Korea" to begin, by negotiation, a termination of the war.

Eventually, Eisenhower brought the war to a close, but several times war in other places threatened to engulf his own Presidency. In the Far East, islands controlled by the National Chinese

President Truman and General Eisenhower. *National Park Service, Courtesy National Archives*

government off the coast of China were suddenly threatened by the Communist Chinese. Another time, a Middle East crisis brewed, with the independence of Lebanon imperiled. In both situations, Eisenhower applied a formula aimed at using his commander-in-chief power without sustaining the political costs suffered by Truman. He requested and secured from Congress a "blank check" resolution by which the legislature expressed its approval in advance of whatever action the President deemed necessary for coping with the crisis as it ensued, including the use of force. By involving Congress in the possible initiation of war, Eisenhower hoped to spread any political blame that might follow between the two branches. He secured his resolutions, but, fortunately, neither crisis became serious. Again, Eisenhower was faced with incipient crisis when the French position in Indochina began to deteriorate rapidly. Key advisers, including the chairman of the Joint Chiefs of Staff, pressed him to send American forces in relief, but the President declined and sidestepped an awaiting morass. His decision went far toward qualifying him as the holder of one of the better track records among contemporary Presidents in managing the awesome power with prudence, discretion, and restraint.

John Kennedy added new dimensions to the autonomous power of the Presidency. In 1961, he approved the invasion of the Bay of Pigs, Cuba, by forces of Cuban refugees, who had begun training under auspices of the United States government during the Eisenhower administration. The invasion proved a disaster, one of the most embarrassing military rebuffs ever sustained by a President. A year later, Kennedy added a further dimension when he became the first President to experience a nuclear confrontation with the Soviet Union. After installing missile bases, the Russians dispatched missiles to Cuba in their own ships and those of satellite countries. Missiles in Cuba meant the reduction of time and distance for Soviet missiles targeted at American cities and enhanced accuracy, compared with missiles dispatched from the distant Soviet mainland. The Soviet's bold gamble in Cuba jeopardized the credibility of the United States's commitment to its allies; if it did not respond when its own interests were at stake in Cuba, it was unlikely to defend an imperiled friend. Kennedy's management of the crisis was a model of prudence and firmness. In carefully controlled negotiations, he avoided backing his adversary into a corner, where going to war might become a likely choice.

All the post–World War II Presidents contributed to American involvement in the Vietnam War, with the first substantial commitment occurring under Kennedy. Despite his 1964 campaign as a peace candidate, Lyndon Johnson escalated American involvement, but again the possessor of the awesome power paid an awesome political price. After the early primaries of 1968 disclosed deep popular discontent with the war policies of his administration, Johnson decided not to run for reelection.

In his early stances toward the Vietnam War, Richard Nixon too was an expansionist. Unlike Johnson, who limited American combat to North Vietnam, Nixon carried the war into Laos and Cambodia, both neutral countries. Like all other Vietnam decisions, Nixon's enlargement of the war was undertaken by autonomous Presidential decision. Ultimately, however, Nixon accomplished

President Johnson addresses troops in Vietnam. *Lyndon B. Johnson Library*

what had eluded his predecessors, when he finally extricated American forces from the war. The independent Presidency can diminish and terminate conflicts as well as commence them. Nixon also promulgated the "Nixon Doctrine," which placed upon other nations greater responsibility for their own defense, presumably decreasing the necessity for American armed interventions. By relying more on foreign aid to strengthen other countries, and by providing good offices of negotiation to halt erupting warfare, in the fashion of the arrangement of a 1974 truce in the Middle East War, the Chief Executive is developing means of peace-keeping by diplomacy that diminishes the likely use of awesome military power.

However, particularly during the unrest and debate over the Indochina War in the Johnson and Nixon years, the autonomous Presidency came under bitter attack. The concentration of monopolistic power in a President who could determine questions of war and peace contradicts a basic tenet of a democratic political system—that the making of highly consequential decisions must be shared. Concentrated Presidential power violates the Constitution, which clearly empowers Congress to declare war. The quality of Presidential military decisions is also questionable: the Chief Executive acts imprudently when, for example, he makes the prolonged and costly commitment in Vietnam and gains only meager results. Finally, the argument often made in behalf of the autonomous Presidency, that the office's monopoly of power and decision is necessary to permit swift action in the brief time frame of international crisis, is specious; in fact, Vietnam, Korea, and other crises afforded ample time for the President to consult with Congress, instead of making heavily consequential decisions in privacy and secrecy.

What can be done to bring the President's military function more into harmony with the democratic ideal of shared power? There could be a return to the constitutional principle of substantial military roles for both Congress and the President. Congress's role is well structured and elaborated; what is required is heightened Presidential awareness that it can be profitable to consult Congress before committing armed forces to combat. As Eisenhower perceived, for the President to associate Congress with his decision is to broaden the base of support; if in time, the resulting war should become costly or unpopular, the President can divide the blame with the legislators.

However, the tenuous character of the Eisenhower formula was revealed by the experience of the Gulf of Tonkin resolution (1964), which Congress adopted, at President Johnson's urging, expressing virtually unlimited support of future Presidential actions in the Vietnam War. But as the war dragged on and sank in popularity, the Presidents concerned, Johnson and Nixon, found the resolution to be a paper shield against the torrential criticism that fell upon them more than upon any other political figures, including Congress, despite its overwhelming adoption of the resolution. The Tonkin resolution became an object of derision, was often cited as an example of Presidential deceit, and the severest critics of these Presidents derived from the Congressional floor managers and other leading exponents of the resolution during its enactment.

If the President does not voluntarily share power, Congress has ample means to force him even to terminate combat actions he has undertaken. Since military machines and war require endless infusions of money, Congress, by wielding its appropriations power, can slow the President down or bring him to a halt. By providing appropriations each year during the lengthy Vietnam War, Congress, in fact, expressed its approval annually of the President's war decisions. Not until 1973 did Congress choose to check the President by barring the use of funds to support the air war in Cambodia.

Also in 1973, Congress adopted a War Powers Act, by which the President must report to the legislature in writing his decision to commit armed forces to combat. Within sixty days, or ninety days if the safety of the forces requires, Congress can intervene, by concurrent resolution, which does not require Presidential approval, to terminate the American involvement, whereupon the forces are to be withdrawn. The statute is useful chiefly as a reminder to the President of Congress's presence and of the wisdom of consulting with it. On the negative side, the act also injects an element of uncertainty, which other nations might exploit, of a sudden Congressional veto. The act conjures up an improbable scenario of American forces fighting one day and withdrawing the next, conduct that would confound both enemies and allies.

In using his military power, the President can be constrained by allies whose approval and support are valued, and whose opposition compounds his task. The United Nations is available as an alternative recourse of debate and negotiation and as a peace-keeping intervenor in lieu of Presidential military action. Presidents faced with crises in the Middle East, in Cyprus, in the Congo, and in Cuba (1962), valued the UN and its resources as a means of avoiding international violence.

Finally, the President can be a constraint upon himself. If peace and respect for human life number high among his values, if he is conscious of the potentialities of international negotiation, and can tolerate its concomitants of patience, sympathy, and hard work, the likelihood is that such a President will be a more responsible steward of the awesome power than a President deficient in those values. History too must become more generous in awarding its accolades to Presidents who excel as peace keepers. It has been overindulgent of the war makers.

18

THE INVISIBLE PRESIDENCY:
GROWTH of the
WHITE HOUSE STAFF
by Louis W. Koenig

"The White House Staff" triggers in many minds configurations of the Watergate scandals that destroyed the Nixon Presidency. But in a larger historical overview, the White House staff has an ample record of positive accomplishment, and it possesses several regular characteristics. It is the most private and confidential part of the Presidency, conducted with a secrecy that the courts and Congress generally respect, though not in the instance of Watergate. Repeatedly, Presidents have protected the confidentiality of their White House staffs by claiming executive privilege for its counsel and activity, and Congress acquiesces to far broader confidentiality for the White House staff than for the Cabinet. Only rarely do staff members testify before Congress, while, in contrast, Cabinet heads and their aides are busily engaged in Congressional appearances.

In the era since Franklin Roosevelt's Presidency, the White House staff has expanded dramatically in size and power, in tandem with the sharp growth of the President's personal power. The precise size of the staff is unknown, since some personnel are "borrowed" from various departments, toiling in the White House while remaining on the departmental payroll. Some White House staff members may not be included in official listings in the *United States Government Manual* and the *Congressional Directory*. Though President Kennedy resolved to reduce the White House staff, which he believed oversized, the staff increased slightly during his tenure. President Nixon, committed to economy in government through reducing the numbers of executive personnel, amassed the largest White House staff in history. In the Kennedy, Johnson, and Nixon Presidencies, some members of the White House staff were as powerful as, if not more powerful than, the most prestigious Cabinet Secretaries, including the Secretary of State and the Secretary of Defense. And in those Presidencies, the staff as a whole exceeded the Cabinet in impact on policy.

For all of its extraordinary power, the White House staff has been slow to develop and appeared in the outline it bears today only in the modern Presidency. Nineteenth-century Presidents, and even those of the earlier twentieth century, had staffs that hardly foreshadowed the contemporary model. In the very beginning, President George Washington considered his chief helpers to be his small outstanding Cabinet, which included Jefferson and Hamilton. Sometimes, in seeking advice outside his Cabinet, Washington turned to the Chief Justice, John Jay, or to Congressman James Madison. For more ordinary duties, he had several clerks.

With minor variation, the staff pattern of Washington endured in the nineteenth century. Near the end of the century there was typically a secretary to the President, a kind of administrative major domo, plus a handful of clerks. The secretary to the President, in addition to overseeing the President's correspondence, dealt with the press and handled patronage and middle-range business between the President and members of Congress and his party. The President's aides and clerks worked on the second floor of the White House, where the President's family also lived.

One reason for the slow development of the White House staff was that some Presidents used persons in the executive branch, Congress, or in private life for counsel or for undertaking special missions, such as a diplomatic negotiation and promoting important litigation. A more structured rendering of informal, part-time Presidential assistants is the Kitchen Cabinet, a phenomenon of Andrew Jackson's Presidency. His Kitchen Cabinet, whose members changed periodically, comprised four or five adviser-assistants at any one time. In all, historians identify twelve individuals—all of whom were close to Jackson—with his Kitchen Cabinet. They included the politically astute Martin Van Buren, who entered the administration as Secretary of State and subsequently became Vice-President. Another major figure was Amos Kendall, fourth auditor of the Treasury and subsequently Secretary of the Treasury. Called "the Deacon," Kendall was tall, emaciated, funereal in expression, a skillful journalist, and master of written argument. In Jackson's battles over the Bank of the United States and other leading issues, Kendall was an invaluable warrior. But the Kitchen Cabinet was much less a cabinet than a collection of individual aides whose common bond was personal rapport with Jackson.

In the twentieth century, Theodore Roosevelt's Tennis Cabinet was devoted to the sport but was never concerned, as an entity, with policy. Harding's Poker Cabinet and Hoover's Medicine-Ball Cabinet were in that tradition. The advent of the modern informal cabinet into the policy arena was signaled by Franklin Roosevelt's Brain Trust, a group that originated in his New York governorship, when, with the economic recession erupting, he sought ideas to carry the state through rising unemployment. His counsel, Samuel Rosenman, a Columbia alumnus, brought together a group of professors from that university to supply policy ideas. After becoming President, Roosevelt called on such members of the Albany group as Raymond Moley, Rexford Tugwell, and Adolf Berle, who quickly became important advisers to the new President and draftsmen of speeches and legislation. Soon, however, each Brain Truster moved on to individual administrative assignments in the departments and agencies, with occasional summonses to White House assignments.

In creating the modern White House staff, Roosevelt established what is known formally as the White House Office and its occupants, the White House staff. Initially, he created the Brownlow Committee to study the executive branch, including the White House, and to recommend administrative improvements. Concerning Presidential administration, the Brownlow Committee proposed, and Roosevelt and Congress approved, the establishment of the White House Office to house the President's secretaries, such as those for press relations and appointments, and his rapidly expanding clerical force, plus six administrative assistants, appointed solely by the President and performing such assignments as he directed. With their titles and flexible assignments, the new appointees became the prototypes of the contemporary staff. Soon the expanded staff overflowed the White House's West Wing and took quarters in the executive-office building next door.

The White House staff tells many things about a Presidential administration, its values, the depth of its commitment to its professed objectives or to others that are unarticulated, and the President's priorities. The President's style is stamped on the White House staff; it reflects his character, and its activities indicate to which problems the President is prepared to commit the resources of his office. Above all, the White House staff gives identity to an administration. Next to the President, and possibly a member or two of his Cabinet, one's impression and evaluation of a Presidency are apt to be based on appraisals of the White House staff. Just as each President is different, so each White House staff is different, because the latter is largely a mirror of the former.

Franklin Roosevelt prized informality, contrasting viewpoints and overlapping jurisdictions among his staff. While this frequently led to intense conflict among staff members, it mirrored Roosevelt's pragmatic approach to most issues. FDR also demanded great flexibility from his advisers. Harry Hopkins, for instance, was a key figure in the New Deal domestic programs of the 1930s, serving as an administrator of relief programs and as a White House adviser. With the advent of World War II, Roosevelt's priorities shifted from the New Deal to the task of winning the war. Hopkins, his spare body afflicted by illness, moved into the White House, initially to convalesce, but he quickly took on vital tasks of the war. In the Lincoln bedroom, where his desk was a broken-down card table, he oversaw the movement of American arms to the Soviet Union and Britain and undertook crucial negotiations with Churchill and Stalin. The Yalta conference, which developed plans for concluding the war and structuring the looming postwar settlement, was arranged by Hopkins, who also attended as Roosevelt's adviser.

Harry Truman believed that Roosevelt had been too casual in matters of organization and he moved to tidy up the Presidency, including the White House staff. His staff's jurisdictions were more clearly delineated and staff members had full-time duties in the White House, since Truman scaled down Roosevelt's practice of utilizing part-time advisers and assistants from other departments. Truman also utilized certain members of his Cabinet more than

Roosevelt had, especially in the area of foreign affairs, where General George Marshall and Dean Acheson were his principal advisers. Yet the White House staff remained important during the Truman Presidency especially in domestic policy and political matters. In fact, it was a young staff member, Clark Clifford, who boldly designed Truman's 1948 whistle-stop Presidential campaign, which featured a rousing new speechmaking technique, the combativeness of which was conveyed to delighted crowds who in return cried, "Give 'em Hell, Harry!" Truman valued friendship in many cases above expertise and this was reflected in a number of appointments he made to the White House staff. Old army buddies, cronies from his days in Missouri politics or the United States Senate were men with whom he could relax. Unfortunately, Truman's loyalty to such individuals made him tolerant, even permissive, toward his subordinates. The Truman Presidency passed through a series of scandals of mink coats and deep freezers, the inducements proffered by private entrepreneurs seeking government favors, usually a loan or access to materials still scarce in the newly reconverted economy. Prominent among the White House figures caught up in the scandals were his military aide, General Harry Vaughan, and his appointments secretary, Matthew Connelly.

Truman's successor, Dwight Eisenhower, a hero of World War II, who at one time or another could have been the Presidential nominee of both major parties, donned the role of healer and restorer of national unity to a people divided by the Korean War and alarmed by the scandals which marred the Truman Presidency. With no previous record of civil candidacy or officeholding, Eisenhower was free of conflicts, enmities, and public commitment on issues, valuable assets of a national unifier.

In structuring his White House staff, Eisenhower appeared to assume that national unity could not transpire unless there was administrative unity in the executive branch, an avoidance of the quarreling agencies of the Roosevelt-Truman era. Eisenhower's pivotal means for securing administrative unity was to adapt the military-staff system, which he knew over a professional lifetime, to the civilian White House staff. The principal concept borrowed from the military was the chief of staff, a figure prominent in Eisenhower's own military commands during and after World War II. As White House chief of staff, he brought in Sherman Adams, a former governor and a key figure in his nomination and campaign.

Adams's task was to assure that working papers requiring Presidential decision were "coordinated" before reaching the Chief Executive, that all agencies with information, opinion, and interest concerning a decision contributed to its preparation. When conflicts flared between agencies, Adams or others on the White House staff endeavored to resolve them before the President was called upon to act. Ideally, all that would be asked of him was a yes or no decision. Similarly, for the sake of administrative unity, the Cabinet, historically an informal body, was put on a more "businesslike" or organized footing. A Cabinet secretary and secretariat was added to the White House staff. Cabinet meetings were guided by an agenda: decisions taken were recorded; and periodic checks were made of accomplishments, obstacles, and the need to reconsider policy.

In his climb to the Presidency, John Kennedy's rallying slogan was the need to "get the country moving again" through Presidential leadership, to shake off the torpor of the comfortable fifties, and to confront problems long building at home and abroad. As President, Kennedy was therefore eager for ideas and innovation, and, just as Roosevelt had done, he turned for his White House aides and advisers to academic sources, and particularly to his alma mater, Harvard. A key recruit was McGeorge Bundy, dean of Harvard College, who became the first powerful assistant for national security affairs. In time, Bundy rivaled, if he did not exceed, the Secretaries of State and Defense in influence on policy. Into his hands flowed copies of the incoming cables of the State and Defense departments, which increased his ability to counsel the President. Bundy was influential in the two Cuban crises, the Bay of Pigs disaster, and the nuclear missile confrontation with the Soviet Union, and in the administration's growing commitment to the Vietnam War.

Another key figure in the Kennedy Presidency was Theodore Sorensen, the President's counsel, who ranged across the board of the Presidency, and whose association with Kennedy began in his Senate days. Intellectually attuned to the President, Sorensen was gifted as a speech writer and at evaluating and improving departmental proposals. Getting the country moving again meant getting the bureaucracy moving, and Sorensen and others of the White

House staff excelled at extracting ideas from the normally slow-moving bureaucracy and prodding it into action.

Lyndon Johnson, the Senate leader who became President, adopted for himself and his White House staff the style of consensus politics he had pursued in his legislative career. As a broker in political consensus, Johnson as President would withhold his own

President Kennedy with the Executive Committee. *John F. Kennedy Library*

commitment until the differences of others such as interest groups and their proponents in the federal bureaucracy, were reconciled, or in effect, until a majority attained a consensus. In this kind of politics, Johnson prized the retention of his own freedom of decision in order to "keep his options open." He preferred to disperse power; consequently no one on his staff approached the power of a

Hopkins or a Sorensen. Those of substantial power, such as Bill D. Moyers, whose role in developing the Great Society domestic program was major, shared his duties with Douglass Cater, a former editor. In recruiting his White House staff, Johnson was partial to writers and to others with public-relations backgrounds, which afforded a staff of high adaptability, a prized value in the workings of Johnson's consensus politics. An imaginative and enterprising President and staff discovered or formulated common denominators of agreement that opened the door to policy and action. For years, for example, quests for comprehensive national-education legislation had stumbled on the issue of aid to parochial schools, but Johnson and his White House and departmental aides devised the concept of aid to the student, whether he received public or private instruction, and a landmark national-education act resulted in 1965.

For his successor, Richard Nixon, the White House staff was the route to his well-defined preference for seclusion and he gladly left the hurly-burly of the Presidency to his White House aides. A major protector of Nixon's privacy was his chief of staff, H. R. Haldeman, whose background was advertising and service in Nixon's earlier California campaigns, including activity in "dirty politics." With a Marine drill-sergeant's manner, Haldeman guarded Nixon's door and privacy, and those he kept away included governors, Senators, and Cabinet members, and their most pained complaints brought no relaxation of the austerely selective access to the President.

To Nixon, as the Watergate tapes make clear, the world outside the White House, including the bureaucracy, was infested with "enemies." The President's chief defense was to centralize, as much as possible, power and operations in the White House staff. A Seattle land-use lawyer, with no particular background in national policy, John Ehrlichman became chief Presidential assistant for domestic affairs, and was overseer of the Domestic Council, a newly created interdepartmental structure, intended as the domestic counterpart to the National Security Council in foreign affairs. Budgets for domestic programs, proposals for new legislation, reviews of the efficiency of existing programs passed under Ehrlichman's authoritative scrutiny.

Centralized power also belonged to the assistant for national security affairs, Henry Kissinger. Unlike his predecessors, Bundy and Walt W. Rostow in the Kennedy and Johnson Presidencies, Kissinger conducted the operations necessary to effectuate the advice he rendered the President. It was Kissinger who conducted the crucial negotiations that extricated American armed forces from the Vietnam War and who prepared the way for Nixon's summit meetings in Peking and Moscow. Even after he became Secretary of State, Kissinger's influence in such areas as arms control and foreign

President Nixon discusses the budget with (left to right) Henry Kissinger, John Ehrlichman, and Budget Director Robert Mayo. *Wide World Photos*

aid, and his success in negotiating the Middle East cease-fire in 1974 were facilitated by his dual officeholding at the State Department and the White House.

Other members of the White House staff, as investigations of the Watergate scandals made clear, were youthful helpers, ambitious, little interested in specific programs and policies, defective in ethics and in understanding of democratic values and processes, and ready indulgers in "dirty politics." Ultimately, the Watergate crimes, committed under the aegis of White House staff chiefs, entrapped the President in the criminal activity of their coverup and led to his resignation from the Presidency in the face of his imminent impeachment.

An early act of his successor, Gerald Ford, was the movement of his administration and the White House staff away from the narrow base of advertising from which many of Nixon's chief aides were recruited—Ziegler as press secretary, Haldeman, and many of the younger staff. Ford conveyed that resolve when he appointed J. F. ter Horst and later Ron Nessen as press secretary. He also established a committee of former Congressmen who had served with him in the House of Representatives to advise on appointments.

In contrast to the secluded Nixon White House, Ford promised an "open" and "candid" administration. A clue to his determination in this respect was the diversity of public and private figures at his swearing-in ceremony, many of whom were persona non grata in the Nixon White House. Mindful of the debacles of the Nixon White House staff, Ford appeared resolved to reduce its power and to shunt initiatives and responsibilities back to the departments. But Presidents, the historical record is clear, show poor effectiveness in seeking to reduce the numbers or the power of the White House staff.

Clearly the White House staff was invaluable to Roosevelt, Kennedy, Johnson, and others as a formulator and promoter of policies and programs. The staff provided much of the administrative unity that Eisenhower prized, and Ford's quest for an administration open to a diversity of views and interests could be readily furthered by the White House staff.

But the White House staff has an underside. It is a fertile source of lapses that can be costly and even disastrous to the President. Since World War II, most Presidents have been tripped or embarrassed by the staff's occasional malfunctioning. Truman paid a high political price for corruption that touched his White House staff. After pledging an administration that would be as "clean as a hound's tooth," Eisenhower was contradicted by his chief aide, Sherman Adams, who interceded with regulatory agencies in behalf of an industrialist and accepted from his grateful friend the gift of a vicuna coat, a lapse for which he soon went into exile.

In approving the disastrous Bay of Pigs invasion, John Kennedy was badly advised by a White House staff that was young and green and that accepted too readily grossly optimistic reports by the Defense Department and the CIA. Most often, however, advisers articulated the instincts and preferences of their Presidents. Consequently, Johnson, who promptly resolved, after becoming President, not to preside over the loss of Vietnam, immediately entertained views that more or less coincided with the dominant opinions of his advisers, and he readily and repeatedly approved their requests for increasing American forces in Vietnam.

But at several crucial junctures in the lengthy history of the war, Presidents rejected the counsel of their principal advisers. Eisenhower, confronted with the recommendations of his leading foreign-affairs and national-security advisers that he inject American forces into the Southeast Asian mainland, rejected their counsel, anticipating, far better than they, the costly dangers lurking in that course. Likewise, Lyndon Johnson was faced, in 1968, with the recommendations of his military advisers that he increase substantially American forces in Vietnam. Instead, he launched policies to deescalate the war.

Why must such a high incidence of trouble, sometimes their worst trouble, befall Presidents from their staffs? Do inherent weaknesses lurk in the nature and functioning of the staff that makes it trouble-prone? One characteristic on which attention has focused is the close secrecy in which the staff's work is shrouded. Its personal and confidential relationship with the President is protected by the ready application of the doctrine of executive privilege, a shield that was penetrated only with the greatest difficulty even when the staff was clearly implicated in the Watergate crimes.

Some former members of the White House staff contend that to function in that capacity is to pursue the life of the courtier, that all too frequently the staff tell its boss only what it thinks he likes to hear. The staff, therefore, is adept at bringing him good news, but loathe to report bad news or anything else unwelcome to the Chief Executive. History-conscious staff members well remember that kings of old expressed their gratitude to messengers from the battlefield who reported that the fight was going badly by slaying them.

Too many staff members know little about democracy, and care less for its values and processes, a fatal fault of the Nixon staff. If staff members are mostly concerned with political power and have little interest in program or policy, the evidence suggests, they are more susceptible to sliding into acts of criminality and subversion of the democratic order, than those committed to policy.

To control these difficulties, attention should be given to possible Senate confirmation of White House staff members who engage substantially in operations—Henry Kissinger, for example in his pre-Secretary of State service as Assistant for National Security Affairs. Normally the advice a staff member gives the President is confidential, but administrative operations ensuing from that advice are carried on by a department or agency, subject to Congressional review. If both advice and operations are concentrated in a White House figure, that executive activity is removed from external review and debate, a condition hardly in accord with democracy. Senate confirmation of this type of staff member would permit a probing of his views and a review of his background and competence, which might make the President more careful in selecting staff, and shun appointments of the weakly qualified.

A danger to be avoided is the White House staff heavily loaded with individuals of the same background or with a common outlook. A healthier arrangement would be a mixed staff, of varied backgrounds and expertise, that might include some appointees with program competence and others with political experience in national, state, or local public affairs, through officeholding, campaign management, or incumbency in party posts. Still others might be drawn from private enterprise, the law firms, and universities, and others from the civil service, whose knowledge of the workings of the federal bureaucracy could be invaluable to Presidents. Some staff members should possess a kind of occupational independence, who can quit at any time for other employment, an option that is apt to foster self-confidence and greater candor with the President. In Johnson's Presidency, Bill Moyers, with an awaiting journalistic career, was of this genre, and he was able to function as one of a few of the staff who could speak more frankly to the President on the Vietnam War and other issues. (Of course, since the White House staff is largely a mirror of the President, it follows that the readiest way to acquire a well-functioning White House staff, compatible with democracy, is to elect good Presidents.)

19

THE PRESIDENCY
and CIVIL RIGHTS
by Roy Wilkins

The civil-rights movement for black American citizens is based, as are civil rights for all citizens, directly upon the Declaration of Independence, written, in large part, by Thomas Jefferson. In these days of sophistication and cynicism, many Americans are inclined not to believe fully in what has been called the American Dream. It may well be, as the United States celebrates its second centennial, that Negro citizens, as a class, still believe, more fervently than most, in Jefferson's immortal prose. From the earliest days they have built their arguments for equal treatment on the principles of the Declaration of Independence. The moral argument is the core of their moves to achieve equality.

Some liberal blacks, largely intellectuals, detect a variety of unflattering motives for President Abraham Lincoln's Emancipation Proclamation of 1863. Yet these theories do not contradict the fact that Lincoln's action ultimately led to freedom for some four million black slaves. The President who freed these slaves did so regardless of his motivation, and historians have taken full advantage of the high moral purpose of this move. Needless to say, the millions of descendants of the slaves of that day are unconcerned with the niceties of motivation. They know that their ancestors were chattel property one day and free men the next—with all the headaches that freedom brings with it.

The years after President Abraham Lincoln's assassination

were dark ones for the civil-rights movement. There was the rise of the Ku Klux Klan and of widespread lynching. There were the Black Codes, which were a group of vagrancy and apprenticeship laws binding the freedmen to the land in the Southern states. The Hayes-Tilden compromise, so-called, took federal troops away from the Southern states and thereby allowed elements of the Southern population to solve their race problem as they saw fit. In the decades after Reconstruction, most Southern states effectively disenfranchised blacks by passing a literacy test, poll-tax, and even grandfather-clause laws. In effect, these actions and laws were an attempt to nullify the Thirteenth, Fourteenth, and Fifteenth Amendments to the Constitution and the emancipation itself.

Permissive interpretation of the Constitution was given the blessing of the United States Supreme Court in the 1896 opinion in the case of *Plessy* v. *Ferguson*. The opinion held, simply, that the Constitution was not violated by the Louisiana law which required the two races to be separated on railroad trains. In his lone and vigorous dissenting opinion, Mr. Justice John M. Harlan prophetically stated that the enforcement of the interpretation would "place in a condition of legal inferiority a large body of American citizens."

The *Plessy* doctrine of "separate but equal" did in fact force a legal inferiority upon black citizens. The doctrine spread from railroad Jim Crow coaches to voting, to public education, to employment and pay rates, to housing, to the administration of justice, and to virtually every facet of American life. In none of these was there equality. The black population would spend the next fifty-eight years (until 1954) striving to throw off the evil effects of *Plessy*. This period, until about World War I, has been described as "the nadir" of race relations in the United States.

President Woodrow Wilson, however much he declared for peace between nations, did little to solve the race problem at home. What little he did was negative and was rooted in the strict separatism of the day. For instance, he instituted separate toilets for the races in every federal building in Washington.

President Hoover did nothing to upset the racial apple cart of his predecessors. In a nation faced by worldwide depression, he never conferred with a single black delegation, except one of the Negro political figures near the end of his administration. Hoover's nomination of Judge John J. Parker of North Carolina for the United

States Supreme Court was viewed as an insult to black Americans. It was generally believed that Judge Parker was opposed to Negro suffrage. As a gubernatorial candidate in 1920, he stated that "the participation of the Negro in politics is a source of evil and danger to both races and is not desired by the wise men in either race or by the Republican Party of North Carolina." The Senate rejected Parker's nomination and this signaled the emergence of the black vote in the North.

President Franklin D. Roosevelt, while thoroughly neutral on the Negro question, made a bow to the growing political strength of the Negro voter through his Black Cabinet. This was made up of advisers, assistants, consultants, and others who dealt with the racial aspects of the various projects of the administration. President Roosevelt was not a Negro partisan and had not named any to important offices in New York State, but he had the task of fighting his nation out of a great depression. He included the blacks in the steps to national recovery, although some of the recovery codes called for wages to be lower in sections of the country where blacks were employed in substantial numbers than where whites formed the majority. President Roosevelt, of course, had Mrs. Eleanor Roosevelt as his ace on political, social, and racial questions. She was a remarkable woman and had almost a one-hundred-percent following among black citizens. She not only addressed the big Negro organizations but could be found as the speaker for many small black groups. She served several terms as a member of the national board of the NAACP.

It is fair to state that President Roosevelt gave impetus to the civil-rights movement through his pragmatic recognition of the growth and importance of the black vote. The Negro voter was an integral part of the big-city vote, which in turn was basic to the FDR strategy. FDR welcomed him, made no moves calculated to alienate him, and upon FDR's death in 1945 black voting strength was a part of the coalition.

President Harry S. Truman added to the pragmatism of the FDR machine a personal warmth on civil rights. He named a commission to report on a riot at Columbia, Tennessee, in 1946. Its report, "To Secure These Rights," used for the first time the sentence "Segregation must be barred from American life." Shortly after he sent the legislative proposals to the Congress in a special message on February 2, 1948, President Truman was chatting with a woman at a White House function who said that she was the Democratic national committeewoman from a Southern state. She chided him about the Columbia report, saying that he surely must have been joking. The President shut off all further chitchat by saying, "Madam, I do not joke about the Constitution."

President Truman further put himself on record with a speech to the NAACP convention in 1947 when he declared, "We can no longer afford the luxury of a leisurely attack upon prejudice and discrimination. . . . We cannot, any longer, await the growth of a will to action in the slowest state or the most backward community. Our national government must show the way."

The true courage of the man on this issue is found in his executive order "The Use of Negro Manpower," issued July 26, 1948. This order was the beginning of the end of segregation by race in the U.S. armed services. Truman had just been nominated by the Democratic convention in Philadelphia, where four Deep South states had withdrawn and set up a third party. His party had just adopted a civil-rights plank, strong for that day although weaker in today's language. There was little need, except to make clear his beliefs, for the issuance of the manpower order at that time. He could have waited, but he chose not to do so. He won by seventeen thousand strategic votes in Illinois after first causing a Chicago newspaper to print that wishful headline "Dewey Defeats Truman."

One did not make casual contact with General Dwight Eisenhower, even before he became President. I well remember the contrast between my meeting with the two Presidential candidates in the summer and fall of 1952. In August, the Democratic candidate, Governor Adlai Stevenson of Illinois, had been issuing from Springfield some analyses of current issues before the heavy campaign began. We in the Leadership Conference on Civil Rights, including the NAACP, were afraid that he did not have sufficient information and that he might confine his judgments and his published conclusions to his experiences in Illinois. A conference was arranged and he and I talked for two hours in a "feet-on-the-desk" meeting. The only other person in the room was Averell Harriman, who had asked to listen in. The only interruptions were connected with his campaign tour that was being put together. All others and all telephone calls were excluded. We had a wide-ranging exchange of ideas on minorities.

Several weeks later (some members of the NAACP board were anxious that our nonpartisan stand be maintained) I met with General Eisenhower in New York City. He came in flanked by an adviser and a public-relations man. The "feet-on-the-desk" air was definitely out. The answers to all questions were as correct as could be. Everything was formal, although I received the impression that his political party and not the general wanted it so.

President Eisenhower, however, continued in one small and important sector the efforts of those Presidents before him. He measured up to the needs of the hour when in 1957 he refused to permit the orders of a federal court, and of the federal government itself, to bow down to state power in Arkansas. Governor Orval Faubus had defied an order of a United States district court to desegregate Central High School in Little Rock. He had used the ultimate in state power, the Arkansas National Guard. Troopers used drawn and fixed bayonets to bar nine Negro students from the school. President Eisenhower was not about to have the federal courts met with defiance, especially in a military setting the general knew by heart. After Faubus conferred at the White House, the President federalized the Arkansas National Guard. Thereafter the order of the federal court system was carried out.

The decade of the sixties, when the civil-rights issue exploded in city after city across the nation, began with the election campaign of John Fitzgerald Kennedy and his inauguration in January 1961. The causes of the unrest had been sown years before with the disillusionment of all blacks, but particularly the youth, by the stubborn resistance to the implementation of the Supreme Court ruling in the famous case of *Brown* v. *Board of Education of Topeka* (1954). In that unanimous opinion the Court had held that segregated education, by law, was unconstitutional. Despite the confrontation in Little Rock, the black population had become impatient with the slow pace of desegregation (less than one percent a year in 1960) and began nationwide sit-ins, marches, peaceful protests, violence, burning, and rioting.

President Kennedy excited among blacks the same hope for a new day and a new generation for social change that was manifest among whites. He dashed the expectations of many blacks, however, when he announced before his inauguration that he would ask for no civil-rights legislation. His attitude against requesting civil-rights legislation was maintained for a time with firmness, but with the well-known Kennedy charm. President Kennedy met the members of the NAACP national board in the White House in 1961, part of a special train delegation of twenty-two hundred persons

President Kennedy meets with leaders of the NAACP. *NAACP*

taking one day from the Philadelphia convention to lobby in Washington. JFK listened carefully to a brief statement read by the chairman of the board, Bishop Stephen G. Spottswood. He smiled affably, gallantly saw to it that every woman in the delegation had a comfortable chair, and then proceeded calmly and in good humor to explain why he was persisting in his course and why no legislation would be introduced.

He toyed with the idea until the spring of 1963. The events of

May 1963 in Birmingham, Alabama, where the followers of the Rev. Dr. Martin Luther King, Jr., had their experiences with water hoses and police dogs, caused him to waver. The final straw was the assassination of Medgar W. Evers, NAACP state director for Mississippi. Evers was slain June 12. On June 19, President Kennedy used a television speech to ask the nation and the Congress for enactment of an omnibus civil-rights bill.

That summer of 1963 was to be a crowded one. More than 220,000 persons, an estimated 40,000 of them white, came in person to the March on Washington, which was held on August 28, 1963. No one who was there will forget the occasion. President Kennedy had endorsed the march against the advice of those who thought the day would end in violence. After hearing the last speech of the day, Dr. Martin Luther King's "I Have a Dream," the huge crowd went home without violence.

The President was pleased that his judgment had been vindicated. More than two hundred members of both houses of the Congress had been present at one time or another before the huge throng at the Lincoln Memorial. Government employees who had the day off came, ignoring the "warnings" issued by some federal agencies (which had a nasty tone) to "stay in their homes and lock their doors." The plain implication was that thousands of black people would be in town and no one could tell what they might do. President Kennedy invited the leaders of ten civil-rights organizations to the White House and served refreshments as they rested and reviewed the events of the day that would go down in American history. Hardly had the March on Washington passed, when four little black girls were bombed to death in a Birmingham church. Then came the tragic assassination of President Kennedy himself on November 22, 1963.

As soon as the funeral was held, President Lyndon Johnson asked a joint session of the Congress to enact the JFK tax bill and omnibus civil-rights bill without delay. Both passed in the House and Senate.

At best Mr. Johnson had a modest record on the issue of civil rights during his long political career in the House and Senate, although he did vote for the 1957 civil-rights bill, and this raised questions about the reasons for his sudden intense interest in the voting rights of Negro Americans. I do not know what Johnson's exact reasons were, but his concern seemed genuine. Perhaps it was that he started life as a poor man and generally speaking a poor population is better understood by a poor man than a rich one.

During the early 1960s he gave much thought to the Negro question. As Vice-President, his address to the Tufts College commencement and especially his address at the Gettysburg battlefield were what any civil-rights activist might have wished to be said. When I saw him after he had returned from Senegal, he was looking over a book of photographs presented to him by photographers who accompanied him on the trip. Suddenly he said, "You know, Roy, I saw the same wish for the black babies by the black mothers of Senegal that I had seen in the eyes of the blue-eyed Texas mothers. All mothers everywhere want the best for their children."

Maybe the realization of this truth helped LBJ in his work to widen the opportunities for blacks. It made him, indeed, the Southern President who did the most for the Negro. Johnson's concern was amply demonstrated in his personally sponsored Voting Rights Act of 1965. No other President in history had introduced a civil-rights bill with such fanfare. First he requested prime time on evening television. Second, he himself addressed a joint session of both houses of the Congress during that time. The Cabinet was there, as were the members of the Supreme Court. The leaders of civil-rights organizations and other prominent and interested citizens were in the gallery. Finally, the American people were present through their television sets. And, of course, the marchers from Selma, Alabama, were there in spirit.

The President said, "This was the first nation in the history of the world to be founded with a purpose. The great phrases of that purpose still sound in every American heart, North and South: 'All men are created equal'—'Government by consent of the governed.' Those are not just clever words. Those are not just empty theories. Those words are a promise to every citizen that he shall share in the dignity of man."

The Voting Rights Act of 1965 was passed and signed into law. The Fair Housing Act of 1968 rounded out the civil-rights legislation. As a result of the Voting Rights Act, black Americans have already elected more than 110 black mayors, including those in Los Angeles, Detroit, Atlanta, Gary, Newark, Raleigh, and

Tuskegee. They now have about 3,000 black elected officials, including 16 Congressmen and Congresswomen, one U.S. Senator, and many state legislators. The violence, which caused President Johnson to appoint a Presidential Commission on Civil Disorders in 1967, has been channeled into political activity.

President Johnson and Roy Wilkins. *NAACP*

President Nixon's record was a disappointment to black Americans. He exhibited a coldness, even an active hostility toward civil rights. His successor, Gerald Ford, ended this closed-door policy when he invited a group of local and national civil-rights leaders along with a sprinkling of black elected officials to the White House and assured them of his desire to listen to their problems.

However, Ford had only a passable voting record on civil rights while he was a member of the House of Representatives. Like many of his former Michigan Congressional colleagues, Ford was against the busing of children to desegregate the public schools. He bluntly but not truculently has maintained this position even after becoming Chief Executive. Most black citizens also were dismayed at his approach to employment, prices, and inflation. There seemed to be no recognition in Washington that unemployment among blacks is two or three times the national rate, while black teenage unemployment is around forty percent.

President Ford is a "good guy" with a cheery greeting but he does not seem to do much. Black citizens who get it "in the neck" for just being black are cheered genuinely by a job and a paycheck rather than a greeting. Blacks have a few words for their President: "He mean so good, but do so po'."

Despite recent disappointments, black citizens feel that these dark days are but an interlude that, like Wilson's administration, will be followed by the forward surge under Truman, Kennedy, Johnson, and even Eisenhower. The civil-rights cause has paused at one of its peaks to acknowledge what drives us forward toward this goal: "Our lives," said President Johnson, "have been marked with debate about great issues. . . . But rarely in any time does an issue lay bare the secret heart of America itself. Rarely are we met with a challenge, not to our growth or abundance, our welfare or our security, but rather to the values and the purposes and the meaning of our beloved nation."

20

PRESIDENTIAL ATTITUDES
and POLICIES TOWARD
CITY and SUBURB
by Stanley Buder

The American Presidency, though over one hundred and eighty-five years old, has had significant influence on the shaping of the American city and suburb only for the last few decades. For the first century and a half, then, as American cities grew to be major metropolitan areas and acted as the forging ground for a new urban-industrial order, their development was a matter of official indifference not only to the Presidents, but also to the entire federal system of government.

This is indeed startling—more so when compared to countries such as Britain in the nineteenth century. There Parliament appointed select committees and royal commissions to investigate urban conditions, while passing a rich skein of legislation pertaining to housing, sanitary-reform, and slum-clearance projects. Nothing comparable would occur in the United States until the 1930s, and even then only as the result of the added pressures brought about by a serious depression.

Part of the explanation is to be found in a federal system, which began with the premise that community problems should and would be left completely to local government without interference from Washington. Such an approach, reflected in a constitution of enumerated and delegated powers, did not receive initial challenge until after the Civil War, and then only briefly.

Even local government, however, was reluctant to act in

community matters when they involved private property. This was especially true of issues related to land and buildings, the most typical and useful forms of private wealth in a precapitalistic society. The absence of Presidential involvement in nineteenth-century urban problems is understandable in the context of this laissez faire attitude that prevailed for most of the century among municipal governments. Thus land developers and speculative builders were allowed to develop the nineteenth-century city without effective checks or restraints from any form of government.

American institutions and values at the nation's start reflected the fact that less than five percent of the population lived in cities. This being the case, existing institutions were obviously inadequate to cope with the coming century's unprecedented urban growth. Only with great reluctance would they be adjusted to meet the new needs of a transformed nation.

Thomas Jefferson, in his inaugural address of March 1805, predicted that the nation would enjoy a virtually limitless supply of unsettled land that would suffice to meet the needs of countless generations; such abundance of space would allow, Jefferson hoped, for the avoidance of the congested cities of Europe with their stark contrast between the rich and the poor. Jefferson's animadversion to the city is, of course, well known. In 1800 he asserted, "I view great cities as pestilential to the morals, the health and the liberties of man." As American cities grew, and New York in the 1820s became the first to exceed a population of one hundred thousand, he found no reason to modify his views. In 1823 Jefferson wrote, "New York . . . seems to be a cloacena of all the depravities of human nature," while in rural Virginia "crime is scarcely heard of, breaches of order rare and our societies, if not refined, are rational, moral and affectionate at least."

Many Americans have shared with Jefferson the belief that the presence of large cities presaged ill for the continuing existence of American society and democracy. Starting in 1820, however, the growth of the urban population began to exceed that of the population as a whole. This trend once started would never be reversed. Towns in the West became cities as their boosters celebrated the wealth associated with rapid growth, while the older cities of the East swelled with the continuous influx of new arrivals. Chicago, a trading post on the shore of Lake Michigan with a few hundred settlers when it was incorporated as a city in 1832, had over a million and a half inhabitants seven decades later: a record of growth without precedent. By 1900 already three of the world's twelve cities with over a million population—New York, Chicago, and Philadelphia—were in the United States. The announcement by the Bureau of the Census that there was no longer an official frontier line, combined with the obvious massing of population in cities, made Americans aware of a changed nation. As the twentieth century opened, it could no longer be stated with pride, as Andrew Jackson had in 1829, that the nation was a happy countryside of "flocks and herds and cultivated farms, worked in seasonal rhythm and linked in republican community."

By 1860 sixteen percent of the population of the United States lived in cities; by 1900 it was thirty-five percent, and twenty years later it was over half the population. Increasingly the cities dominated the marketplace and reached out to influence the life styles of those beyond its borders. The relatively decentralized economy and self-contained communities of early nineteenth-century America was superseded by an urban-industrial society whose keynote was the complex and intricate interdependence of individuals and communities.

The problems of cities demanded attention, and slowly the federal government responded. In 1892 Congress appropriated a small sum of money, twenty thousand dollars, to investigate tenement conditions in cities of two hundred thousand or more population. With turbulent, poorly housed immigrant masses filling the cities, another byproduct of growing concern was the passage in 1896 of a literacy test for newcomers. In his last days of office President Grover Cleveland vetoed the measure, explaining that it was a repudiation of our historic role as an asylum for the oppressed. An immigration law was enacted in February 1917, however, over Woodrow Wilson's veto. After the war, the Johnson-Read Act became law in 1924 with the support of Calvin Coolidge. Its avowed intention was to maintain the "racial preponderance [of] the basic strain of our people" by setting national quotas designed to discriminate against southern and eastern Europeans.

One consequence of this legislation was to encourage American blacks, who started the century as an essentially Southern rural group, to migrate northward to the cities to replace the immigrant as a reservoir of cheap, unskilled urban labor. Federal action would thus have grave, albeit unintended, consequences for the cities. As immigrant neighborhoods began to change into black ghettos, the stage would be set for group conflict and white flight. John F. Kennedy, himself the grandson of immigrants and author of *A Nation of Immigrants*, made reform of the national quotas a major goal of his administration. In 1965 under President Lyndon Johnson a more liberal and nondiscriminatory bill was passed.

Calvin Coolidge epitomized the traditional rural identification of the Presidency. *U.S. Information Agency, Courtesy National Archives*

In the early years of the twentieth century, until entry into World War I, the United States experienced a period of intensive interest in reform that historians have entitled the "Progressive Era." This marked the end of laissez faire and its replacement with an approach that has been characterized as social engineering. Interest by the federal government in influencing community development, however, would only become manifest in the 1920s.

It was the encouragement and assistance offered by the federal government that explains the speedy acceptance of zoning and planning regulations by American communities in that decade.

The emergence of modern city planning occurred during the Progressive Era. As an expression of a new concern with imposing a rational order on land use, New York City in 1916 adopted a zoning ordinance specifying the use, height, and bulk of new buildings. This was the first instance of zoning by an American city. Appointed Secretary of Commerce by Warren Harding in 1921, Herbert Hoover strongly supported zoning as a way that communities could guarantee that the public interest would be protected against overbuilding. In 1924 and again in 1928, Hoover called together experts to draft model enabling acts and also model zoning ordinances. By 1928 over sixteen hundred local governments had followed New York's lead. Zoning, contrary to expectations, had little impact on land-use patterns of the already built-up great American cities, except to offer an imprimatur to what had already occurred. Instead, its significance would be in shaping the smaller, newer communities—especially the American suburbs.

With the advent of various forms of mass transportation in the second half of the nineteenth century there developed an increasing tendency to build suburbs for the more affluent middle class. As metropolitan growth began to occur increasingly beyond the city's political boundaries, these middle-class communities resisted annexation to neighboring cities. The term *suburb*, which had initially suggested only an extension of the city, acquired its modern connotation as the physical and sociological antithesis of the great city.

By the 1920s, the rate of growth of the suburbs began to exceed that of the cities. By the 1970 census 76.3 million Americans lived in the metropolitan area outside the city, while only 63.9 million resided in core cities. In 1972 suburb and city had almost an equal number of jobs. Thus, the nineteenth-century trend toward urban concentration gave way to a new pattern of suburban diffusion. Unlike the process of urban increase, suburban growth received considerable federal support.

In 1931, Edith Elmer Wood published *Recent Trends in American Housing*, in which she asked for programs of financial assistance by government to erect model housing estates of garden apartments for the working class similar to those being built in Europe for the working class. Such an approach was too radical for Herbert Hoover. He was only interested in constructing privately owned, single-family, detached houses for the middle class. At a conference on Home Building and Home Ownership that he called in 1931, Hoover spoke of the pressing need to "make a home available for installment purchase on terms that dignify the name credit."

Hoover's attitude might well be compared to that of his opponent in 1928. Both Hoover and Al Smith were self-made men, but while Hoover started life in rural Iowa, Smith was a product of New York's Lower East Side. His jauntily angled derby, omnipresent cigar, and heavily inflected speech were the hallmarks of the Tammany politician. As his state's governor, Smith pursued a course charted by Bella Moskowitz, the social worker, which made New York a pioneer in a program of tax abatements for multifamily housing.

The 1931 conference foreshadowed the enactment of the Federal Home Loan Bank, the reform of mortgage-lending practices, and the establishment of the Federal Housing Administration. FDR in an early message to Congress stated that "the Nation required that special safeguards should be thrown around home ownership as a guarantee of social and economic stability." The consequential lengthening of time needed to amortize a mortgage and lowering of interest rates has significantly increased home ownership in the United States.

Federal mortgage subsidy programs combined with tax advantages have been a strong support to home ownership, but they have also reflected American values and influenced the development of city and suburb in other important ways. Federal mortgage policies until 1961 reflected a conservative, businesslike approach. To be eligible housing had to be relatively new, in good condition, and in a stable neighborhood. This meant that houses in racially mixed or blighted neighborhoods were viewed as bad risks. Most eligible housing, then, tended to be located in the new suburbs outside of the city lines. Thus, the drift of the white middle class to the suburbs was considerably accelerated by federal programs.

In the central city, as early as World War I, the federal government had erected sixteen thousand dwelling units for war workers, but this was looked upon as an emergency action. Unlike most European nations, where housing since the late nineteenth century has been thought of as a public utility and hence a suitable subject for governmental financing, the American government had looked toward the private market to remedy an inadequate housing situation. Then in the 1930s, the depression brought about a change of attitude.

Library of Congress

Roosevelt's administration, committed to economic relief and recovery, viewed experimentation as necessary. The Public Works Administration, to help the housing industry, built over fifty housing projects which were eventually turned over to local control in thirty cities. A coalition of social reformers, spearheaded by settlement-house workers and enlisting the assistance of Senator Robert

Wagner and Eleanor Roosevelt, pushed through the National Housing Act of 1937, though FDR had not extended it full support. Under this act over 170,000 units of public low-rent housing were constructed by 1942, when wartime needs forced the program to a halt.

In 1949, during the second term of the Truman administration, Congress enacted a second housing act. Its goals—"a decent home and a suitable living environment for every American family"—significantly broadened federal involvement in community affairs. By 1954, according to this act, 810,000 more units of public housing were to be constructed. However, the number actually built was only half that figure. By the early 1950s public housing had become embroiled in the politically sensitive issue of racially changing neighborhoods and the related controversy over whether projects should be located on vacant sites or in conjunction with slum clearance. Politically controversial, public housing became unpopular with Congress, city governments, and especially the Eisenhower administration. Even its former proponents began to have second thoughts about its desirability, at least as it was then administered. The 1949 Housing Act also included the highly important Title I, a program of federal subsidies for private redevelopment of blighted areas, known as "urban renewal" since 1954. By the early 1960s this program was also coming under fire.

The most important legislation to affect city and suburb during the Eisenhower years was the Federal-Aid Highway Act of 1956. Authorizing the outlay of over one hundred billion dollars to build intricate networks of limited-access expressways about the cities, it has probably done more to change the character and structure of metropolitan areas than any other single piece of federal legislation. Unquestionably, it speeded the "splatterdash growth" of suburbs, usually without adequate controls or planning. In the cities, it frequently led to the indiscriminate bulldozing of great swaths through irreplaceable historic and ethnic neighborhoods.

By 1961, when John F. Kennedy became the youngest elected President, the American city was clearly in trouble. The Democratic party since the New Deal has found much of its strength in the country's great cities with their immigrant and working-class population. JFK's slim victory in 1960 over Richard Nixon was clearly attributable to his great appeal to the population of cities and in his first State of the Union Message, he promised that we would "begin now to lay the foundation for liveable, efficient and attractive communities of the future." Soon Kennedy introduced an ambitious program directed at urban problems, with new approaches to such problems as open spaces and mass transportation, but much of this, including his efforts to create a new Cabinet position for a Secretary of Housing and Urban Development, was stymied by a reluctant Congress. Kennedy, however, by executive order in November 1962, did prohibit any form of discrimination in federally subsidized housing, and after his death the new department, called HUD, was established in late 1965.

In 1966 the Johnson administration launched its "model-cities project" as an effort to foster and finance on the federal level an experimental approach to the multifaceted problems of urban minority neighborhoods. Attempting a comprehensive attack on social ills, this act provided not only housing, but jobs, health- and day-care centers, and improved educational and community facilities. A key feature of the program was to be community involvement. At a time when American cities were gripped with apprehension over urban riots, and with heightened minority consciousness and militancy, the "model-cities" program was designed to avoid the charge of "another ripoff." But attempts to involve the community in decision making often aroused the suspicion of municipal officials who felt bypassed and threatened. Indeed, many in the white community viewed "model cities" as a boondoggle which came at their expense.

Johnson's Housing Act of 1968 set major housing goals for the nation: twenty-six million new housing units—six million of these for the poor—were to be built in a decade. Federal subsidy programs were to encourage various types of nonprofit or limited-profit housing for elements in the population historically short-shrifted by the private-building market, including the elderly and the lower middle class. Though loopholes in the law unquestionably allowed unscrupulous speculators to make millions, and certain programs, such as Section 235 housing—designed to allow the poor to buy homes—bogged down in inefficiency and corruption, the record of the Housing Act of 1968 was not without positive accomplishments.

Between 1969 and 1973, housing starts averaged over 2 million per year, and 1.5 million of these 8 million were designated for low-income families. Then in January 1973 President Nixon's administration placed a freeze on new federal-housing commitments. This moratorium has been lifted during the Ford Presidency, but the money allocated has been meager. Following the lead of his Republican predecessors Eisenhower and Nixon, Ford appears determined to reduce the scope of federal-housing programs. By the summer of 1975 experts were wondering whether the nation would achieve even half the goal of new housing set by the Housing Act of 1968 for the late seventies. Such Johnson programs as the Office of Economic Opportunity and "model cities" survived Nixon's administration, but only at a barely functioning level. The manner preferred by the Nixon administration for dispersal of federal money to state and local governments was "revenue sharing": the issuance of bloc grants that recipients may employ mostly at their own discretion, though some of the monies must be assigned to certain broad categories. A major problem in this approach is the need to establish criteria for determining federal allocations. Are they to be decided on the basis of past use of funds, population, need, or political considerations? Already a struggle between city and suburb over their distribution has occurred, and in the councils of Republican administrations the suburbs exert stronger political influence.

No matter the President or his policies, one fact is clear: local communities will remain in dire need of federal funds, for the federal income tax will continue nonpareil as a generator of governmental revenue. This is particularly true for the older center cities with their limited prospects for an expanding tax base. What remains to be seen is how this federal power will be employed. Kennedy and Johnson hoped to bring about social reform as well as encourage regional forms of land use and environmental planning. Their policies, experimental, often poorly conceived and stated, and coming in a decade troubled by momentous social change as well as involvement in Vietnam, were never permitted to achieve fruition. Nixon, especially after George Romney left as head of HUD, eased federal pressure on local governments for innovation and change. In the main, Gerald Ford has continued the hands-off policy he inherited. The absence of riots in the seventies has allowed Washington the luxury of pretending that the urban crisis is either over, or at least under control, and Ford has remained aloof from the obvious distress caused American communities by the serious economic problems of his first year in office.

Whether a new national mood will emerge, fostering once again strong Presidential leadership in policy making for city and suburb, only time will answer. A highly mobile population means that social ills generated in one geographical context freely cross state lines to cause problems for distant localities. Many environmental issues cannot be attended to even on the state level, and will require forms of controls that can only emanate from Washington and the recently created Environmental Protection Agency. The distinctions once drawn between local problems and national issues by the Founding Fathers of this nation have been unalterably blurred by two centuries of urban and technological development.

The twentieth century has inevitably experienced the extension of federal power to the communities, yet few Presidents—with the exception of Johnson, and perhaps Kennedy if he had lived—have tried to identify their administrations with a program of remaking the physical and social organization of cities and suburbs. Much of importance has been done but, with the exception of federal assistance to the mortgage market, there has been little consistency, commitment, or comprehensiveness.

Part of the explanation for this may be found in the background of the twentieth-century Presidents. Until Kennedy none of these Presidents were born in this century, and almost all had prided themselves on rural and small-town origins. Such a background, though often identified in America with rock-bottom virtues, usually provided little sensitivity to the diverse needs of a metropolitan society. It would not be difficult to demonstrate that the Presidents from Theodore Roosevelt to Dwight Eisenhower shared, as did their predecessors earlier, a Jeffersonian animus to the city. FDR once warned that the "growth of cities, while the country population stands still will . . . bring disaster." Truman as a Senator in 1937 claimed that "a thousand county-seat towns of 7,000 people each are a thousand times more important to this Republic than one city of 7,000,000."

It is only in the last four decades that federal policy has directly and intentionally influenced the destiny of local communities. Even a cursory review of this legislation reveals it in the main piecemeal, short range, and after the fact. The ultimate accomplishment of Presidential policy in the twentieth century, then, is that a commitment to healthy, safe, and open communities offering equal opportunity, decent housing, and an adequate range of social services to all Americans has been made. If this commitment is not honored, we may indeed, in the words of President Johnson's Commission on Crimes of Violence, "expect further social fragmentation of the urban environment, formation of excessively parochial communities, greater segregation of different racial groups and economic classes . . . and polarization of attitudes on a variety of issues."

21

THE PRESIDENTS
and the PRESS
by John W. Tebbel

When George Washington departed for Mount Vernon at the end of his Presidency, he left behind him, among other things, a record of almost unbroken antagonism, even hatred, toward the only medium of any consequence at the time—the newspapers. As a parting shot, he canceled his subscriptions to some thirty papers and gave an exclusive on his Farewell Address to the only newspaper in Philadelphia that had consistently supported him.

Washington got over it, though. He renewed most of his subscriptions in retirement and spent the last evening of his life reading the newspapers and discussing the news with his faithful secretary, Tobias Lear. Other Presidents similarly have recovered from their quarrels with the press, but there has not been one Chief Executive who did not consider himself unfairly used by the media, and only Jefferson fully comprehended the role of the press in the American system, whose creation was so much the product of his intellect.

The multifaceted assault of the Nixon administration on First Amendment freedoms, with the resulting increased hostility toward the press among large numbers of Americans, has brought into sharp focus once more the constitutional role of the press. At the same time it has disclosed the lack of understanding, not only by this President and his supporters in Congress, but by the public generally, of what the Founding Fathers meant that role to be.

In the simplest terms, the First Amendment was added to the Constitution because the American people wanted a guarantee that the press would be wholly free to act as a buffer between the governors and the governed.

The press, it must be added, was not a responsible institution at that time, nor for a long time afterward. Before the Revolution, it had been a propaganda organ for both patriots and Tories, and afterward it was settling into a dark period when it would be the political tool of the Federalists and their opponents. But the citizens, or at least many of them, who were called upon to ratify the Constitution were old enough to remember that the newspapers had been their chief weapon since 1721 in the long struggle for freedom from British rule, and they were determined to keep it free from control by any succeeding government that might be oppressive. Their determination is evident in the wording of the amendment—"Congress shall make no law" abridging freedom of the press, or of speech.

For some time after ratification, the politicians and their parties were too busy using the press as a controlled weapon to advance their interests to think of it in any other terms—that is, as an independent medium. Thus, when Washington railed against the press, as he frequently did, he meant the opposition newspapers. The first President, however, was not even comfortable with the papers of his own party that were supporting him. His was essentially the aristocratic view of the Virginia planter: the press made loud, vulgar noises; it was violent in tone; and it permitted mere printers and the politicians who financed them to attack the work of statesmen whose minds were on higher things.

From the beginning there was a power struggle between the Presidents and the press. Congress could be opposed through the veto and party manipulation. The Supreme Court could be controlled, in a sense, if a President was able to make enough of his own appointments—as witnessed by the conservative cast of the Nixon Court. The press was a different matter. There were the libel laws, of course, and Presidents would try that route and fail. But short of measures that would be obviously unconstitutional, there was no way to prevent the press from being the watchdog over government that the ratifiers of the Bill of Rights intended it to be.

The pattern of the struggle that has continued since Washing-

ton's time was set in his administration in 1795 when John Jay
brought back from London the treaty he had negotiated there. It
was a document that was already highly controversial before anyone
but a few people knew what was in it. Many Jeffersonian
Republicans were prepared to oppose it on principle. Washington
hoped to avoid trouble by conferring secretly with the Senate over
the treaty and trying to reach agreement with that body before the
document was disclosed to the public. But the Republican's leading
publisher, young Benjamin Franklin Bache, affectionately known as
"Lightning Rod Junior" in memory of his illustrious grandfather,
published in his Philadelphia paper, the *General Advertiser*, better
known as the *Aurora*, an account of what the treaty contained. It
was so full of inaccuracies that a Virginia Senator, fearful of the
consequences, leaked a copy of the whole document to Bache, who
not only printed it in full but denounced it in a pamphlet published
separately.

With that a storm of criticism burst upon Washington and the
administration, zealously fed by the Republican newspapers. The
President, said Bache, "had violated the Constitution and made a
treaty with a nation abhorred by our people; that he had answered
the respectful remonstrances of Boston and New York as if he were
the omnipotent director of a seraglio, and had thundered contempt
upon the people with as much confidence as if he had sat upon the
throne of Industan." That was the mildest of the abuse. Tom Paine,
in an open letter, called Washington a "hypocrite in public life" and
questioned whether he ever had any principles.

Washington was outraged but he was not the kind of man to
move against the press directly. He confined himself to angry
outbursts in private and in the pages of his correspondence. John
Adams, who succeeded him, was a different man. The abuse of the
opposition press set him so violently against the media that he
signed into law the infamous Alien and Sedition Acts. Adams
believed the press should present America in the best possible light,
and he was against carrying on political controversies in the papers.
He and the Federalists, however, made a fatal error in supporting
the Alien and Sedition Acts. They were so clearly unconstitutional
that they became a key factor in the collapse of the Federalist party,
which was hastened by the unrelenting assault of the Republican

press. Adams never forgave the newspapers, although he continued to write for them after he left office.

Jefferson was attacked as violently as Washington and Adams had been, but he had learned something from observing the First Amendment in action. He interpreted it as absolute, believing it was more important to be informed than to be governed. He hoped at the beginning to put himself and the Presidency above partisan squabbling. Failing, he defended the right of his press critics to print anything they chose.

One story about Jefferson illustrates perhaps better than anything else the difference between his clear-sighted view of the press and the obfuscation that prevails today. The Prussian ambassador was waiting to see Jefferson one morning and happened to pick up in the President's outer office one of the more vituperative Federalist gazettes. He was so angered by it that when he was admitted to Jefferson's presence, he waved the paper indignantly and exclaimed, "Mr. President, why do you permit such things to be printed?" "Put that paper in your pocket, Baron," Jefferson said, "and should you ever hear the reality of our liberty, the freedom of the press questioned, show them this paper—and tell them where you found it."

By the time James Madison became President, the major papers were paying much more attention to the news. The political parties had largely lost control of them, and independent editors had come into being. There were now newspapers operated by private citizens, not necessarily printers, capable of expressing their dissent against the government and the party in power on behalf of other citizens of like mind, who might be in the minority. Ironically it was Madison, who had done so much to ensure the adoption of First Amendment freedoms, who became the first victim of the new order.

The issue was the War of 1812, which Samuel Eliot Morison has called "the most unpopular war that this country has ever waged, not even excepting the Vietnam conflict." New England was the center of dissent. There elements of the Federalist press were among the prime movers in a plan that would, in effect, have created a new constitution and eliminated New England from the Union through secession.

For the first time, the question was raised: how far should press criticism go in wartime? The war may have been wrong, but for a time it appeared that the British would win it and the survival of the country was threatened. In that context, the kind of opposition proposing nonsupport and secession carried on in New England by the Boston *Columbian Centinal,* a rabid Federalist organ, was treasonous. Yet Madison did not even consider censoring it or closing it down, nor did he move against another dissenter much closer to home, the Georgetown *Republican.* However, in that case his supporters revived the mob rule that had destroyed newspapers and injured editors in previous years. They not only demolished the paper's shop twice, but in the end killed one of its editors, James Lingan, and maimed for life another, "Light Horse Harry" Lee. Both men had been generals and heroes of the Revolution.

These events were followed in time by the paradox of Andrew Jackson. Here was a popular President, elevated to the White House by a grass-roots revolt against the Eastern establishment, who demonstrated his faith in a free press by establishing his own newspaper, operated by his closest intimates, which became the official propaganda organ of the Presidency. The Washington *Globe* was founded by means of a pressure campaign which resulted in six hundred of the President's friends subscribing in advance, and it became the best-read paper both at home and abroad because it was a reliable index to what Jackson might be thinking and planning.

Establishing the *Globe* was only one evidence of Jackson's shrewd awareness of what a controlled press could do for an incumbent President. In distributing patronage, he brazenly gave out jobs to the editors who had supported him, thus guaranteeing their continued help. Thus Jackson's answer to a dissenting press was not to attempt to stifle it, but to create a kept press and overwhelm it with the authority of the Presidency.

As the press continued to evolve toward its present-day pattern, a new phase began in 1835 with the establishment of the *New York Herald* by James Gordon Bennett, Sr. Within little more than fifteen years, he was competing with Horace Greeley's *Tribune* and Henry J. Raymond's *New York Times.* These three papers became the country's leading opinion makers, powerful independent organs, two of whose publishers, Greeley and Raymond, were nevertheless directly involved in party politics. Presidents and other politicians were compelled to take the support or nonsupport of these papers into account, and for the first time people began to talk seriously about the "power of the press."

Yet, in the War of 1812, the dissenting press had shown that it could not bring a President down, nor even, in the case of the Georgetown paper, save itself from the mob. The question of its power was now raised again in the Mexican War of 1846, which offered a preview of the conflict between the Presidency and the press over Vietnam.

In brief, the Mexican War was one of the democratic process's more sordid failures, which divided the country and both parties, whose minorities were unable to stop it. The opposition press could not stop it either, although President James K. Polk was attacked with every weapon in the newspapers' armament. The sheer persistence of the press, however, in mercilessly exposing the Polk administration's efforts to justify the unconscionable, had its ultimate effect. This opposition helped to obtain a treaty that was adopted in a form Polk did not want to accept. There is good reason to believe the treaty would have been even harsher than it was, and much more of Mexico unjustly taken, if it had not been for the dissent which the press brought into focus.

The greatest crisis between the President and the media, before Vietnam and Watergate, occurred during the Civil War. Abraham Lincoln was conscious that his nomination had been achieved by the maneuverings of two Chicago newspaper editors, Joseph Medill and Charles Ray, but as a man of principle he did not hesitate to repudiate the high-level patronage promises they had made on his behalf, and without his knowledge, to get the necessary votes on the convention floor. Once in the White House, he used the newspapers astutely as sounding boards, speaking openly to reporters assigned to cover him and even consulting them during the war if they had firsthand information from the battlefields. In a sense, he began the Presidential press conference, although on a purely informal basis.

But Lincoln had his priorities and the salvation of the Union was at the top of the list. Consequently he permitted widespread censorship and suppression of the press, on a scale not seen since the founding of the republic. There was a thriving "Copperhead" press, as opponents of the war were called, and some of its editors were thrown into jail with no formal charges ever filed against them. Telegraph companies were censored, and Union generals were allowed to suppress papers on their own initiative. Mob censorship appeared again, and Copperhead papers were destroyed and their editors tarred and feathered. Yet Lincoln, with a patience reminiscent of Jefferson, drew back constantly from imposing total control on the media, as it was in his power to do. Most of the Copperhead press continued to function throughout the war.

The white-hot passions of the war deprived newspapers of whatever progress in the direction of objectivity they might have attained. That led not only to the virulent assault on Lincoln in the opposition press, but also to the abuse of the exceptional freedom that correspondents, known as "specials," enjoyed in covering the war's battles. They traveled with the armies, saw the action at firsthand, and wrote whatever they liked until questions arose as to whether their uninhibited reporting was endangering the lives of soldiers by revealing troop movements and other military details. The contest between the press and the military came to a head when General William T. Sherman arrested a *Tribune* correspondent; he would have had him shot as a spy if Lincoln himself had not intervened. That event had the sobering effect of bringing both sides together to work out a system of accreditation, much as exists today.

The power of the Presidency and the newly found power of the press was at a standoff, then, when the war ended. Until that time, however, the newspapers had been playing only two roles in American life: first as propaganda weapons in the hands of the political parties, and, with the coming of the Civil War, as collectors and purveyors of news on a scale not seen before.

With the accession of Ulysses S. Grant to the Presidency, the media began to develop the function for which they are presently celebrated—investigative reporting. Grant was no sooner in the White House than the newspapers began to report a series of events which the President took no particular pains to conceal. In the usual list of patronage appointments were forty-eight of his kinsmen. His rich friends who had helped finance his way to the White House began to shower him with expensive gifts, notably three houses, one worth sixty thousand dollars, and another worth one hundred thousand dollars. Since this kind of corruption had been going on for so long, it did not at once disturb the consciences of many in the electorate. The papers also were reporting that the husband of Grant's sister was involved in a conspiracy to rig the gold market, and the President was made a part of the plot, although that could not be proved. In any case, this fraud led to a disastrous collapse in the market. Even then, in an era of unregulated boom-and-bust finance, many voters were inclined to put the whole episode down to bad luck, and in fact most of the country's newspapers presumed the President to be innocent as he prepared to run for reelection in 1872. In spite of the evidence accumulating almost daily in the news columns, the voters agreed and sent Grant back to the White House.

In his second inaugural address, the President declared that he had been "the subject of abuse and slander scarcely ever equaled in political history." While these words were still ringing down the editorial pages, investigative reporters disclosed that the Vice-President and others in the administration had accepted stock in return for helping the dishonest promoters of the Union Pacific Railway. In 1876, the *New York Herald*, soon joined by other papers, began to dissect the corruption in the War Department which resulted in the impeachment of Secretary of War William W. Belknap for taking bribes. He resigned to avoid trial, but the Senate acquitted him anyway. Almost incidentally, it was revealed that the President's brother Orvil was involved in this affair.

Then came the exposure by the *St. Louis Democrat* of the Whiskey Ring fraud, a conspiracy of revenue officials, led by a Grant appointee, to defraud the government of tax money. A total of 238 people were indicted, including the President's private secretary, who was saved only by Grant's personal intervention. After all this, in his final message to Congress, Grant referred to the criminal events of his administration as "errors of judgment," wrapping himself in the Presidency and blaming others for the nearly total corruption.

By the time William McKinley was elected, the lines were clearly drawn and the press had assumed its role as the people's watchdog over government which the architects of the First Amendment had envisioned. It was a power once again abused, however, as a large segment of the press, reflecting the wave of national jingoism, helped push McKinley slowly and reluctantly into the war with Spain. The flamboyant, sensational coverage given the war by Joseph Pulitzer's *New York World* and William Randolph Hearst's *New York Journal*, was a further abuse in itself. But the press in general redeemed itself with its investigative exposure of American atrocities in the Philippines (recalling the Mylai massacre), which the administration and the Army had assiduously tried to suppress.

The crusading that had begun with Grant reached its climax in the years of Theodore Roosevelt's White House tenure. Roosevelt made considerable political capital of the role in which he cast himself as a "trustbuster," but when the crusading newspapers and magazines attacked the evils of these same trusts, the President called them "muckrakers," and so they came to be known.

On the eve of the election of 1908, Pulitzer's *World* disclosed the results of its investigation of the Panama Canal financing, involving administration figures and possibly the President himself. Roosevelt had hated this newspaper since his glory days in the Spanish-American War, when one of the *World's* correspondents, Stephen Crane, wrote a somewhat less than complimentary account of the famed charge up San Juan Hill. Now the President was so outraged by the canal story that he tried to get Pulitzer indicted and thrown into jail.

Once again the question was raised: how far could the press go in criticizing a President? In the several actions resulting from this test, the courts, including the Supreme Court on appeal, ruled in effect that the federal government could not sue a newspaper for criminal libel in its own courts. Nevertheless, and for the first time, a President had attempted to assert the doctrine that the rights of the Chief Executive superseded the First Amendment or any other law that happened to interfere with Presidential authority.

The gulf between that authority, which had been steadily growing, and the right of the press to challenge it appeared to be increasing. No President, regardless of party, seemed to understand or accept the press's freedom. Woodrow Wilson, presumably a liberal Democrat, began his term in office by declaring that he believed in "pitiless publicity" for public business, and indeed he instituted the first formal White House press conferences. But he ended by writing a friend, "Don't believe anything you read in the newspapers." That could certainly have been said with truth in the years of World War I, when civil liberties and the First Amendment were virtually suspended and the press became little more than a propaganda arm of the government, as it had been a hundred years before. Before America's entry, however, Wilson could not tolerate the interest of the press in his private life, which he seemed to think was no different from that of any other citizen, and afterward he was shocked and angered by the attack of the opposition press on the League of Nations.

FDR broadcasts via radio. *Franklin D. Roosevelt Library*

The modern era of press-government relations is often said to have begun with the accession of Warren Harding, the only publisher ever to occupy the White House. He began with the best press relations any President ever enjoyed and ended by demanding that the administration, and particularly the Cabinet, rocked by the

Teapot Dome scandal, be given good publicity by the newspapers or else offending journalists and their newspapers would be excommunicated by the White House.

With the advent of radio and television, a new dimension was added to the relationship between the Presidency and the media. Presidents were quick to seize broadcasting as a political weapon,

President Truman holds a press conference. *National Park Service Photograph, courtesy Harry S. Truman Library*

beginning with Franklin Roosevelt, who was the first to demonstrate with his Fireside Chats how a popular President could extend and reinforce his popularity.

Even Roosevelt, however, who enjoyed the affection of most newsmen and was called by them "the best managing editor in the country," nevertheless ended, as the *Emporia Gazette's* great editor, William Allen White, put it, in a stance where he "utterly misunderstood and entirely misconstrued and misconstructed the motives underlying the presentation of the news."

General Eisenhower was so popular he scarcely needed the media and experienced the barest minimum of dissent from them, yet he came to believe that the press was often unfair to him and his administration and that it did not always reflect public opinion. Harry Truman shared this belief. Yet, like Eisenhower, his personal feelings did not often seriously hamper his relationships with the press.

With President Kennedy, a new era of press relations began. Young, politically tough, more culturally knowledgeable than the others, and once a working newspaperman himself, he used the media as a political weapon with an adroitness not seen before. As unsuccessful as the Bay of Pigs affair may have been, Kennedy's manipulation of the press, sometimes with its willing knowledge and cooperation, was so masterful that only recently have we come to know how extensive it was. The President also well understood how to employ the "favored nation" idea of trade relations in the extraordinary access he permitted some newspaper and magazine people, nearly always with the purpose of creating favorable media attitudes or even specifically planting stories. It was difficult to tell sometimes, as in the case of his friendship with Benjamin Bradlee, editor of the *Washington Post*, who disclosed their relationship in a recent book, where public relations stopped and friendship began.

Lyndon Johnson carried these personal relationships to an even greater extreme, which sometimes had a tendency to backfire when they became *too* personal. The contrast between the Johnsonian approach and the Nixon administration's open hostility toward the press was sharp, although it was a long time before the media began to understand how they were being used to divide the nation for Mr. Nixon's political purposes, and even then they were reluctant to accept it.

President Gerald Ford's midwestern friendliness and relatively open approach to the press represented another marked swing, but with his first press secretary's almost immediate resignation and his successor's growing confrontations with the White House press corps on the same kind of issues that had cost Ronald Ziegler his credibility, it was clear that Presidential attitudes toward the press had not changed as much as the personality contrast between Nixon and Ford had led many people to believe. Beneath the smile and the easy manner lay the old problem: the tendency of the politician to conceal, to cover up, to manipulate for his own ends, and the skeptical persistence of the press in trying to prevent him from doing so.

President Kennedy holds a press conference. *National Park Service Photograph, courtesy John F. Kennedy Library*

The promoters and framers of the First Amendment, fearing the tyranny of a government able to control the free expression of opinion, devised what they conceived to be an absolute freedom for the media within the framework of the American system. It was a response to the clearly and forcibly expressed will of the people who consented to be governed under that system. But rulers everywhere, including Presidents, have never liked or willingly accepted the concept of press freedom because it subjects them to constant examination and criticism, which may result in the removal of themselves or their party from power. That is why American Presidents of both parties, without exception, have been hostile in some degree toward the media. The Nixon administration, however, understood, better than preceding administrations, that the freedom guaranteed by the First Amendment is, in the end, dependent on the willingness of the people to uphold it.

Alexander Hamilton fully understood this situation. In 1788, when Jefferson took the comfortable position that it was only necessary to embody the principle of press freedom in a constitution to make it viable, he wrote, scornfully and prophetically:

> What signifies a declaration, that "the liberty of the press shall be inviolably preserved"? What is the liberty of the press? Who can give it any definition which would not leave the utmost latitude for evasion? I hold it to be impracticable; and from this I infer that its security, whatever fine declaration may be inserted in any constitution respecting it, must altogether depend on public opinion, and on the general spirit of the people and of the government.

PART IV

VIEWS of the TOP

22

PRACTICAL ASPECTS of
PRESIDENTIAL NOMINATIONS:
AN INSIDE VIEW

by Richard C. Wade

PHILIP C. DOLCE: Dr. Wade, you have held important positions in every Democratic party campaign since 1952. From your experience, how much money is needed to win a Presidential nomination or even to mount a serious campaign?

RICHARD C. WADE: In the 1972 election Senator George McGovern raised about thirty-eight million dollars. President Nixon spent at least fifty million dollars that we know about. But the fact of the matter is that it was not the money that counted in the end. Nixon could have run the same campaign with half the money that he used; actually even McGovern could have run the campaign with a good deal less than he used. The trouble now is that people have the idea that you can run for President only if you are rich and have a great deal of money. Then you mount a drive for the nomination, and, if nominated, you can get elected by some kind of high spending. I think it is one of the myths of political life. McGovern, after all, came from a very small state, South Dakota; he had no money at the outset and yet he went through all the primaries, raised thirty-eight million dollars, and when it was all over, he could say as William Jennings Bryan did in 1896, "I wasn't beaten by the money; people knew my views, they simply weren't yet ready to accept them." It was not the money that did it; he had enough money to publicize his views but then the voters decide. I think that we could cut our spending in half without affecting the outcome. The spending we do now is much inflated. In New York City, people have spent one hundred thousand to two hundred thousand dollars just running for offices like assemblyman, when in fact it could be done easily with thirty or forty thousand dollars. But people have the notion that you have to buy television time, print literature, pay bar bills, and things like that, none of which is essential to winning an election at all.

PCD: Well, one thinks of the charges that Joseph Kennedy bought the nomination for his son in 1960. Was his father's money the most influential factor in John F. Kennedy's nomination?

RCW: No. Money can carry a candidate only so far. Senator Robert Kerr from Oklahoma was one of the richest men who ever ran for the Presidency in the United States. He tried to get the Democratic party nomination in 1952. He spent more money than anyone else, but he received only a handful of votes at the convention. Money will help, but you must have a candidate whom you can project. In Kennedy's case, the money was very helpful, but he could have had all that money and still not have won. If you have a great deal of money and an inferior candidate, you may not get the nomination. What happened in 1960 was the conjunction of a first-class candidate with adequate financing. In 1964, or if Bobby had run in 1968, the escalation of spending was such that even the Kennedys would have had to worry about money. Even Nelson Rockefeller would have to worry for the first time in his life about money if he ever ran for the Presidency again.

PCD: Another factor that worries people about the nomination process is the effect of public-relations men who surround a candidate. Do you think the image makers mold candidates?

RCW: Once again, I think you can do only so much with a candidate. Image makers can take somebody who is unknown and make him well known. In the long run, however, the man himself emerges. Of course, he may get away with one election, but the image makers cannot really transform a candidate. What they can do is make him more adjustable to important trends in the electorate. I think there has been too much emphasis placed on money and image makers, largely by the people who are involved in both. The people who give money to a party or try to buy a candidate, and the image makers who receive the money to make the candidate, always say that they are essential to electing a man President or governor. I do not think it happens that way. If they have a good product, they can help it, but I don't know of any case where a candidate was simply invented by money and image makers.

PCD: What do you consider to be the most important ingredient in winning a Presidential nomination?

RCW: The quality of the candidate and his relationship with the trends of the time. Often good candidates do not win, and bad candidates do, as we saw in 1972. Nonetheless, the combination of the character of the candidate and the broad trends of the time are the delicate ingredients of victory. I do not care how good the candidate is; if he is running against the grain of the day, he will lose. Conversely, no matter how bad a candidate is, if he is in tune with the times, he cannot lose. I think that Nixon suited the temper of this country perfectly in 1972. There had been no student riots, there had been no flames in the cities for four years. There had been a détente with Russia, a winding down of the war. In short, a big backlash against everything that happened in the 1960s. Nixon had nothing to do with the calm, but he was a beneficiary of the trend. That is what made him President. He was a perfect embodiment of what people wanted at the moment. In retrospect, people will change their minds. McGovern was, I think, an obviously superior character—a man of obvious honesty and decency. But he was ahead of his times on the issues. He would do better in 1976 or 1980.

PCD: Do political bosses still play an important role in deciding who will win the Presidential nomination?

RCW: In the Republican party, the political bosses are still important. There are about a dozen Republicans in the country who can sit down and determine who is going to get the Presidential nomination. There are no comparable twelve Democrats whom you could put in a room to make that decision. Moreover, if they did, they could not make their will stick. In the Democratic party, the candidate has to go through a whole series of primaries. If he cannot win them, whether the bosses want him or not, he cannot win. This situation really began in 1968 when the traditional process sort of unraveled. In 1972, there was no boss in Miami because the people had become the boss. They sent down delegates who were committed to McGovern. I know there is a great deal of nostalgia for the "good old boss days." However, there are no real bosses left. Richard Daley of Chicago is over seventy years old and not in the best of health and the same is true of Dan O'Connell of Albany. They are all that is left of the bosses.

PCD: Then what meaning does a political party have? Has the Democratic party become so fragmented that there is no organization left? Can anybody walk off with the Presidential nomination if he can get dedicated workers outside the party?

RCW: That is exactly the way you get nominated today. You get yourself a group of committed people who will stick with you for about two years; if others cannot get the same kind of dedication, they cannot win. The last election is a good example of this. What McGovern had going for him from the very beginning was about a couple of hundred thousand people around the country who had watched him on the war issue, had watched him on food for peace, watched his campaigns, and thought he would make a great President. They stuck with him through a long eighteen months until he won the nomination. No other candidate had that kind of dedicated following behind him. It is the edge of commitment that makes the difference. I remember in New York during debates between Muskie and McGovern supporters, the Muskie people would always say, "well, I think Muskie is popular in the party because he would have been the best candidate in 1968," or "he made a very good speech in 1970 on the eve of the election," or "he's Catholic, and a moderate." But nobody ever said that Muskie would make a great President. And because Muskie did not have enough people who thought he would make a great President, his campaign floundered and collapsed. When McGovern started his campaign Muskie was ahead by forty-one percent to three percent in the polls—but the three percent was more important than the forty-one percent, because it represented hard-core support. These dedicated supporters proved to be crucial as the candidates moved through the long historical corridor of primaries where Muskie's campaign started to collapse.

PCD: Then, to win the Democratic nomination for President, you do not even have to go through the party anymore, do you?

RCW: In fact, you are probably better off not going to the party. I remember Senator Edward Kennedy once responding to a question, "What happened to Ken O'Donnell when he ran for governor in Massachusetts?" He replied that O'Donnell's trouble was that he received the nomination of the state party. As a result he was

Senator George McGovern proclaims victory in the New York state primary. His family and Richard Wade are with him. *United Press International Photo*

defeated in the primaries. People are so suspicious of parties and of politicians that the man who runs on the outside is in a much stronger position than the man who attempts to win a nomination by putting together little coalitions of mayors, Congressmen, and city councilmen.

PCD: Is this trend dangerous to our historic two-party system? If the party organization is so weak that outsiders can win its Presidential designation, then are the independents the real force in national politics?

RCW: Well, the party system is in trouble. And it is in trouble because the people no longer believe in the parties. The last political-preference polls I have seen show the Democrats at about thirty-seven percent; Independents at about thirty-two percent; and Republicans at about twenty-six percent. Therefore, the second "party" in the nation now are the independents, and if you take the

The 1968 Wallace campaign showed the strength of the Independent vote. *Wallace Campaign Committee*

projections of the last five years, the first "party" is going to be an independent one very soon. Neither the Republicans nor the Democrats have really adjusted to that fact. They still think their nominations are crucial. But somewhere along the line, somebody is going to run outside both parties and is going to do well. That fact will further disintegrate the party structure. There simply is no national Democratic party. The Republican party is an association of a small number of people who see each other all the time and who share a certain ideology, resources, and commitments, and hence influence it. The Democratic party is very fragmented, and I see no way of bringing it together again.

PCD: Then, how does a candidate mount a national drive for the party's Presidential nomination?

RCW: You have to begin by assuming that the National Democratic Committee does not mean much. That is the first step. Secondly, because it does not mean much, you go state by state. There is a historical corridor of primaries that has developed over the last twenty years. The corridor begins with New Hampshire in the first week of March and it runs through Wisconsin, Nebraska, Oregon, California, and New York. With each election new primaries are added and some others become crucial. We added West Virginia in 1960 and Florida in 1972. But generally speaking, the public watches what they consider to be a fair representation of states. And that is how you win. If you win those states, the public thinks you deserve the nomination. And no party is going to turn you out. Now McGovern finished the primaries about two hundred votes short of the nomination, but how could the party have nominated anyone else after the man had won so many primaries? The primaries give a presumption of the nomination. Each state is different. Campaigning in New Hampshire compared with California is different; any shrewd campaign operation knows that. It puts certain kinds of people in New Hampshire; other kinds of people in California or New York or Nebraska.

Inside the states, there is virtually no organization either; you can come in from the outside. Otherwise your candidate gets involved in internal party warfare. The great asset McGovern had in New York in 1972 was that there was no faction within the party for him at the outset. This permitted him to keep out of the factional fights and to remain above them. The same thing was true in Nebraska and in California. In some places you will find a local party organization whose support is valuable in a primary. The Democratic organization in Wisconsin under Pat Lucey is a good example of this. Normally, though, it is much better to run from the outside.

PCD: Are all those primaries really necessary? Should we have a national primary?

RCW: Historically, the primaries are essential. I think that some part of the primary system we now have should be kept, even if we can reform it. Primaries test the person in front of the voting public. The public sees a man running in several states in different environments. They have an opportunity to find out more about him. Moreover, primaries are brutal on people. Harold Stassen was destroyed in Oregon in 1944; George Romney was destroyed in 1968 in New Hampshire; Muskie was destroyed because he just could not manage a campaign even in a neighboring state like New Hampshire. The public gets a focus on the candidate; they watch him, and he has to last. Beyond that they test the candidates over a period of time, not at just one particular moment. I think that is very important, for the public can see a man grow or shrink. Also, as the staff emerges, they find out what kind of people he is going to bring around him; that is something the public wants to know.

But we now have twenty-six primaries for the 1976 election, and there will be even more by election time. I have a suggestion which would keep part of both the convention and the primary systems, while, at the same time, maintaining the integrity of the party. We should do in the future exactly what we do now. Delegates would be chosen state by state. But a candidate at the convention would be eligible for the nomination if he got twenty percent of the delegates' votes. He would then automatically go on the ballot for a preferential primary across the country three weeks after the convention. It would mean that a candidate would not have to go through every state to get a majority of delegates. As soon as he was assured of twenty percent, he could stop.

Secondly, party platforms unfortunately have become less and less important. If, however, you had a system like this—the delegates would go to the convention and make up their minds on issues without calculating the impact on their own candidate. This would produce a genuine platform convention.

I would go even further. When a candidate went before the convention to accept a place on the primary ballot, he would select a Vice-Presidential running mate. The two of them would constitute a slate. Three weeks later, Democrats all over the country, on the same day, would determine which slate they would want to carry the Democratic banner for the next election. This would be a comparatively cheap system. No candidate would have to go through thirty primaries. In addition, a three-week national campaign would be inexpensive because the newspapers and the media would be focused on the candidates, and it would be unnecessary to buy time. Each candidate could get his views widely circulated. Since the ultimate decision would be in the hands of Democratic voters, this would reduce divisions in the party.

PCD: An interesting example of a candidate who secured the Democratic Presidential nomination in different ways is Adlai Stevenson. In 1952 he won the Democratic nomination without the primaries, but in 1956 he won by going into the primaries. Did this fact change his campaign or image in the two elections?

RCW: Well, there is a very strange paradox in all this because in 1952 Stevenson was in fact handed the nomination by the bosses, but the bosses needed him very badly. They wanted to keep the nomination away from Senator Estes Kefauver of Tennessee, and so he went in as a very free man; they had to take him. In fact, he was not too keen on running and they virtually had to draft him at the convention. In 1956, he really wanted the nomination; but he was now weak and they were stronger. In 1956 he ran as a Democrat. What is interesting in this is that in 1952 he ran a much better campaign because he was freer and he appealed to many different kinds of people. By 1956 he had been pictured as *the* Democratic nominee and therefore did not do very well. His campaign was not as good and the results were worse, though it is fair to say that no candidate, no matter how independent and well financed his candidacy was, could have defeated General Eisenhower.

PCD: More recently, in 1968, Eugene McCarthy managed to extinguish Lyndon Johnson's reelection hopes by challenging him in the primaries. Why did McCarthy attempt this?

RCW: McCarthy's candidacy was a mutiny. A lot of people for a variety of reasons, mostly the Vietnam War, focused their attention, indeed hatred, on Lyndon Johnson. The primary system gave them the opportunity to knock him out. In the process, however, he demonstrated what was wrong with the party: neither of the candidates who won every primary was nominated by the convention, hence hurting Hubert Humphrey's chances of winning. It looked as though the convention overturned the results of the primaries. When McGovern got to Miami in 1972, it was clear that he was going to be nominated even though he was two hundred votes short, because no convention would ever again turn over the nomination to someone who had not won the primaries.

PCD: The Republicans do not seem to have much trouble in nominating a Presidential candidate. Why is that so?

RCW: The Republican party is, first of all, smaller; that is a very great advantage in politics. The smaller a party is, the more tightly organized it becomes. Their registration is about twenty-five percent of the voters. They have few blacks, Puerto Ricans, or activist youths. They have a monolithic party of white, middle-class people with an ideological cohesion. Historically, it has been the party of business. The business community, by and large, directs the platform, directs the fund raising, and chooses delegates and nominees. In that sense, it has always been much more cohesive. But when a split really comes in the GOP as in 1964, it eats as deep as—indeed much deeper than—in the Democratic party. Secondly, no Republican as yet has decided to take advantage of the state laws permitting primaries to select delegates to the national convention. When some Republican decides to take the historical corridor from New Hampshire on through New York and wins it, that will be the end of peaceful Republican conventions.

23

PRESIDENTIAL GREATNESS

by R. Gordon Hoxie

PHILIP C. DOLCE: Dr. Hoxie, what yardsticks are used to measure Presidential greatness?

R. GORDON HOXIE: In the final analysis the basic yardstick is the achievement of that individual and his (or her) administration. The measure is the influence each President has had on history, and that is why it is so extremely difficult to do it other than from the perspective of considerable time. Of course, there are many ingredients which one does consider, such basic things as ethics and integrity on the one hand, and, on the other, blunders.

You have to ask the question, was he a great leader? Leadership in this case is multidimensional. For instance, the President is a leader of the people in both peace and war, and also a leader of his party. Take for example Andrew Jackson, who is placed fairly high in polls of Presidential greatness. Certainly one of the reasons for his high marks was effective leadership of his party. He and Thomas Jefferson were of the Democratic party, and they certainly utilized the party well in achieving their goals.

PCD: While Jackson ranks fairly high on these polls, which Presidents consistently receive the highest ranking?

RGH: The two giants who stand head and shoulders above all others are the founder of our country, our first President, George

Washington, and the man who served during those most trying years of the Civil War answering the question whether the Union would be preserved—Abraham Lincoln. Three other Presidents who are usually considered in the same category are Franklin Delano Roosevelt, Woodrow Wilson, and Thomas Jefferson. Thomas Jefferson is really there in the final analysis because he was one of the greatest Americans. Actually, the last two years of his second administration were extremely unhappy, when he sought to steer a neutral course between Britain and France and declared an embargo on all foreign trade. Jefferson virtually retreated into exile in his last weeks in office to his beloved home, Monticello. In the final days in the Presidency, Jefferson wrote, "Never did a prisoner released from his chains feel such relief as I shall on shaking off the shackles of power." But he is rightly among the greatest Americans. Apart from the Presidency, he was the author of the Declaration of Independence and the Bill for Religious Freedom in Virginia, and the founder of the University of Virginia. He wanted to be remembered for these services rather than for his Presidency.

PCD: Do the times in which they lived influence our evaluation of Presidents? For instance, a President during a crisis or war is most familiar. Does that influence our evaluation?

RGH: It certainly does, both for high marks and for low. One of the things which we cherish above all is peace, but three of our greatest Presidents led the nation during wartime: Abraham Lincoln, Woodrow Wilson, and Franklin Delano Roosevelt.

But crisis does not necessarily assure that notch of greatness. James Madison, for example, certainly one of the best prepared of all to be President, did not benefit from a wartime crisis. Mr. Madison's War, as the War of 1812 is derisively referred to, brought him extremely low marks. This was in part due to our lack of preparedness, and in part due to the war's unpopularity. As for other types of crises, the depression certainly did not bring Herbert Hoover high marks. Only in retrospect, forty years later, do we recognize Hoover as the first of the modern Presidents and the creator of much new and reform legislation. Harry S. Truman handled many crises exceedingly, indeed surprisingly, well. But his last two years in office were unhappy ones in what looked like a stalemated war in Korea. High marks are, therefore, not necessarily related to wartime Presidents. But it is true that among our greatest Presidents are those who have handled crises effectively.

PCD: Is there not a tendency to give high marks to activist Presidents who have expanded Presidential power and to give rather low marks to those who took a restrained view of their office? For instance, William Howard Taft and John Quincy Adams both had very restrained constitutional views of the Presidential office.

RGH: That is certainly true. Moreover, if they follow or precede an extremely active President, we seem to rank them relatively lower. In the case of John Quincy Adams, preceding an extremely active Andrew Jackson, that of itself seems to negate him. The same may be said of William Howard Taft, having followed Theodore Roosevelt. In fact, Roosevelt, who had practically made Taft President, felt Taft should have followed his policies exactly. However, Taft had a different and more circumspect view of the Presidency. While not as dynamic as Roosevelt, Taft's administration was not without merit. TR was noted for "busting" trusts, but there were more trusts "busted" in the Taft administration, although it is true that many of the cases were started under TR. Nevertheless, the activist President just seems to loom larger on the historical horizon. We yearn for vigorous leadership, and are charmed by charisma. Hence FDR's trial-and-error methods generally bring higher marks than Hoover's more considered actions.

PCD: Do you believe that the general public would rank the Presidents differently than the experts?

RGH: There is no doubt about it! Certain of our Presidents who have not been given too high a rating in these polls were among the most popular Presidents. Let me give you a couple of examples. Calvin Coolidge could have been elected to another term if he desired it. He was extremely popular with the people, but he comes off very low on the polls. Certainly one of the most beloved Presidents in our time was Dwight David Eisenhower. Again he does not come off as high on the polls. There is a great differentiation between popularity with the people and the evaluation by scholars, and there again, with all due respect to them, I do believe a part of it is due to a certain built-in prejudice. I hasten to say that I am not suggesting that Calvin Coolidge would emerge as one of the greatest of our Presidents. I was only giving an example of his great popularity.

PCD: Can Presidents who lived one hundred years apart and occupied the White House under entirely different circumstances really be evaluated and measured against one another?

RGH: I do not think they can be. Times change, and attitudes toward the Congress and the President change. By and large the nineteenth century was a period when there was Congressional leadership in the nation. Lincoln was a notable exception as an outstandingly strong President. The twentieth century, beginning with Theodore Roosevelt, has been characterized by activist Presidents, strong Presidents. Indeed, when General Eisenhower came along and seemingly did not have that same activism, many people assumed that he was not a strong President. Thus, you have to consider the attitudes, the times in which the man lived—that makes it extremely difficult to try to compare various Presidential administrations over these spans of years. However, there is no way to deny the greatness of character, the greatness of strength, the greatness of leadership, of both Washington and Lincoln. We always come back to that.

PCD: Do you think there is a built-in prejudice on the part of those historians and political scientists who rank the Presidents?

RGH: There is no question about it! As Professor Thomas Bailey, of Stanford University, pointed out in his book *Presidential Greatness*, the vast majority of historians and political scientists are Democrats of liberal persuasion. He did a poll of the American Political Science Association and found that only about one-fourth of the members were of Republican persuasion, and he said, in essence, that most of the historians and political scientists feel that the Democratic party is identifiable with the activist kind of President which they want. Probably if you conducted a poll of the college presidents, their political views would be somewhat different and so would those in schools of business administration and engineering. But they are not asked to make these evaluations. Historians and political scientists are and they do so with the best sense of personal integrity, but they do have a bent toward the liberal Democratic persuasion.

PCD: Does a man who is elected to the Presidency think about his historical reputation?

RGH: Every President looks over his shoulder in terms of what history is going to record. George Reedy, President Johnson's press secretary, has emphasized that so many of the things that are said, even in the press conferences, and certainly in Presidential papers, are spoken with an eye on history. That is human, and certainly every President somehow wonders how history will finally evaluate him . . . or maybe someday . . . her! Perhaps Reedy was a bit harsh in one of our Center's symposia when he declared, "Presidents like to talk about their press problems. It's a way of preparing an alibi for history."

PCD: When you look at the Presidential office, the first President, Washington, added prestige to it. But subsequently has not almost every man who occupied the Presidential office been transformed by it?

RGH: No question about that. They generally have risen to the occasion. One of the best examples of that is President Chester Arthur. When President James Garfield was assassinated, people were horrified at the thought of his Vice-President, Chester Arthur, entering the White House. They felt that Arthur, the former Collector of the Port of New York, was at best a most astute politician but certainly not a person of stature. Chester Arthur emerged as a capable President and an able administrator. To the surprise of most people this veteran of political patronage became a firm, constructive advocate of civil-service reform. Presidents have, in brief, risen to the position.

Of course, the greatest example of all is Abraham Lincoln: his humble origin, a very unspectacular short period in the Congress of the United States, a not too successful law firm, and a failure in his early life in business. Despite this modest background, Lincoln had an inner strength which emerged fully during his Presidency. Again in more recent times, we have the example of Harry Truman. People derisively asked how that "little haberdasher from Independence" was going to fill the shoes of FDR. He filled them exceedingly well!

PCD: At the other end of the spectrum, only two Presidents have been classified as "failures," and they were Ulysses S. Grant and Warren G. Harding. Do you agree with these evaluations?

RGH: I would not label them as "failures." Harding was not a direct party to the scandals that burst over the land after his death. He generally is viewed as a "do-nothing" President, but this is too simple an evaluation. Harding had campaigned vigorously for better working conditions and for reducing the twelve-hour day, which with all the liberalism of Woodrow Wilson who had preceded him, was still the workingman's day. He campaigned for the eight-hour day and did a great deal to reduce it to that length. Harding showed a great deal of compassion for some of our political troublemakers and some people of a radical bent. Eugene Debs had been languishing in jail and this so-called do-nothing President said in essence that this was not helping the American image or our way of life in any way, and he got Eugene Debs out of prison. Harding is not going to emerge as a great President, but he is not a "failure."

Grant came into office during an extremely difficult period in American history. The bitterness of the Civil War was still fresh and the reconstruction of the nation had not been achieved. Moreover, his predecessor, Andrew Johnson, had barely been able to survive impeachment. By contrast, Grant worked well with the Congress. Moreover, he had one of the best Secretaries of State, Hamilton Fish. Grant's critics say that was just an accident, but such appointments are never entirely accidental. In retrospect, Grant was a most able soldier, but he lacked the political arts and civilian administrative experience. However, given the problems he had to face, I would certainly not put him in the "failure" category. In that splendid biography of Grant by his grandson, the story is recounted of how Secretary of War James D. Cameron read to Grant an abusive account, after which Grant observed, "That is pretty bad." "Yes," Cameron responded, "that was . . . about George Washington."

PCD: Which other President has been underrated?

RGH: You may say I am not entirely objective, since this man inspired the founding of the Center for the Study of the Presidency, which I now head. Moreover, I had an opportunity to serve him when he was President of Columbia University. Despite this, I am firmly convinced that Dwight David Eisenhower has been rated too low by historians and political scientists. Indeed he is listed as an "average" President, just above Andrew Johnson, a most obstinate man who had considerable difficulty in his relations with the Congress. By contrast, Eisenhower had established the first Congressional liaison office at the White House and was most effective in his relationships with that body. To use Al Smith's term, "Let's take a look at the record."

First, he kept his campaign promise to end the Korean War and he did so with adroitness and firmness which the Communists respected. Thereafter, for perhaps the first peacetime period in our history, we maintained adequate defenses. His administration virtually stopped the rampant inflation which had been going on since the beginning of World War II and also substantially reduced taxes. What Presidency introduced the first substantial civil-rights legislation in eighty years—that is, going back until just after the Civil War? The Eisenhower Presidency. What Presidency brought Hawaii and Alaska into the Union? The Eisenhower Presidency. What Presidency reorganized—and it really needed reorganizing to make it work more effectively—the Department of the Defense? The Eisenhower Presidency. What Presidency founded the Department of Health, Education and Welfare and introduced many educational programs? The Eisenhower Presidency.

Other accomplishments included the largest road-building program in American history and the building of the St. Lawrence Seaway. Desegregation was completed in both the District of Columbia and the Armed Services without the passage of any law for the purpose. President Eisenhower worked most effectively with Congresses which he did not control. The Republicans held a slim majority in Congress for only two of his eight years in office. Lyndon Baines Johnson was the leader of the Democratic side. Eisenhower worked with the Democratic leadership extremely well; indeed Senator Johnson felt that these were his own programs! George Reedy, who later became Mr. Johnson's Presidential press secretary, had also served as Johnson's assistant during those Senatorial years. Reedy recently declared, "I really believe today that he [Eisenhower] was a master politician. . . . He conducted himself masterfully. . . ." One thing which Eisenhower used so very skillfully was the veto. He used it 201 times in eight years. The Democratic majority in Congress only overrode three of these vetoes. This is only one example which demonstrates President Eisenhower's leadership ability. I believe history inevitably is going to bring Dwight Eisenhower a considerably higher mark than he has received to date.

PCD: It is quite obvious that Presidential greatness is a subjective evaluation that not only depends on the man and an evaluation of his career but also on the times in which the polls are taken, the bias of those polled, and the mood of the people. Probably how a man ranks in a Presidential poll will vary from generation to generation.

24

THE IMPERIAL PRESIDENCY

by Arthur M. Schlesinger, Jr.

PHILIP C. DOLCE: Professor Schlesinger, for many years you have been a chronicler of famous Presidential administrations. One thinks of *The Age of Jackson, The Age of Roosevelt,* and *A Thousand Days: John F. Kennedy in the White House.* In these books you were a firm advocate of Presidential power. You saw Presidential power as necessary to overcome government inertia and to enable the nation to meet crises. Now you are plainly worried about the growth of Presidential power. In fact you use the term "imperial Presidency" to describe it. Do you still retain your faith in the strong Presidency?

ARTHUR M. SCHLESINGER, JR.: I still believe in a strong Presidency. I really do not see how a system based on the separation of powers can move and act without leadership from one of the branches, and historically the President has provided that leadership. But I think that some of us, I among them, were a little uncritical in the past in the way we have defended the strong Presidency. We should have said, "A strong Presidency *within the constitution.*" The men who made the Constitution wanted a strong and energetic national government. They expected the President to be a leader. But they expected him to operate within an equally strong and effective system of accountability. What has happened in recent years is that a state of imbalance has developed between the President's power and his accountability. Presidential power has grown, and Presidential accountability has weakened. This produces the situation I have described as the "imperial Presidency."

PCD: You state that the "imperial Presidency" is essentially the creation of foreign policy after World War II. Could you explain why you think that is where the "imperial Presidency" grew from?

AMS, JR.: I mentioned the system of accountability. That system has historically embraced certain formal modes of accountability—the written restraints on Presidential power in the Constitution, the President's accountability to law, to Congress, to the courts. Then there evolved in the early republic various informal modes of accountability: accountability to one's colleagues in the Cabinet and the executive branch, to one's political party, to the media of opinion, to public opinion in general. But the historic system of accountability has had one grave weakness, and this is in the field of foreign affairs. In foreign policy Presidents often had to take, or thought they had to take, actions on their own initiative and without Congressional authorization, actions they thought necessary to preserve the safety of the republic. Confronted by such Presidential initiatives, Congress, the courts, and public opinion had much less confidence in their own information and judgment, felt much less sure of their ground, and therefore were much less inclined to challenge and check and balance as they were accustomed to doing in domestic policy. Thus, international crisis increased Presidential power and weakened the system of accountability. Since 1939 or thereabouts we have been in a state of protracted international crisis. Moreover, this age of crisis was preceded by a period between the two world wars of active Congressional intervention in foreign affairs—intervention which even members of Congress themselves later agreed to have been unfortunate and mistaken. With that background our contemporary international crisis has carried power faster than ever to the Presidency. For Congress has readily abdicated its responsibilities in the international field because of its own inferiority complex. This has laid the basis for the "imperial Presidency." More particularly, the "imperial Presidency" is the compulsion to use against American citizens the powers that have flowed to the Presidency to meet international emergency. That happened very freely in the Nixon administration, where, under the all-purpose incantation of national security, powers that had been bestowed on the Presidency to meet foreign crises began to be turned against Americans at home.

PCD: How has the "imperial Presidency" permeated the domestic scene?

AMS, JR.: There have, of course, been occasions when Presidents have received unusual powers to cope with domestic crises. For example, Congress gave Franklin D. Roosevelt unprecedented powers to deal with the depression in the 1930s. But powers bestowed on Presidents to meet domestic crises do not have a spill-over effect into foreign affairs. Roosevelt used the powers he had been granted in the domestic field with great skill. He was an exceptionally popular President. Nonetheless, Congress tied him hand and foot in foreign affairs through the neutrality acts. Roosevelt was still struggling to get out of those knots weeks before Pearl Harbor. On the other hand, power given to the Presidency for foreign affairs does spill over into domestic policy. President Truman could hardly have been lower in the polls than he was in 1952. Yet he seized the steel industry on the ground that it was necessary to prevent a steel strike which might stop the flow of ammunition to our troops in Korea. This was a case in which the Supreme Court declared Truman's actions unconstitutional, and he immediately complied with the action. In the Nixon case, you had a President threatening the liberties of the people far more directly in the belief that he could do almost anything in the name of national security—that he could, for example, privately declare a state of national emergency which, he felt, empowered him to create a secret posse in the White House and to release it to break the laws and the Constitution. This is a very clear case, it seems to me, of the way power flowing to the Presidency for foreign reasons is turned against the republic itself.

PCD: Less than a decade ago, there was no cry against the growth of the strong Presidency by Congress, by public opinion, or even by the media. Most intellectuals sang the praises of the strong Presidency and sought to increase its power. Was this uncritical national attitude in part responsible for the growth of the "imperial Presidency"?

AMS, JR.: I am sure you are right. The growth of the "imperial Presidency" is not so much the result of the rapacity of Presidents for power as it is of Congressional abdication and popular acquiescence or even popular demand. This is, after all, a turbulent and baffling world. It is much easier to have the weight of responsibility taken off one's shoulders and let the President make the decisions. For a time, we elected Presidents who, on the whole, made fairly good decisions and, on the whole, did not abuse their power, Presidents who operated within the system of accountability. That is why there was no great criticism of Presidential power. But, when Presidents began to abuse their power and reject their accountability, then we suddenly realized where the uncritical cult of Presidential power had led us.

PCD: The federal government has been taking powers away from the states and cities for years. Is the "imperial Presidency" part of a great centralization of power that this nation has undergone in the twentieth century?

AMS, JR.: I would agree that Franklin D. Roosevelt, for example, was a very strong President and that the centralization of authority which took place under the New Deal was certainly part of that larger wave of institutional centralization you mention. But on the whole Roosevelt was a President who respected the system of accountability. He held Cabinet meetings twice a week. He held press conferences twice a week—more during his first three months than Nixon held in his first four years. He was very accessible to members of Congress. He liked to see them and talk to them individually; he did not just receive them en masse as has become the recent Presidential fashion. In other words he did not run a "closed Presidency." I think the peculiar characteristic of the "imperial Presidency" is that it is a "closed Presidency." It rejects the system of accountability. I think we must have strong Presidents. We must have a measure of centralization. But strong Presidents must be open, they must want to be legal and they must respect the system of accountability.

PDC: You mention the word "accountability" and I wonder what that means. While it is true that FDR did speak informally to members of Congress, does that mean he was truly accountable—

the way the Constitution would have had it? What I am really making a distinction between is informal consultation and formal accountability.

AMS, JR.: Well I would think in FDR's case he was probably good at both of them—except during the time of national emergency he proclaimed in 1941. The essence of the thing was well put by Theodore Roosevelt when he said that the President ought to be a very strong man and he ought to use all the powers the office yields but because of that he should be sharply watched and held to the strictest accountability. I think Nixon's view was rather different. Obviously he did not like to be sharply watched or held to strict accountability. His view was essentially that a President is accountable only once every four years—that an election confers a mandate and the mandate empowers the President to do what he thinks best for the safety and welfare of the country: to spend money appropriated by Congress or to impound it, to give out information requested by Congress or withhold it, to make war or to make peace; and that between elections the mandate ought to protect the President from harassment from Congress or by the press or by political opposition and so on. It is essentially a plebiscitary theory, well summed up in that wretched phrase one used to hear during the Nixon Presidency: "Let's all get off his back and let him do his job." That idea, of course, is quite contrary to the conception of the Constitution, which is that the country should always be in a sense on the President's back, and that accountability is a continuous matter, not a quadrennial matter.

PCD: For years conservatives have been crying out against the extension of governmental power and now they see some of their cries of anguish recognized by others. At least one of them has said that the "imperial Presidency" is really a creature of the "welfare state," that we have entrusted too much power to government to solve social and economic problems and in doing so have created the "imperial Presidency." Do you think that is true?

AMS, JR.: I do not see that because it seems to me that the Presidency on the whole does not have a great deal of power in domestic affairs, particularly in economic affairs. American Presidents probably have much less power over economic policy than the head of any other democratic country in the world. Take the question of taxes. I can well remember in 1962 when President Kennedy had gone to Congress with a tax-reduction bill which he considered necessary to reduce unemployment and stimulate growth. About the same time Harold Macmillan went to the British Parliament with a tax-reduction bill of his own. In the English case the bill was voted on in a few weeks, but in the American case it was introduced in the spring of 1963 and passed about a year later. In that respect I think American Presidents do not have a great deal of power. As for the relationship between the "imperial Presidency" and the "welfare state," I see none at all—that seems mythological. If there are American institutions on which the "imperial Presidency" has drawn heavily, I would say that they are institutions like the FBI—and the CIA—and these are hardly institutions of the "welfare state." One of the oddities is that the conservatives, who are to some degree justifiably smug for having warned against Presidential power, have never been notable for their criticism of the FBI.

PCD: You have drawn an interesting distinction between the domestic Presidency and the foreign-policy Presidency. In your book *The Imperial Presidency* you mention that in foreign policy the American President has more power over war and peace than any other leader in the world with the possible exception of Mao Tse-tung. In domestic policy you say the President has much less power. Since World War II, however, are not most issues so intertwined that you cannot separate them into these categories?

AMS, JR.: In many cases they are. It is an artificial distinction and there are many issues which involve both foreign and domestic policy. Nonetheless, when one makes an analysis of Presidential recommendations to Congress, those that fell clearly in the field of foreign policy in the period say from 1946 to 1966 had a much better chance of acceptance than those that fell in the field of domestic policy. It seems to me that since World War II the President has enjoyed much more scope and discretion in the field of foreign policy than he has in the field of domestic policy.

PCD: Many people have claimed that the growth of Presidential power was in response to emergency or crisis. Should the President be able to go beyond constitutional limits in the times of crisis?

AMS, JR.: Obviously one cannot say that there are no conceivable circumstances in which a President might have to move beyond or even against the Constitution. John Locke, in his famous chapter "Of Prerogative" in his *Second Treatise of Government*, argued that this might be necessary. When the life of the nation is involved, Presidents have acted on their own. But responsible Presidents must declare publicly what the reasons are for the emergency and for the

President Nixon and Mao Tse-tung. *Wide World Photos*

unconstitutional acts they may have taken, and in general they try to get retrospective Congressional sanction for what they have done. Moreover, the times and occasions when the life of a nation is really at stake are damned few. There have been only two, in my judgment, in American history. One was the Civil War, and the other was World War II. These were both periods of clear and present danger to the United States. Lincoln and FDR both did things they were not authorized to do by the Constitution. But they proclaimed national emergencies, they explained why they thought the life of the country was in danger, and on the whole Congress and the people supported them in those acts. Such situations occurred in the past and may occur in the future, and I would not for a moment argue for any conception of Presidential power that would deny Presidents the power to act in an emergency.

On the other hand it is plainly essential to have criteria for what constitutes a genuine emergency. You cannot allow the President to make such a judgment on his own personal say-so and expect everyone to surrender automatically to that judgment. One criterion certainly is to proclaim the emergency as Lincoln did and as FDR did. Nixon went into a private panic in 1970 because of the Weathermen or something and in 1971 because of the Pentagon Papers. But he proclaimed no national emergency. He did not go to the country and say, "I think the life of the republic is in danger." He just sat in the White House and communed with himself and set up the Plumbers and let them commit robberies and forge cables and so on. So one criterion is that the President is under an obligation to state plainly and publicly what the emergency is. Second, he can act himself only if Congress is unable or unwilling to prescribe a course of action. Then he must go to Congress and get retroactive sanction for what he has done. There are other criteria. He must never, for example, commit acts against the political process itself, as Nixon did. Presidents who ignore these criteria get into trouble.

Take the case of Jefferson. Jefferson acted, as he said, "beyond the Constitution" in the case of the Louisiana Purchase, but the Congress and the nation agreed that this was an emergency and that he was justified in his action. When he took things into his own hands in the case of the Burr conspiracy, the courts resisted. Congress and the people did not think it was an emergency, and Jefferson's course was rejected. I have mentioned Truman and the steel-seizure case. Both Jefferson and Truman at least sent messages to the Congress explaining why they thought the Burr conspiracy and the steel strike were going to threaten the life of the nation. What Nixon did was to reject all the criteria by which the emergency power has been exercised in the past—and still claim the right to exercise that power.

PCD: You make an interesting distinction between the usurpation and abuse of Presidential power. In times of emergency the President might have to usurp power, but this should never be institutionalized. Is that correct?

AMS, JR.: Yes, because if usurpation is recognized as usurpation it does not create a precedent and therefore does not legalize that kind of use of power for future Presidents.

Richard Nixon bids farewell to those who served under him in his administration. *Wide World Photos*

PCD: Does the increase of Presidential power and Presidential responsibility show that the office is just too much for any one man to handle, either psychologically or physically?

AMS, JR.: I do not think so. I think the problem of the Presidential work load has been much exaggerated. Presidents never have to worry about the things that take up time for people like you and me. They have every convenience of life. They are surrounded by people who want to do things for them. No ordinary citizen spent as much time in his vacation places as Nixon did. All Presidents appear to have a great deal of leisure time. Their psychological burden is much more wearing than the physical work load. But I think one man can handle the Presidency better than two. In addition, if you have more than one man, the problem of accountability becomes much more difficult, which is why people like Alexander Hamilton opposed the idea of the plural executive when it was first brought up in the Constitutional Convention.

PCD: One of your principal concerns is that the revolution against the "imperial Presidency" might lead to institutional limits on the office. After all the abuse we have seen, should there not be institutional limits on the Presidency?

AMS, JR.: On the whole, my view is that the office has served the republic well. I think the problem is not so much that of reducing the power of the Presidency as of rehabilitating and enforcing the system of accountability. The great virtue of strengthening the system of accountability is that it will preserve Presidential power and at the same time will discourage future Presidents from abusing that power. The great virtue of impeachment, for example, is that it punishes the offender without punishing the office.

PCD: What are some of your suggestions for reforming the office itself?

AMS, JR.: The important approach, it seems to me, lies in the realm of consciousness-raising rather than of structural reform. We must raise the consciousness of future Congresses so they will begin to acknowledge and meet their responsibilities. This is far more important than structural reforms. There are some structural reforms of consequence. Cleaning up campaign financing would be very useful. Congress might well increase its own research and analysis capacity by setting up a Congressional counterpart of the bureau of the budget. Congress should establish effective oversight committees for the FBI and CIA. But all this is essentially marginal. Congress has only to exercise the powers given it in the Constitution to restore the balance of the system. The real question, it seems to me, is not one of structure but of will. It is the question whether Congress really wants to contain the "imperial Presidency" and it is the question whether the American people really want to contain the "imperial Presidency." If they do, the way to do it is within the Constitution by invoking the remedy prescribed by the Founding Fathers.

25

PRESIDENTIAL and
PARLIAMENTARY GOVERNMENT
in PERSPECTIVE
by Frank J. Coppa

American political institutions have enjoyed an extraordinary prestige at home and abroad. The Constitution and the institutions it provides have assured the country a certain stability enabling it to endure a bloody Civil War, several economic depressions, and two world wars. Under this governmental scheme the United States has broken out of the ranks of the small states to attain superpower status with a standard of living envied throughout the world. At the same time individual liberty has been guaranteed and the tradition that government exists to serve its citizens maintained.

Despite these achievements, some have always felt that the American political system should be improved and many of the suggested changes center upon its Chief Executive. Criticism of the Presidency, which reached a high point during the Watergate scandal and the subsequent disclosure of the alleged misuse of the Internal Revenue Service, the Central Intelligence Agency, and the Federal Bureau of Investigation, is neither a new nor an extraordinary phenomenon. As early as 1789 Patrick Henry lamented the growing power of the office and warned that if it was left unchecked, despotism would ensue.

In the past as at present, all responsible parties who have called for a reform of the presidential system have stressed the need to preserve democratic principles. This, in turn, has led to the attempt to determine what is essential for the perpetuation of democracy and what is peripheral. A number of studies, especially those of a comparative nature, reveal that many established aspects of American political life are not always necessary for democracy. Among these one might cite: a written constitution, judicial review, bicameralism and federalism, the notion of the separation of powers, and even the presidential form of government. For several hundred years parliamentary government has provided the English with benevolent traditions of law and limited government.

Both the presidential and parliamentary systems have shown themselves capable of preserving democracy, but one might ask which is more appropriate in the nuclear age? Which provides greater efficiency, more dynamic leadership, greater accountability? Finally, can governmental arrangements developed in one area be transferred to another and operate as well?

Central to the presidential system is the doctrine of the separation of powers, which maintains that the function of the legislature is to make the laws, that of the executive is to see that they are carried out, and the one should be independent of the other. Thus in the presidential or monocratic type of executive, one finds parallel with the legislature a single, independent individual responsible for executive functions. Usually this post is entrusted to the person who holds the office of president as a result of election by the people. Although he is surrounded by a team of helpers, they are clearly his subordinates. The president's position is enhanced by the fact that he is at once head of the state and head of the government. This system is the one that prevails in the Philippines, the Republic of Korea, Egypt, Brazil, Argentina, and most notably the United States, where it evolved.

The collegiate or parliamentary executive, which prevails throughout most of Western Europe and England's former colonies, has its own unique characteristics. Among these is the division of the executive function between two powers more or less independent of one another. On the one hand there is a head of state represented by a monarch—as is the case in Great Britain—or an honorific president—as in the case of Italy, West Germany, and a number of other states—and on the other, a cabinet, which is responsible for the management of affairs.

While there is a kind of division in the exercise of the executive power between the president and the prime minister, there is no separation between the legislative and executive branches of government. Members of the cabinet are drawn from the parliament and guide it in implementing the ministry's program. Indeed, their close collaboration is one of the most useful features of parliamentary government. Since the cabinet can only govern with the support of parliament, possession of a majority therein usually assures the government that its policies will be approved without the delay or deadlock that occurs in countries having a separation of power.

This feature of parliamentary government helps to account for European bewilderment at the recent American Congressional intrusion in foreign policy. Congressional action which tied trade with Russia to the emigration of Jews from this Communist state and the Congressional ban of arms sales to Turkey against the wishes of President Gerald Ford and Secretary of State Henry Kissinger, have stunned the current generation of European leaders. These men are accustomed to the parliamentary system under which the foreign policy decisions of the executive are seldom if ever challenged by the legislature, for this would be tantamount to a vote of no confidence and sufficient to overturn the regime.

Most important of all, the collegiate executive is more easily restrained because it does not receive its mandate directly from the people for a fixed period of time as does the presidential executive. Rather it has to rely on the support of the legislature, which is popularly elected and which can withdraw its confidence from the cabinet at almost any moment. This is known as ministerial responsibility and serves to keep the plural executive under close scrutiny and control. It enables Europeans quickly and painlessly to bring about dramatic changes in leadership. Consequently, while Watergate troubled the United States for over a year, rendering its government less efficient and its people demoralized, a spy scandal in West Germany in May 1974 led almost immediately to the resignation of Chancellor Willy Brandt; and within a month a new government was installed and the incident largely forgotten.

It is this feature of parliamentary government that appeals to critics of the American presidential system and figures prominently in their schemes for reform. They decry the fact that executives under the presidential system can be removed only with the passage of time and another election or by the traumatic experience of impeachment.

Despite the greater and more immediate accountability of the parliamentary executive, the Founding Fathers deliberately rejected this system. They agreed with Montesquieu, who in his *Spirit of the Laws* had argued that when the legislative and executive powers were united, liberty was jeopardized. In fact they condemned King George III for creating his own party in Parliament and held him responsible for undermining the country's liberty by blurring the distinction between the executive and the legislature. Meanwhile, their unfortunate experience with the Articles of Confederation during the "Critical Period" of American history, led them to associate the union of legislative and executive authority with instability, intrigue, and executive weakness. This sentiment was confirmed by their knowledge of European history and the fact that states such as the Holy Roman Empire and Poland, which did not develop strong and independent executives, fell prey to foreign influence and counted for very little in Europe.

The Founding Fathers also seemed to sense better than their European contemporaries that the viability of a parliamentary regime rested upon the existence of a two-party system, which the United States with its already vast geographical expanse, sectional interests, and diversity of views did not possess. In order to disprove the old maxim that republicanism was not suitable for a large country because the chief magistracy could not preserve order, men such as Gouverneur Morris and James Wilson called for a powerful and singular head of state.

Much of their position was adopted in the federal Constitution. It provides for an independent executive with a veto—the word is from the Latin meaning "I forbid!"—and the separation of power. Although the attempt to saddle the President with an executive council which would have curtailed his power was abortive, his power to appoint was somewhat circumscribed by making it subject to the Senate's advice and consent.

The Constitution does not specify if the Chief Executive has the obligation of consulting the Senate when removing officials it had to confirm. However, when the first departments were set up—those of War, Foreign Affairs, and Finance—Congress decided that the Senate should not hinder the President in removing department heads from their posts. James Madison championed this position, arguing that administrative integration was necessary to assure full executive responsibility. In this manner all would know that the President and he alone was responsible for the good behavior of his officials. Madison also shied away from creating a situation that sanctioned a type of ministerial responsibility to the Senate which would have undoubtedly occurred if the upper house had the power to control removals.

The Presidency faced a serious challenge during the Reconstruction era when the House voted to impeach Andrew Johnson for having disregarded the Tenure of Office Act. With the passage of this act in 1867, the interpretation of the First Congress that the power of removal of executive appointees rested with the President alone, was overturned. Until 1887, when it was repealed, the power of removal was to be exercised only in concurrence with the Senate. Specifically designed by the Radical Republicans to restrict the freedom of Andrew Johnson and compel his retention of Secretary of War Edwin Stanton in the Cabinet, this act was of little use after his acquittal in 1868 following a sensational trial before the Senate.

In the 1860s a bill introduced by Representative George Hunt Pendleton sought to reverse the growth of Presidential power at the expense of Congress by permitting secretaries of the executive departments to occupy seats in the House of Representatives. This legislation would have increased the power of Cabinet members by providing them with some input into the legislative process while subjecting them to Congressional scrutiny, thus rendering them far less the creatures of the White House. This measure, which was a first step in attempting to transform the American presidential system into a European, parliamentary one, failed to secure enactment.

For the next fifteen years the notion that heads of the executive departments should be allowed to sit in Congress in parliamentary style remained dormant until Pendleton reintroduced the principle, following his election to the Senate in 1879. As before, the proposal failed to secure legislature approval. In the last decades of the nineteenth century, Congressional domination and a string of weak Presidents allayed the fears of many that the executive would overpower the legislature. Hence in the twenty-two years after

Pendleton's last endeavors in 1881, only one bill was presented in the House, which suggested that Cabinet members be allowed to participate in Congressional debates.

With the reemergence of strong executive leadership and the end of Presidential eclipse in the twentieth century, the desire to curtail the chief magistrate's influence reappeared. During Franklin D. Roosevelt's administration, one of the frequent charges launched against the President was that he undermined the balance of power in government by infringing upon the rights of Congress and attempting to "pack the Court." In 1940, when he broke the tradition against a third term of office, some accused him of establishing a personal dictatorship, a fear that alarmed more Americans when Roosevelt was elected for a historic fourth term. This prompted passage of the Twenty-second amendment to the Constitution, which prescribes that no person shall be elected to the office of President more than twice.

Roosevelt's successor, Harry Truman, was denounced for involving American troops in Korea without Congressional approval and was accused of undermining its constitutional authority to declare war. More recently the Vietnam War and the Watergate tragedy have led an increasing number of Americans to question their political process and some have sounded the call for substantial reform of the executive power.

Early in 1974, Representative Henry S. Reuss, Democrat of Wisconsin, proposed an amendment to the Constitution that would enable Congress, in parliamentary fashion, to issue a vote of no-confidence in the Chief Executive—it would require a three-fifths' majority of both houses—and call for a special election to select a successor. This feature of the proposed amendment is clearly inspired by Western European political developments and the parliamentary system of government. Its supporters, desirous of restoring some parity between the legislative and executive branches of government in the United States, point to its effectiveness in England.

Unquestionably, while events in the United States have led to a strengthening of the Presidency and rendered the office increasingly the center of government, a different solution evolved in Great Britain. There Parliament gradually established control over the crown. Central in the attempts to render the king subordinate was the House of Commons's determination to control royal advisers. In addition to the power of the purse, the most powerful weapon the House employed was impeachment, and eventually an intolerable situation developed for the ministers. If they did not do the bidding of the king they were dismissed by him; if they followed the royal will against the wishes of the House they were in serious danger of impeachment. A solution to the dilemma was found in the establishment of parliamentary control over the ministers. This assured that though the king would reign he would not rule.

The ministry experienced some reversals in its attempt to impose parliamentary control upon the crown. However, by the reign of Queen Victoria, parliamentarianism in England assumed its modern form. Under this system the crown in theory retains all the executive powers that are vested in the President of the United States, if not more. In reality, all of its powers are implemented by the prime minister and his colleagues who control the government, subject to the approval of the House of Commons.

In England, the ministers of the crown must not only have the support of the House of Commons, they must also be members of it or the House of Lords. While all members of Parliament who hold important administrative posts of a political character (and relinquish these when the cabinet resigns) are ministers, only the eighteen or twenty most important officials of the crown are members of the cabinet. It is their collective function to formulate the policy of the state and legislative program for each session of Parliament.

The prime minister, as the name implies, is the leading minister, but he is not the commander in the American sense. He must persuade the other ministers who are his colleagues, not his subordinates, if he wishes to maintain their support and that of their friends in the legislature. The cabinet remains extremely important in the drafting and implementation of legislation as well as in making important decisions. During the American Civil War recognition of the Southern Confederacy was averted by a majority vote of the cabinet against the wishes of three of its most important members: the prime minister, the foreign secretary, and the chancellor of the exchequer.

In the United States, however, the Cabinet does not have any official responsibility for lawmaking. Unable to sit in the legislature as their English counterparts do, American Cabinet members are unable to direct debates and influence policy in the Senate or the House of Representatives. Furthermore, they enjoy very little independence vis-à-vis the President. Even the most competent Secretaries legally remain Presidential aides rather than integral and independent parts of the executive power as in England. An American President can unilaterally dismiss one or several of his Secretaries without provoking the ministerial crisis which would very likely occur under a parliamentary system.

Some have argued that this provision renders the American executive more important and therefore has attracted stronger figures. Not all would concur with this conclusion. In the nineteenth century Lord Bryce, in his work *The American Commonwealth*, examined the Presidency and cited its failure to attract great men. An objective analysis of parliamentary and presidential executives reveals that both have produced their share of outstanding, competent, and mediocre leaders. The parliamentary executive does have the advantage of being more readily controlled by the legislature while providing a concentration of power which facilitates the implementation of programs.

Indeed, in England the Parliament is supreme to the point that there exists no charter or statute Parliament does not have the power to change. There is in fact no legal difference between constituent authority and lawmaking authority. Under emergency conditions the Parliament, which normally must be elected every five years, even has the power to prolong its own life and did so during the course of both world wars. The President and Congress, in comparison, cannot prolong their terms in office for a single day, no matter what the circumstances.

The collegiate or parliamentary executive developed first in England has provided that country with prestige, power, and stability as well as responsible leadership and has exerted an undeniable fascination elsewhere. The countries of the Continent, understandably envious of the good government enjoyed by the English, looked to the mother of parliaments for inspiration. Camillo di Cavour, the creator of the unitary state, was instrumental in promoting the development of ministerial responsibility in Italy as it existed in England. Influenced by the governmental system of the island kingdom, which he regarded as the best in the world, Cavour did not take into account the political and social realities of the Italian peninsula. It was soon apparent that political manipulation as well as electoral engineering were required to make the English parliamentary system work in Italy.

France, likewise, has not been too successful in its attempts to imitate the political institutions of others. When the revolution overturned the *ancien régime* in 1789, the French quite naturally looked to the British for direction in establishing constitutional government. They were soon to learn that it was easier to transport armies than transpose institutions.

Undeterred, the French subsequently attempted to combine aspects of parliamentary and presidential government as Woodrow Wilson suggested at the turn of the century and as currently proposed by Representative Reuss. The constitution of the short-lived Second Republic sought to synthesize the two systems, borrowing what it deemed best from both worlds. Thus France was to have a president elected directly by the people and he, in turn, was given the responsibility of naming his ministers. Under this constitution the relationship between the president and the legislature was uncertain since both were designed to represent the popular will.

One deputy in analyzing the document acknowledged that the executive and legislative branches would clash, but he hoped that they would balance each other under the scrutiny of the press and thus work to preserve liberty. His was an optimistic appraisal. Critics of the constitution of the Second Republic were quick to enumerate its flaws. It was difficult to revise, as is that of the United States. Even more serious, the ministers were not only secretaries of the president and responsible to him, they were accountable to the assembly whose agents they were. It soon became apparent that ministers like other men cannot serve two masters. This contributed to the collapse of the republic.

Despite this failure the French repeated the attempt to combine parliamentary and presidential government with the establishment of the Fifth French Republic. Under its constitution the locus of power shifted from the assembly to the president, who appoints the prime minister with the concurrence of parliament. Furthermore, in the Fifth Republic, unlike the Third and Fourth, there is maintained the principle of the separation of power so that no member of the cabinet can hold a seat in the chamber. This separation is an aspect of presidential government and a bold departure from traditional parliamentary government.

General de Gaulle, the founder and first president of the Fifth Republic, could not resist the allure of getting votes of confidence, not from the parliament but from the people. When one such plebescite disagreed with his policy, the general resigned although he was under no constitutional mandate to do so. In many ways he was the victim of the political schizophrenia of the Fifth Republic, that attempts to reconcile parliamentary and presidential government. Whether the incumbent president, Giscard d'Estaing, can do so remains to be seen. It is not only his political career but the fate of the republic which hangs in the balance.

Aside from the technical problems the French have encountered in attempting to reconcile these rather different forms of government, various examples reveal that one cannot transfer institutions from one area to another and expect them to operate in the same manner. The Italians and the French, as well as the Germans who established parliamentary government with ministerial responsibility after World War I, failed to realize that the parliamentary system worked so well in Britain because it had evolved there out of a far greater consensus on political issues in that country. The English also enjoyed the advantages of a two-party system. The multiparty system of the Third and Fourth Republics in France as well as the Weimar Republic in Germany contributed to their instability and eventual collapse.

Despite the best of intentions, Britain's former African colonies have not been successful in adopting the mother country's parliamentary government and developing viable democratic institutions. Nor have the countries of Latin America been any more successful in their attempts to attain political stability and assure democracy by adopting the presidential system of government that has worked so well in the United States. In many of these South American republics what has emerged is not only a strengthened executive but an outright dictatorship. For example, in Argentina, where the Constitution of 1853—which provides for a separation of powers into executive, legislative, and judicial branches—is supposedly still in effect, its provisions have been altered by the military coup of 1966. Under the Statutes of the Revolution, both the executive and legislative functions have been combined in the office of the presidency.

Likewise, the United States presence in the Philippines and its impact upon its governmental institutions have not been sufficient to prevent that democracy from sliding into a type of personal dictatorship in recent years. The bitter harvest reaped by the American investment in South Vietnam—which copied the American presidential system—as well as the disappointing results obtained in South Korea provide further proof that political ideas and experience are not easily transported elsewhere.

Paradoxically, while earlier attempts to reconcile parliamentary and presidential governments have proved less than successful and the attempts to transplant institutions have witnessed far fewer triumphs than failures, some Americans liberated from the shadow of domestic uncertainty by the resignation of President Nixon continue to look to the parliamentary system for inspiration. Undeniably the impeachment process is cumbersome when compared to the procedure employed in some parliamentary regimes, but one cannot be certain that this feature would operate as well in the United States if it were suddenly grafted onto the existing political structure.

Furthermore, parliamentary government does not always resolve conflict in the best possible manner. In the summer of 1975 when Prime Minister Indira Gandhi was stripped of her right to vote in Parliament as a result of her conviction on charges of electoral corruption, the daughter of former Prime Minister Nehru imposed a sweeping state of emergency upon her country, jailed some twenty members of the parliamentary opposition, curtailed a series of basic civil rights, and had these steps legitimized by parliamentary approval.

The United States, with its presidential system and its lack of immediate accountability, fared much better in the Watergate crisis. Despite the rigidity of its forms and the relatively slow pace at which the corrective mechanism moved, eventually its own institutions gained sufficient momentum to contain the excessive power of the Presidency, restrain the actions of those who would have subverted the Constitution, and aroused the conscience of its citizenry. The presidential system in the United States survived the "national nightmare" in such a manner as to show that the republic "is a government of laws and not of men."

Under the presidential system developed in the United States the country has enjoyed strong leadership and has preserved its democratic ideals. In the words of Edmund Burke, "It is with infinite caution that any man ought to venture upon pulling down an edifice which has answered in any tolerable degree for ages the common purposes of society, or on building up again without having models and patterns of approved utility before his eyes."

26

THE SCOPE and LIMITS
of PRESIDENTIAL
POWER
by Robert S. Hirschfield

The Watergate affair and the unprecedented resignation of a President have focused attention on the oldest and most difficult problem of American government: defining the scope and the limits of Presidential power. Although this problem has been a matter of concern since the beginning of the republic, it requires more serious consideration now than ever before because Watergate has made it clear that in the wrong hands the powerful Presidency which we have come to accept over the past forty years can endanger the very foundations of our constitutional democracy.

The power of the Presidency is a complex phenomenon. It cannot be determined simply by reference to the Constitution; nor does it become fully evident by reviewing the history of what Presidents have done or gotten away with. The reason for this elusiveness is that Presidential power *varies*, and that its reality at any given time is the product of a number of factors. The meaning currently attributed to the formal, constitutional sources of executive authority is one of these factors. Another is the state of the political system in which the specific Presidency is operating. The personal attributes and attitudes of the incumbent President comprise still another factor determining his power, while it also depends on the particular set of circumstances, conditions and events presently confronting the nation. Finally, Presidential power varies with the degree of trust ·and confidence the incumbent inspires among the general public. All of these factors change from time to time and from President to President. They are constantly in flux, and since the power of the Presidency is the product of interaction among all of them, the dimensions of that power are continually changing. As a result, no absolute definition of Presidential power is possible, because that power is always in the process of being defined.

When Professor Woodrow Wilson said that "the president is at liberty, both in law and conscience, to be as big a man as he can," he indicated the range of possibilities open to a President in attempting to exercise power, and emphasized that the essential attribute of the constitutional office is its flexibility. For the Presidency under the Constitution is only potentially, not necessarily, powerful. The document's provisions on the executive branch, even more than those on the judicial and legislative, are general, indefinite, and ambiguous. They allow for Presidential energy, resourcefulness, creativity, and aggrandizement; but they also permit passivity, indifference, ineptitude, and possibly worse. Constitutional flexibility—the most distinctive and important feature of American government—has made the Presidency both the most dynamic and the most dangerous of our political institutions.

The basic characteristics of the office—its unitary form, independent functions, and national purview—are clear enough. But Article 2 provides at best only a hint of the potential for Presidential power. In fact, those cryptic provisions raise more questions than they answer. The President is "commander in chief of the army and the navy of the United States." But does this make him only the nation's "first general and admiral," as Alexander Hamilton insisted, or does it empower him to use the armed forces in such a way as to commit the nation to war? Does his authority to make treaties by and with the advice and consent of two-thirds of the Senate require a sharing of power in the formulation and control of foreign policy, or does it mean, as the Supreme Court once stated, that the President is America's "sole organ of government" in the field of international relations? The President is to "take care that the laws be faithfully executed," but faithful according to what standard? Congressional intention? Judicial rulings? His own determination of constitutionality or political expediency? The very first words of Article 2 read, "The executive power shall be vested in a

President of the United States of America." But is this simply an introductory statement, or is it a grant of inherent power to act in any way the President deems necessary to protect the national interest?

Ostensibly it is possible in the American governmental system to determine the scope and limits of Presidential power, since interpretation of the Constitution's meaning is the function of the Supreme Court. But despite its vaunted reputation, judicial review

Richard Nixon and Lyndon B. Johnson. *Lyndon B. Johnson Library*

has not been an effective method of defining executive authority. Judicial pronouncements on the subject are rare, and in virtually every instance they have involved acquiescence in extraordinary actions taken during periods of grave national emergency. Although in its latest major decision on Presidential power the Court rejected Mr. Nixon's claim of absolute "executive privilege" and ordered him to make available information relevant to the Watergate affair, it is the lesson of history that the Supreme Court usually restrains itself rather than the President. If, as in the executive-privilege case, the misuse of power is clear and the political climate compels, the Court may go further and attempt to impose limits on specific exercises of authority. But in relation to strong Presidents the judiciary has generally functioned only as a symbol of restraint, a moral force, and a reminder of established principles. As a result, the powerful Presidency has developed within a framework of legitimacy, its awesome authority accommodated by the almost infinite flexibility of the Constitution.

The American political system is also extremely flexible. Operating simultaneously at two levels—national and local—it is exceedingly complex, allowing for the expansion of executive power when the President can mobilize broad support for himself and his policies, but providing formidable constraints on that power when he cannot. The growth of democracy has made the Presidency a tribunate office so that today the President is politically as well as constitutionally, actually as well as symbolically, "the sole representative of all the people." This development, which had its beginnings in the Jacksonian era, has resulted in a Presidency potentially much more powerful than the monarchical office so feared by its early opponents. But Presidential power is subject to limitation because of its dependence on public attitudes, and because changes in those attitudes can be reflected through institutions (Congress, the media, economic enterprises, state governments) which have countervailing power.

Although the President ostensibly heads his political party both in the country and in Congress, this party leadership does not give him control over the political process. There is no conformance between the President's position of national leadership and the structure of American politics. At the root of this anomaly is the fact that our political system is locally rather than nationally based. Despite the quadrennial appearance of "national parties" to contest for the Presidency, politics in America is essentially local in organization, operation, and orientation.

Unlike parliamentary systems, ours consciously separates the executive and legislative branches of government politically as well as functionally. The President and Congress are selected and elected independently of each other; they represent different constituencies and have different interests. Our national parties are only federations of state and city political organizations which come together in tenuous alliance every four years to seek the substantial rewards of capturing the White House. It is the leaders of the major party organizations, the political chieftains of the largest states and cities, who choose the party's Presidential nominee and mobilize the resources for his campaign. But candidates for local offices—Senators, Representatives, and other officials—are selected separately by local parties and local electorates, entirely without reference to the Presidential nominee and in no way beholden to him. The so-called "national election" is primarily the Presidential election and is in fact only one part of an electoral cycle in which the various participants in national governance are chosen.

The results of this process are as complicated as the system itself. Because our politics is neither national nor disciplined, party and government have little relationship to each other. Since the Presidential and Congressional elections are separate, a party's nominee may capture the White House, while the party as a whole fails to win a majority of seats in one or both legislative houses. But in any event, party control of both the executive and legislative branches does not have the same effect as in parliamentary systems. For whether the President's party does or does not control Congress, independently elected legislators are free to act independently of the President. Any President must bargain, cajole, or threaten to get what he wants in Congress. To achieve his legislative goals he must constantly try to form majority coalitions among members of both his own and the opposition party. As a result, every President finds that leadership of party and Congress is his most difficult and frustrating job, whether it be John Kennedy with a legislature dominated by his own party, Lyndon Johnson with a quarter-century of experience in fashioning working majorities on the Hill, or Richard Nixon lacking party control in either house. Moreover, because Congressmen are extremely sensitive to the views of their own constituents, a President who has lost the confidence of the people finds that loss quickly reflected in Congress, as public criticism or hostility lead to legislative obduracy and opposition.

While it may be difficult for the President to control Congress, the opposite is even more true. Although the legislature is traditionally regarded as the executive's principal antagonist and most effective restrainer, in modern times Congress has had little success in performing this role. The local orientation of Congress results in a structural fragmentation and dispersal of power which leaves the legislature without a cohesive majority or strong leadership. In fact, if the President does not himself assume the role of legislative leader, Congress cannot move on important or controversial issues. Lacking the information-gathering and problem-evaluating apparatus of the Presidency, Congress is not properly equipped to oversee executive operations; on the contrary its supervisory function is to a large extent dependent on the executive's willingness to cooperate. Indeed this limitation on Congressional control extends even to determination of the final plan for governmental expenditures, the budget, which is formulated by the executive branch.

Congress is not impotent in restraining the President, but except for rare occasions when issues of prerogative or policy are clearly drawn, the key to legislative control lies outside the houses in the relationship between the President and the people. The political longevity of Congressional leaders and the absence of party discipline allow for displays of independence which can embarrass or inhibit the executive, and legislative hearings and investigations can focus attention on alleged maladministration or misconduct in the Presidency. But by its nature Congress is attuned to compromise and accommodation rather than decisive action, and it can be mobilized against the President only when he has lost public approval and there is a general and sustained popular demand to impose restraints on him.

Because the political system divides the American people into separate Presidential and Congressional constituencies representing different interests and divergent views, it raises the constant threat of governmental stalemate or dyarchy. And because it is deeply rooted in the basic structural principles of American government—federalism and the separation of powers—the system is uncommonly resistant to change. Nonetheless it is resilient enough to permit unity, leadership, and action when necessary. As the depression and wartime experiences demonstrate, the executive and legislative powers can be fused, partisanship has been sublimated, and Presidential primacy is accepted under the pressure of crisis.

The third element that must be considered in attempting to

ascertain the scope and limits of executive authority is not systemic but human: the personal attributes and attitudes of the President himself. Because the Presidency is a personal office, the incumbent's personality—his capacity for generating positive (or negative) public feelings and responses toward himself—is essential to his leadership role. While this personality factor involves the mysterious chemistry that develops between a President and the people, it is closely related to the incumbent's attitude regarding his office, its authority, and the way in which he believes that authority should be used. In fact, a President's own view of his power plays an important part in shaping the dimensions of that power.

Presidents do not often indulge in theoretical exposition of their ideas, and only occasionally has one expressed himself clearly or systematically on the subject of his authority. But such formal statements are not necessary, since a President's views are revealed in the way he conducts his Presidency and confronts the problems of his time. Every President has some conception of the Presidency's power. In at least one instance (Woodrow Wilson) that conception was fully developed before the office was achieved. Among the other Presidents, some (like Lincoln) formulated their views of power under the pressure of events, some (like Kennedy) modified their views in accommodating to the realities of their situations, and a few (like Buchanan and Hoover) held to views which circumstances had made untenable. But however a President reaches his concept of Presidential power, and whatever form that concept assumes, his own attitude and behavior are major determinants of the power he in fact possesses. Moreover, the President's conception of his functions and authority is a crucial factor in determining America's destiny, as John Kennedy pointed out in 1960 when he noted that "the history of this nation—its brightest and bleakest pages—has been written largely in terms of the different views our Presidents have had of the Presidency itself."

Here again there are no definite rules, for the office is open to a wide range of background, experience, and temperament. But in attempting to assess the Presidents, observers have developed criteria and classifications—the "weak" and "strong" Presidents and Presidencies—which reflect the different ways that Presidential power has been conceived and exercised.

The weak Presidents are those who regard the exercise of

power as distasteful and the avoidance of decisive action as a virtue. This view is translated into a literalist conception of the American constitutional and political systems, and a strict-constructionist interpretation of the President's power in those systems. The weak President believes that his office is bound by the principles of federalism and separation of powers. He is reluctant to advocate or enforce policies that expand national government control and impinge on state or local authority. He considers Congress an equal and coordinate, if not superior, organ of government, and often expects the legislature to express the public will and formulate public policy. The Presidency itself he sees as a moderative office, its influence as primarily moral and above partisanship. The weak President takes a narrow view of his independent constitutional authority, even in the field of foreign affairs, and he is comfortable in the political system of widely distributed power and responsibility.

The strong President regards government as the appropriate instrument for achieving change in society and the Presidency as the vital center of government. Historically associated with the development of mass democracy and the growth of social consciousness, the strong Presidency is power-oriented and attuned to assertive, charismatic, and visionary leadership. In terms of the governmental system, this Presidency reflects a latitudinarian attitude toward basic constitutional principles and an expansionist view of Presidential power. National in his outlook, the strong President advocates the extension of national authority and is untroubled by the decline of localism. He attempts to join the political branches of government and to direct the legislative process. If Congress is uncooperative, he may resort—particularly in foreign affairs—to independent measures. Needing widespread support to gain his policy objectives, he seeks to be both a popular and party leader. To the strong President, the Presidency's essential attribute is its power, and his purposes can be achieved only through the use of that power. For him it is the center of action, the only office representing the national interest, the focal position in American government and society.

Caution is required in assessing Presidents, since even those who have been regarded as weak or mediocre were not necessarily untalented or inept. Rather, Presidents and their administrations have almost invariably been reflective of the dominant mood of their times. More important than judging or rating Presidents, therefore, is the fact that the weak and strong Presidencies have generally been associated with different historical conditions—the former with periods of normalcy, of consolidation, of national reconciliation and "good feeling"; the latter with times of tension, movement, change, and crisis. Nor is this surprising, since no

Enlarging the Presidential Chair. *Courtesy of the Chicago Tribune and the Chicago Historical Society*

President operates in a vacuum, and since his own conception of the Presidency's power is not alone sufficient to determine the reality of that power. A President may conceive of his authority in the broadest terms and yet be unable to use it, or he may view his authority narrowly and still be compelled to act in a vigorous manner.

Two factors in addition to the President's own proclivities determine whether or not power can or will be used: the existence of circumstances or conditions perceived by the nation as requiring action and the nation's willingness to support the President if he chooses to act. While events, and particularly crises, can make vast authority available to the President, only a President who is prepared to act and whose popular support is firm can make the decision to use it. And conversely, no such Presidential decision can assure the availability of power without the existence of conditions which justify and legitimize its use. Harry Truman was able to act on his own initiative and according to his broad view of inherent executive authority when the Cold War turned hot in Korea, but when the crisis atmosphere and public approval passed he could not apply the same concept to seizure of the steel industry. John Kennedy could not move the country or Congress during a period of ostensible normalcy which he regarded as unperceived emergency, but he encountered no resistance when he alone decided the issue of national survival in the Cuban missile crisis. And while Lyndon Johnson found widespread support in 1964 for his attack on America's most critical domestic problems, by 1968 his ability to lead the nation had been dissipated by grave doubts regarding both the morality and the necessity of the war in Vietnam.

Only when it is apparent that the nation's fate is at stake does extraordinary power flow to the President; but in times of crisis his authority reaches its zenith, as illustrated by Lincoln's "dictatorial" regime during the Civil War, by Wilson's highly centralized World War I administration, and by Franklin Roosevelt's executive-dominated government during the emergencies of domestic depression and global conflict. National peril creates conditions—psychological as well as constitutional and political—for the use of power by a power-oriented President. Partisanship and localism are sublimated, and Congress and the country alike turn to the President for leadership in time of evident emergency. It is not surprising, therefore, that all of the "great Presidents" have held office during periods of great crisis.

Although theoretically the twin fountainheads of executive authority are "the Constitution and the laws," in fact the sources of this prodigious power are democracy and necessity. The public need for clearly identified and deeply trusted leadership and the governmental need for focus, initiative, and action form the dual base of the powerful contemporary Presidency. Given this foundation, the edifice of Presidential power is constructed through a combination of popular attraction to the President as a person and popular support for his policies as national leader.

The President's role as "tribune of the people" is essential to the acceptance of a need for action in defense of the national interest and to the exercise of whatever authority may be latent in the Presidential office. Neither Lincoln nor Roosevelt could have acted with such spectacular independence in meeting the challenges confronting them had they lacked solid public support, but with that support they could push their powers to the limits of constitutionality and beyond. Indeed a number of strong Presidents have received object lessons regarding the dependence of power on popular approval: Wilson during the fight over the League of Nations, Truman in the steel dispute, Roosevelt when he presented his plan to "pack" the Supreme Court. The power of a power-oriented President is virtually unlimited if he enjoys the trust of the people, but if a President loses the public's confidence his authority as Chief Executive is seriously impaired and his position as acknowledged leader of the nation may be jeopardized.

Depending on how intense, widespread, and sustained is the public reaction against a President, the consequences of popular disapproval cover a broad range of constraints. Inevitably a President who cannot mobilize national support finds his leverage in Congress and his effectiveness in areas requiring Congressional consent or cooperation curtailed. At a more serious level of confrontation, the legislature and other centers of countervailing power may assert their authority and rebuff the President, as the Supreme Court did in declaring Truman's seizure of the steel mills unconstitutional and as Congress did by refusing to enact additional New Deal legislation in the wake of Roosevelt's abortive Court-packing plan. Public pressure can become so great that a beleaguered President may be compelled to "campaign" for popular support or he may attempt, as Lyndon Johnson did, to calm the situation by announcing that he will not seek another term in office.

Ultimately, if public reaction to the President reaches a crescendo of outrage and opposition, Congress may turn to the only remedy for involuntary executive change provided by the Constitution—impeachment by a majority vote of the House of Representatives, followed by trial before the Senate with the Chief Justice presiding, in which a two-thirds' vote for conviction results in the President's removal from office. This process, often threatened, has been carried to conclusion only once in the nation's history—against Lincoln's successor, Andrew Johnson—and in that single instance the Senate failed to convict by one vote. Thus no President has as yet ever been removed from office, and only Mr. Nixon has ever resigned under pressure. But the power of any discredited President declines in direct proportion to his loss of popular approval, and if public sentiment remains overwhelmingly negative, he cannot function effectively as the country's leader.

In a governmental system noted for its pragmatism, the Presidency is our most pragmatic institution. The office is truly a mirror of our national life, reflecting accurately the events that have made our history, the men we have chosen, for better or worse, to deal with those events, and our own willingness to entrust them with enormous authority over the nation's destiny. It is a flexible and resilient office, whose form has remained undisturbed for almost two hundred years, although its substance—that is, its power—has constantly varied.

Presidential power is now under attack because the misconduct in office of an aberrant incumbent threatened to undermine the fundamental principles of our constitutional democratic system. But the nation should remember that a strong executive has been its indispensable instrument in meeting crises at home and abroad since the republic's inception. That the vast power of the office creates real danger we know, now more clearly than ever before, but the answer to the problem of Presidential power is not an emasculated Presidency. The uncertainties of our time still demand an executive capable of leadership and action. There is no alternative to the strong Presidency as the keystone of American government and the Western alliance. There is no substitute for the President as the sole representative of the national interest, as the focus of our political system, as the major initiator of change in our society.

Watergate should make every one of us more aware of our own responsibility for the defense of constitutional democratic government. But nothing that we have experienced changes the fact that America needs a powerful Presidency.

SELECTED BIBLIOGRAPHY

GENERAL WORKS

An excellent introductory book for the student or general reader is Clinton Rossiter, *The American Presidency* (rev. ed., New York, 1960). The best analytical work on the Presidency is Edward S. Corwin, *The President: Office and Powers* (4th rev. ed., New York, 1957). Both of these outstanding works are somewhat dated since they do not deal with Presidents after Eisenhower. A first-rate volume that discusses the various functions and roles of the President with a contemporary emphasis is Louis W. Koenig, *The Chief Executive* (3rd ed., New York, 1975). Among the many short volumes on the Presidency, one of the better ones is Wilfred Binkley, *The Man in the White House: His Powers and Duties* (rev. ed., New York, 1964). A good standard textbook is Joseph Kallenbach, *The American Chief Executive* (New York, 1966). A fine collection of perceptive essays on aspects of the Presidency is Aaron Wildavsky, ed., *The Presidency* (Boston, 1969); Nelson W. Polsby, ed., *The Modern Presidency* (New York, 1973), is a collection of essays on Presidents from Franklin D. Roosevelt to Richard Nixon.

An informative and lively discussion dealing with rating the Presidents is Thomas A. Bailey, *Presidential Greatness* (New York, 1966). Important and pivotal Presidential decisions have been collected in Richard Morris, ed., *Great Presidential Decisions* (enlarged ed., New York, 1973). Two perceptive works which discuss the President and Congress are Wilfred Binkley, *The President and Congress* (3rd rev. ed., New York, 1962), and Louis Fischer, *President and Congress: Power and Policy* (New York, 1972). The latter work gives more attention to more contemporary relationships between the two branches.

A provocative study of Presidential character and personality discussing Presidents from Taft to Nixon is James David Barber, *The Presidential Character: Predicting Performance in the White House* (Englewood Cliffs, N.J., 1972). Another perceptive personality study of twentieth-century Presidents is Erwin C. Hargrove, *Presidential Leadership: Personality and Political Style* (New York, 1966). An excellent collection which portrays the growth of Presidential power is Robert S. Hirschfield, ed., *The Power of* the Presidency (2nd ed., Chicago, 1973). Other works which analyze the contemporary Presidency and discuss Presidential power are Richard E. Neustadt, *Presidential Power: The Politics of Leadership* (New York, 1960); James MacGregor Burns, *Presidential Government: The Crucible of Leadership* (Boston, 1965); Emmet John Hughes, *The Living Presidency* (New York, 1973); and Arthur M. Schlesinger, Jr., *The Imperial Presidency* (Boston, 1973). The latter work includes an interpretive study of the Nixon Presidency and aspects of Watergate. A probing and arresting work which analyzes the atmosphere of royalty surrounding the Presidency is George Reedy, *Twilight of the Presidency* (New York, 1970). This work was written by one of Lyndon Johnson's press secretaries and in many ways it predicted some of the problems involved in Watergate.

A collection of essays which reexamines the Presidency is Rexford Tugwell and Thomas E. Cronin, eds., *The Presidency Reappraised* (New York, 1974). The proceedings of one of the symposia sponsored by the Center for the Study of the Presidency is R. Gordon Hoxie, ed., *The Presidency of the 1970's* (New York, 1973). This compilation includes discussions by members of various Presidential administrations as well as scholars and journalists. Other valuable books on the contemporary Presidency are Erwin C. Hargrove, *The Power of the Modern Presidency* (New York, 1974), and Thomas E. Cronin, *The State of the Presidency* (Boston, 1975). For a comprehensive bibliographical essay on the American Presidency see Kenneth Davison, "The American Presidency: A Bibliographical Essay," *American Studies: An International Newsletter* 12 (Autumn, 1973), pp. 16–23, and (Winter, 1973) pp. 29–44; this essay, with some revisions, also appears in *The Center House Bulletin* 4 (Winter, 1974), pp. 10–12 and *Presidential Studies Quarterly* (Spring, 1974), pp. 23–34.

THE PRESIDENCY
FROM WASHINGTON TO McKINLEY

An excellent starting point for a study of the early development of the executive is Charles C. Thach, Jr., *The Creation of the Presidency, 1775–1789: A Study in Constitutional History* (Baltimore, 1923). A fine study of the colonial governors is Evarts B. Greene, *The Provincial Governor in the English Colonies of North America* (New York, 1898). The factors shaping New York's 1777 Constitution are described very well in Bernard Mason, *The Road to Independence: The Revolutionary Movement in New York, 1773–1777* (Lexington, Ky., 1966). Ernest W. Spaulding, *His Excellency George Clinton (1739–1812): Critic of the Constitution* (New

York, 1938), describes the successful political career of New York State's first governor. Some of the better treatments of the Philadelphia Convention of 1787 are: Max Farrand, *The Framing of the Constitution* (New Haven, 1913); Charles Van Doren, *The Great Rehearsal* (New York, 1948); Charles Warren, *The Making of the Constitution* (Boston, 1928); and Clinton Rossiter, *1787, The Grand Convention* (New York, 1966). A convenient, condensed version of the debates of the convention is found in Charles Callan Tansill, ed., *Documents Illustrative of the Formation of the Union of the American States* (Washington, D.C., 1927). *The Federalist Papers* are essential reading and have been printed in numerous editions. Cecelia Kenyon gives a sampling of Antifederalist arguments against the Constitution's ratification in her collection of documents, *The Antifederalists* (Indianapolis, 1966). An overall view of the ideology of the period, set within a republican framework, is Gordon Wood, *The Creation of the American Republic, 1776–1787* (Chapel Hill, 1969).

An excellent detailed study of President Washington's first year in office is James Hart, *The American Presidency in Action, 1789* (New York, 1948). The sixth and seventh volumes of Douglas Southall Freeman's life of Washington, *George Washington: Patriot and President, 1784–1793* (New York, 1954) and *George Washington: First in Peace, March 1793–December 1799* (New York, 1957), completed by John Alexander Carroll and Mary Wells Ashworth, furnish an excellent and exhaustive narrative of Washington's administration. James Thomas Flexner, *George Washington and the New Nation, 1783–1793* (Boston, 1970) and *George Washington: Anguish and Farewell, 1793–1799* (Boston, 1972), are less detailed but quite good. Biographies of Washington's principal collaborators in the executive branch include: John C. Miller, *Alexander Hamilton: Portrait in Paradox* (New York, 1959); Dumas Malone, *Jefferson and the Rights of Man* (Boston, 1951) and *Jefferson and the Ordeal of Liberty* (Boston, 1962); volumes two and three of Malone's *Jefferson and His Time* (Boston, 1951, 1962); and Irving Brant, *James Madison: Father of the Constitution, 1787–1800* (Indianapolis, 1950). Leonard White, *The Federalists: An Administrative History* (New York, 1948), is invaluable for studying how the executive departments were set up and how Washington supervised their work. A good general treatment of the Federalist Period is John C. Miller, *The Federalist Era, 1789–1801* (New York, 1960). A valuable primary source which includes the story of Washington's attempt to fully implement the "advice and consent" clause is Edgar S. Maclay, ed., *The Journal of William Maclay* (New York, 1923). Consult Richard H. Kohn, "The Washington Administration's Decision to Crush the Whiskey Rebellion," *The Journal of American History* 59 (1972), pp. 567–84, for a detailed study of the President's handling of the crisis. Burton Ira

Kaufman, ed., *Washington's Farewell Address: The View From the 20th Century* (Chicago, 1969), is a convenient compilation of differing articles.

There are two useful histories of American political parties: Roy F. Nichols, *The Invention of the American Political Parties* (New York, 1967), and Wilfred E. Binkley, *American Political Parties* (New York, 1947). An excellent history of Presidential elections is Arthur M. Schlesinger, Jr., and Fred Israel, eds., *History of American Presidential Elections*, 4 vols. (New York, 1971). An older and less comprehensive study is Eugene H. Roseboom, *A History of Presidential Elections* (New York, 1964). Also valuable, although limited to the nineteenth century, is Edward Stanwood, *A History of Presidential Elections* (Cambridge, Mass., 1888). For a superb treatment of the changing attitudes toward parties during the early days of the Republic see Richard Hofstadter, *The Idea of a Party System: The Rise of Legitimate Opposition in the United States, 1780–1840* (Berkeley, 1969). The development of the Republican and Federalist parties are described in several valuable studies. These include Morton Borden, *Parties and Politics in the Early Republic* (New York, 1967); William M. Chambers, *Political Parties in a New Nation* (New York, 1963); Joseph Charles, *The Origins of the American Party System* (Williamsburg, 1956); Noble E. Cunningham, Jr., *The Jeffersonian Republicans: The Formation of Party Organization, 1789–1801* (Chapel Hill, 1957); and *The Jeffersonian Republicans in Power: Party Operations, 1801–1809* (Chapel Hill, 1963). A classic in the study of American parties is M. Ostrogorski, *Democracy and the Organization of Political Parties*, 2 vols. (New York, 1902). The evolution of a one-party system and the subsequent reemergence of the two-party system can be studied from two important books: George Dangerfield, *The Era of Good Feelings* (New York, 1952), and Richard P. McCormick, *The Second American Party System: Party Formation in the Jacksonian Era* (Chapel Hill, 1966). The early formation of the Democratic party is the subject of two studies by Robert V. Remini, *Martin Van Buren and the Making of the Democratic Party* (New York, 1959) and *The Election of Andrew Jackson* (Philadelphia, 1963). The beginning of the Whig party is the subject of Eber M. Carroll's *Origins of the Whig Party* (Durham, 1925). A valuable monograph is James S. Chase, *Emergence of the Presidential Nominating Convention, 1789–1832* (Urbana, Ill., 1973).

Outstanding on the administrative aspects of the Jackson Presidency is Leonard E. White, *The Jacksonians: A Study in Administrative History, 1829–1861* (New York, 1954). More sympathetic to Jackson than White is Carl R. Fish, *The Civil Service and the Patronage* (New York, 1905). The literature on the "great issues" of the Jacksonian era is vast; useful leads to it appear in Edward Pessen, *Jacksonian America: Society, Personality, and Politics* (Homewood, Ill., 1969), and Alfred A. Cave, *Jacksonian Democ-*

racy and the Historians (Gainesville, Fla., 1964). For a sympathetic evaluation of Jackson's administration almost diametrically unlike Pessen's, see Arthur M. Schlesinger, Jr., *The Age of Jackson* (Boston, 1945), an influential book which soon after its publication stimulated many dozens of criticial studies. Among the best of the latter see Bray Hammond, *Banks and Politics in America from the Revolution to the Civil War* (Princeton, 1957), and Richard P. McCormick, *The Second American Party System: Party Formation in the Jacksonian Era* (Chapel Hill, 1966). Overviews on the unideological nature of the issues dividing the major parties are, on the national level, Joel H. Silbey, *The Shrine of Party: Congressional Voting Behavior, 1841–1852* (Pittsburgh, 1967); on the state level, Herbert Ershkowitz and William G. Shade, "Consensus or Conflict? Political Behavior in the State Legislatures during the Jacksonian Era," *Journal of American History* 58 (December 1971), pp. 591–621; and on the municpal level, Edward Pessen, "Who Governed the Nation's Cities in the 'Era of the Common Man'?" *Political Science Quarterly* 87 (December 1972), pp. 591–614. Worthy of special mention is Sidney H. Aronson, *Status and Kinship in the Higher Civil Service: Standards of Selection in the Administrations of John Adams, Thomas Jefferson, and Andrew Jackson* (Cambridge, Mass., 1964), which points up the gulf between Jacksonian theory and practice with regard to civil service appointments. Robert V. Remini's *Andrew Jackson and the Bank War* (New York, 1967) is a readable discussion of the issues which is noteworthy for the fair-mindedness of its judgments.

There are two good but somewhat outdated one-volume biographies of Lincoln, one by Benjamin P. Thomas, *Abraham Lincoln* (New York, 1952), and the other by Reinhard H. Luthin, *The Real Abraham Lincoln* (Englewood Cliffs, N.J., 1960). Ray P. Basler, ed., *The Collected Works of Abraham Lincoln,* 9 vols. (New Brunswick, N.J., 1953–1955) is an important source for any Lincoln scholar. It supplants the earlier work compiled by John G. Nicolay and John Hay. These two secretaries to the President also wrote a ten-volume biography, *Abraham Lincoln: A History* (New York, 1890), which has merit despite its age. Two books by T. Harry Williams, *Lincoln and the Radicals* (Madison, Wis., 1941) and *Lincoln and His Generals* (New York, 1952), cover two significant topics of the war years. Other works that deal with the politics of the Civil War are Burton J. Hendrick, *Lincoln's War Cabinet* (Boston, 1946), and William B. Hesseltine, *Lincoln and the War Governors* (New York, 1948). The fullest treatment of Lincoln's Presidency is the four-volume work by James G. Randall, *Lincoln the President* (New York, 1945–1955). Richard N. Current completed the fourth volume. Provocative commentary on Lincoln and related Civil War topics can be found in David Donald,

Lincoln Reconsidered (New York, 1956). Donald's chapter, "Abraham Lincoln: Whig in the White House," is especially pertinent. Other books that encompass a number of different subjects related to the Lincoln theme are Richard N. Current, *The Lincoln Nobody Knows* (New York, 1958); James G. Randall, *Lincoln the Liberal Statesman* (New York, 1947); and Allan Nevins, *The Statesmanship of the Civil War* (new enlarged ed., New York, 1962). Richard Hofstadter has contributed an important chapter on Lincoln in his *The American Political Tradition and the Men Who Made It* (New York, 1949). Significant issues during Lincoln's Presidency are covered in William B. Hesseltine's *Lincoln's Plan of Reconstruction* (Tuscaloosa, Ala., 1960), James G. Randall's *Constitutional Problems Under Lincoln* (rev. ed., Urbana, Ill., 1951), and John Hope Franklin, *The Emancipation Proclamation* (New York, 1963).

Leonard D. White, *The Republican Era, 1869–1901* (New York, 1958), is required reading for anyone interested in the Gilded Age Presidency. Also valuable are the relevant sections of Loren Beth, *Development of the American Constitution* (New York, 1971); Marcus Cunliffe, *American Presidents and the Presidency* (New York, 1972); John A. Garraty, *The New Commonwealth* (New York, 1968); and Norman C. Thomas and Hans W. Baade, eds., *The Institutionalized Presidency* (Dobbs Ferry, 1972). The domestic politics of the period is covered in H. Wayne Morgan, *From Hayes to McKinley* (Syracuse, 1969). Shorter and somewhat differently focused treatments of Gilded Age politics can be found in John A. Garraty, *The New Commonwealth*, and Harold U. Faulkner, *Politics, Reform and Expansion* (New York, 1959). For an interesting and critical assessment of Cleveland's second term, consult J. R. Hollingsworth, *The Whirligig of Politics* (Chicago, 1963). The outstanding biography of a Gilded Age President is the prize-winning study by Allan Nevins, *Grover Cleveland: A Study in Courage* (New York, 1932). Other important biographies include Kenneth E. Davison, *The Presidency of Rutherford B. Hayes* (Westport, Conn., 1972); Harry J. Sievers, *Benjamin Harrison*, 3 vols. (Chicago, 1952–1968); H. Wayne Morgan, *William McKinley and His America* (Syracuse, 1963); and Margaret Leech, *In the Days of McKinley* (New York, 1959). Classic contemporary commentaries on politics and government in the Gilded Age will be found in Woodrow Wilson, *Congressional Government* (New York, 1885); James Bryce, *The American Commonwealth* (New York, 1888); and Henry Adams, *The Education of Henry Adams* (Boston, 1918).

THE PRESIDENCY IN THE CONTEMPORARY AGE

Theodore Roosevelt, considered by many the first of the modern Presidents, has been well served by his recent biographers. For his early years, there is Carleton Putnam's formidable *Theodore Roosevelt: The Formative Years, 1858–1886* (New York, 1958). The best one-volume biography is William H. Harbaugh, *Power and Responsibility* (New York, 1961). *Theodore Roosevelt and the Politics of Power* (Boston, 1968), by G. Wallace Chessman, is a sturdy, compact study. An insightful slim volume by John Blum, *The Republican Roosevelt* (Cambridge, Mass., 1954), evaluates Roosevelt as a political leader. The best history of the Roosevelt years is George E. Mowry, *The Era of Theodore Roosevelt, 1900–1912* (New York, 1958). No one interested in Roosevelt and his times should miss the lively volumes of Mark Sullivan, *Our Times, The United States, 1900–1925*, 6 vols. (New York, 1926–1935). In assessing the meaning of the progressive reform movement, two books merit special mention: Richard Hofstadter, *The Age of Reform* (New York, 1955), and the New Left analysis by Gabriel Kolko, *The Triumph of Conservatism: A Reinterpretation of American History, 1900–1916* (New York, 1963). An impressively researched, thoughtful, and, on balance, critical study of TR's foreign policy is Howard K. Beale, *Theodore Roosevelt and the Rise of America to World Power* (Baltimore, 1956). There is also a stimulating essay on Roosevelt in Erwin S. Hargrove, *Presidential Leadership* (New York, 1966). On TR as a leader of public opinion, see Elmer E. Cornwell, Jr., *Presidential Leadership of Public Opinion* (Bloomington, Ind., 1965).

Serious students of Woodrow Wilson should consult the projected forty-five volume collection, Arthur S. Link, ed., *The Papers of Woodrow Wilson* (Princeton, 1966–   ); thus far over twenty volumes have been published; the editor is the most distinguished and prolific Wilson scholar. A more selective source is Ray Stannard Baker and William E. Dodd, eds., *The Public Papers of Woodrow Wilson*, 6 vols. (New York, 1925–1927). The two most significant books written by Wilson containing his ideas on the Presidency are *Congressional Government* (Boston, 1885) and *Constitutional Government in the United States* (New York, 1908). Both are still available in paperback editions. Arthur S. Link, *Wilson*, 5 vols. (Princeton, 1947–1966) is an exhaustively researched multivolumed Wilson biography which carries his career to 1917. A sympathetic multivolumed authorized biography of Wilson is Ray Stannard Baker, *Woodrow Wilson: Life and Letters*, 8 vols. (Garden City, N.Y., 1927–1939). The better short biographies of Wilson are Arthur S. Link, *Woodrow Wilson: A Brief Biography* (Cleveland, 1963), and John Garraty, *Woodrow Wilson: A Great Life in Brief* (New York, 1956). Excellent collections of essays are Earl Latham, ed., *The Philosophy and Policies of Woodrow Wilson* (Chicago, 1958), and Arthur S. Link, ed., *The Higher Realism of Woodrow Wilson* (Nashville, 1971). A detailed study of Wilson's early life before he entered politics is Henry Wilkinson Bragdon, *Woodrow Wilson: The Academic Years* (Cambridge, Mass., 1967). An incisive interpretative volume is John Morton Blum, *Woodrow Wilson and the Politics of Morality* (Boston, 1956). An unsuccessful attempt at psychohistory, criticized by both historians and psychologists, is Sigmund Freud and William Bullitt, *Thomas Woodrow Wilson: A Psychological Study* (Boston, 1967). The best single volume on Wilson and progressivism is Arthur S. Link, *Woodrow Wilson and the Progressive Era, 1910–1917* (New York, 1954). A fine analysis of Wilson's ideas on foreign policy is Harley Notter, *The Origins of the Foreign Policy of Woodrow Wilson* (Baltimore, 1937); a penetrating group of essays on Wilson's foreign policy is Arthur S. Link, *Wilson: The Diplomatist* (rev. ed., Baltimore, 1968). This latter edition reveals the author's more sympathetic treatment of Wilson policies. A critical study of Wilson's neutrality policies is Walter Millis, *The Road to War, 1914–1917* (Boston, 1935). Two fine books by Thomas A. Bailey containing balanced interpretations of Wilson and the League episode are *Woodrow Wilson and the Lost Peace* (New York, 1944) and *Woodrow Wilson and the Great Betrayal* (New York, 1945). An analytical and interpretive study of Wilson's foreign policy is N. Gordon Levin, *Woodrow Wilson and World Politics* (New York, 1968). A journalist's fascinating but at times distorted account of Wilson's last and tragic years is Gene Smith, *When the Cheering Stopped* (New York, 1964). Kurt Wimer has written a series of articles on Wilson and the League; these include "The League of Nations: A Victim of Executive-Legislative Rivalry," *Lock Haven Review* 1 (February 1960), pp. 1–12.

There are many biographies of Hoover, the most recent and best of which is by Joan Hoff Wilson, *Herbert Hoover: Forgotten Progressive* (Boston, 1975), a successful synthesis of recent research based upon new sources. The most important piece on Hoover's work and ideas in the 1920s is Ellis W. Hawley's "Herbert Hoover, the Commerce Secretariat, and the Vision of an 'Associative State,' 1921–1928," *Journal of American History* 61 (June 1974), pp. 116–40. The article also contains in its notes the best published bibliography on Hoover in the twenties. Joseph Brandes, *Herbert Hoover and Economic Diplomacy: Department of Commerce Policy, 1921–1928* (Pittsburgh, 1962), though published before the opening of the Hoover Papers is based on National Archives materials and is thorough and reliable for its subject. Jordan A. Schwarz, *The Interregnum of Despair: Hoover, the Congress, and the Depression* (Urbana, Ill., 1970), ably revises the story of Hoover's relations with Congress. The essays, by Ellis Hawley, Robert Himmelberg, Gerald Nash, and Murray Rothbard in *Herbert Hoover and the Crisis of American Capitalism*, edited by J. J. Huthmacher and Warren Susman (Cambridge, Mass., 1973), offer varying and stimulating perspectives on aspects of Hoover's Presidency.

Craig Lloyd in *Aggressive Introvert: A Study of Herbert Hoover and Public Relations Management* (Columbus, Ohio, 1972), has succinctly and very capably related the way Hoover's image was made and unmade. One of the most important events of the Hoover Presidency has been freshly treated from the new sources by Donald Lisio in *The President and Protest: Hoover, Conspiracy and the Bonus Riot* (Columbia, Mo., 1974).

For an elaboration of James MacGregor Burns's ideas, consult his outstanding biography in two volumes, *Roosevelt: The Lion and the Fox* (New York, 1956) and *Roosevelt: The Soldier of Freedom* (New York, 1970). Two useful collections of Roosevelt material can be found in Samuel Rosenman, ed., *The Public Papers of Franklin D. Roosevelt*, 13 vols. (New York, 1938–1950), and Elliott Roosevelt, ed., *F.D.R.: His Personal Letters*, 4 vols. (New York, 1947–1950). A detailed and balanced account of Roosevelt's early life and career which carries him into the first hundred days of his Presidency is Frank Freidel, *Franklin D. Roosevelt*, 4 vols. (Boston, 1952–1973). A penetrating, lively, and sympathetic multivolumed study which takes Roosevelt through the 1936 election is Arthur Schlesinger, Jr., *The Age of Roosevelt*, 3 vols. (Boston, 1957–1960). An exhaustively researched and excellent account of the New Deal is William E. Leuchtenburg, *Franklin D. Roosevelt and the New Deal, 1932–1940* (New York, 1963). Joseph P. Lash in his *Eleanor and Franklin* (New York, 1971) provides an illuminating account of their personal relationship. For a critical work from a conservative point of view, see Edgar E. Robinson, *The Roosevelt Leadership, 1933–1945* (Philadelphia, 1955). A slim provocative study which criticizes Roosevelt's leadership and the New Deal policies is Paul Conkin, *The New Deal* (New York, 1967). One of the best collections of interpretive essays on the New Deal is found in Otis Graham, ed., *The New Deal: The Critical Issues* (Boston, 1971). An authoritative account, generally favorable to Roosevelt, discussing the background to America's involvement in World War II is in William L. Langer and S. Everett Gleason, *The Challenge to Isolation: 1937–1940* and *The Undeclared War, 1940–1941* (New York, 1952–1953). A revealing account of American diplomacy is Robert E. Sherwood, *Roosevelt and Hopkins: An Intimate History* (New York, 1948). Critical works of Roosevelt's neutrality policies which express isolationist sentiments are Charles A. Beard, *American Foreign Policy in the Making, 1932–1940* (New Haven, 1946), and Charles Tansill, *Back Door to War* (Chicago, 1952). A more balanced account is Robert Devine, *The Reluctant Belligerent: American Entry into World War II* (New York, 1965). Of the many works discussing the events leading to the "Day of Infamy," a comprehensive balanced view is given in Herbert Feis, *The Road to Pearl Harbor* (Princeton, 1950). One of the best books on wartime diplomacy is Herbert Feis, *Churchill, Roosevelt, and*

Stalin (Princeton, 1957). A concise volume on the same topic is Gaddis Smith, *American Diplomacy During the Second World War* (New York, 1965). A short analysis of American strategy during the war is found in Samuel E. Morison, *Strategy and Compromise* (Washington, D.C., 1962). Among the better books dealing with Roosevelt and the Yalta Conference are John L. Snell, ed., *Meaning of Yalta: Big Three Diplomacy and the New Balance of Power* (Baton Rouge, 1956), and Diane S. Clemens, *Yalta* (New York, 1970). Of critical interpretative works, one from the "New Left" revisionist viewpoint is Gabriel Kolko, *The Politics of War: The World and United States Foreign Policy, 1943–1945* (New York, 1968); another with a conservative perspective is George Crocker, *Roosevelt's Road to Russia* (Chicago, 1959). A more balanced view which discusses Roosevelt's foreign policy and the coming of the Cold War is John L. Gaddis, *The United States and the Origins of the Cold War, 1941–1947* (New York, 1972). Consult William J. Stewart, ed., *The Era of Franklin D. Roosevelt: A Selected Bibliography of Periodical and Dissertation Literature, 1945–1971* (Hyde Park, N.Y., 1974), for a detailed discussion of the literature on the Roosevelt era.

Harry S. Truman's views are contained in a number of works including: *Mr. President* (New York, 1952); *Memoirs*, 2 vols. (Garden City, N.Y., 1955–1956); and *Mr. Citizen* (New York, 1953). There is not an adequate biography of Truman or an in-depth overview of his administration. Margaret Truman's *Harry S. Truman* (New York, 1973) and Merle Miller's *Plain Speaking: An Oral Biography of Harry S. Truman* (New York, 1973) are uncritical but contain useful information, while Cabell Phillips, *The Truman Presidency: The History of a Triumphant Succession* (New York, 1966), is outdated but still worth reading. Shorter overviews of Truman or his Presidency which are useful, although varying in interpretation, are Richard S. Kirkendall, "Truman's Path to Power," *Social Science* 43 (April 1968), pp. 67–73; his "Harry Truman," in *America's Eleven Greatest Presidents* (Chicago, 1971), edited by Morton Borden; Samuel Lubell's sections on Truman in his *The Future of American Politics* (rev. ed., Garden City, N.Y., 1955); and Richard E. Neustadt's "Congress and the Fair Deal: A Legislative Balance Sheet," *Public Policy* 5 (1954), pp. 351–81. The Truman period is one of the most controversial in American history and the literature reflects the widely diverse views of scholars working in the field. This dispute is best reflected in Richard S. Kirkendall, ed., *The Truman Period as a Research Field: A Reappraisal, 1972* (Columbia, Mo., 1974). There are a number of studies dealing with specialized topics including Allen J. Matusow, *Farm Policies and Politics in the Truman Years* (Cambridge, Mass., 1967); Richard F. Haynes, *The Awesome Power: Harry S. Truman as Commander in Chief* (Baton Rouge,

1973); Donald R. McCoy and Richard T. Ruetten, *Quest and Response: Minority Rights and the Truman Administration* (Lawrence, Kans., 1973); Susan M. Hartmann, *Truman and the 80th Congress* (Columbia, Mo., 1971); Alonzo L. Hamby, *Beyond the New Deal: Harry S. Truman and American Liberalism* (New York, 1973); and Philip C. Dolce, "Conflict over Goals and Leadership in Immigration Policy: The McCarran Walter Act and the Controversy During the Truman Administration," in Frank J. Coppa and Thomas Curran, eds., *The Immigrant in American Life* (Boston, 1976). Athan Theoharis's *Seeds of Repression: Harry S. Truman and the Origins of McCarthyism* (Chicago, 1971) is thought-provoking but overemphasizes its main point. An interesting collection of essays dealing with the Truman period is contained in Barton J. Bernstein, ed., *Politics and Policies of the Truman Administration* (Chicago, 1970). The Cold War has been the subject of many valuable studies. Currently, the best "liberal" interpretation is John Lewis Gaddis, *The United States and the Origins of the Cold War, 1941–1947* (New York, 1972), while varying "revisionist" views are contained in Thomas G. Paterson, *Soviet-American Confrontation: Postwar Reconstruction and the Origins of the Cold War* (Baltimore, 1973), and Walter LaFeber, *America, Russia, and The Cold War, 1945–1975* (New York, 1976).

Herbert S. Parmet, *Eisenhower and the American Crusades* (New York, 1972), offers a comprehensive view of the Eisenhower Presidency and the politics of the 1950s. Robert L. Branyan and Lawrence H. Larsen, *The Eisenhower Administration, 1953–1961: A Documentary History*, 2 vols. (New York, 1971), provides a handy compilation of papers from the Eisenhower Library. One should consult Eisenhower's own two-volume memoir, *The White House Years* (New York, 1963, 1965). James L. Sundquist, *Politics and Policy, The Eisenhower, Kennedy and Johnson Years* (Washington, D.C., 1968), is vital for the formulation of legislation. David A. Frier, *Conflict of Interest in the Eisenhower Administration* (Ames, Iowa, 1969), often sounds like a diatribe but provides a service by questioning the "team's" moral values. Two volumes by persons having close access to the administration are Emmet J. Hughes, *The Ordeal of Power* (New York, 1963), and Robert J. Donovan, *Eisenhower: The Inside Story* (New York, 1956). Richard Rovere, *Affairs of State* (New York, 1956), and I. F. Stone, *The Haunted Fifties* (New York, 1963), offer collections of contemporary insights. William V. Shannon, "Eisenhower as President," *Commentary* (November 26, 1958), pp. 390–98, is an article that does more than any other to seal the liberal indictment. More recent considerations, all tending to give Ike more credit, are Garry Wills, *Nixon Agonistes* (Boston, 1970); Arthur Larson, *Eisenhower: The President Nobody Knew* (New York, 1968); and Richard Rovere, "Eisenhower Revisited," *New*

York Times Magazine, February 7, 1971. John S. D. Eisenhower's *Strictly Personal* (Garden City, N.Y., 1974) tells what it was like to be the general's son.

Arthur M. Schlesinger, Jr., *A Thousand Days: John F. Kennedy in the White House* (Boston, 1965), is an authoritative account of the Kennedy administration written by an aide who is a professional historian and who had responsibility for keeping a record. Based not only on official documents, but also on the author's personal participation, Schlesinger's interpretations and judgments are sympathetic but for the most part persuasive. Theodore C. Sorenson was a long-time speech writer and aide to Kennedy both as Senator and as President. His book, *Kennedy* (New York, 1965), is an invaluable source based on insider materials and personal experience. Roger Hilsman, *To Move a Nation: The Politics of Foreign Policy in the Administration of John F. Kennedy* (New York, 1967), is based on documents and personal participation. It discusses some of the major foreign policy problems and issues of the Kennedy years, such as the Congo, Laos, curbing the CIA, the Bay of Pigs, the Cuban Missile Crisis, China policy, and Vietnam. Theodore H. White, *The Making of the President, 1960* (Boston, 1961), is a journalist's report on the Presidential campaign of 1960, replete with anecdotal detail and shrewd insight. Another excellent journalistic account worth reading is Elie Abel, *The Missile Crisis* (Philadelphia, 1966), which deals with the Cuban Missile Crisis and is based mainly on interviews. Graham T. Allison, *Essence of Decision, Explaining the Cuban Missile Crisis* (Boston, 1971), is a scholarly reconstruction of the Cuban Missile Crisis based on thorough research and interviews. David Halberstam, *The Best and the Brightest* (New York, 1972), is a journalist's account of U.S. involvement in Vietnam during the Kennedy and Johnson administrations. It is full of interesting anecdotal detail and offers a critical assessment of decision-making during these years. A handy collection of essays on the Kennedy years is Earl Latham, *J. F. Kennedy and Presidential Power* (Lexington, Mass., 1972). A foreign assessment can be found in Henry Fairle, *The Kennedy Promise* (Garden City, N.Y., 1973).

Until a documented, full-portrait biography of Lyndon Johnson is written, the richest account based on extensive interviewing is Alfred Steinberg, *Sam Johnson's Boy* (New York, 1968). Johnson's memoirs, *The Vantage Point: Perspectives of the Presidency, 1963–1969* (New York, 1971), is "official" history and the reader searches in it in vain for important personal revelations. In his Presidential campaign book, *My Hope for America* (New York, 1964), Johnson presented his principal political ideas in brief compass. An abundance of fascinating detail about Johnson and his Presidency is in Lady Bird Johnson, *A White House Diary*

(New York, 1970). The most illuminating introduction to the political style of LBJ is William S. White, *The Professional: Lyndon B. Johnson* (Boston, 1964). For a striking look at Johnson's Presidential "style," albeit concentrating on his last days in office, see *The President Steps Down* (New York, 1970) by George Christian, the last of Johnson's White House press secretaries. A perceptive foreigner's view of the Johnson Presidency is *No Hail, No Farewell* (New York, 1970) by Louis Herren, Washington correspondent of the *London Times*. A sharply critical account of the Johnson years, full of firsthand detail, is Eric Goldman, *The Tragedy of Lyndon Johnson* (New York, 1969). Another critical discussion of the people who made the Vietnam debacle is David Halberstam, *The Best and the Brightest* (New York, 1972). An informed general treatment of the American involvement is Chester L. Cooper, *The Lost Crusade: America in Vietnam* (New York, 1970). Capturing through a report of lengthy conversations with Johnson and his chief advisers the flavor of the Vietnam decisions is Henry F. Graff, *The Tuesday Cabinet: Deliberation and Decision on Peace and War under Lyndon B. Johnson* (Englewood Cliffs, N.J., 1973).

John Osborne, *The First Year of the Nixon Watch* (New York, 1970), and the next four "Nixon Watch" books are collections of good reportage on the administration from the weekly journal of opinion *The New Republic*. Gary Wills, *Nixon Agonistes* (Boston, 1970), is long and somewhat diffuse, but the best psychological and geographical analysis of the man done so far. James Barber, *The Presidential Character* (Englewood Cliffs, N.J., 1972), examines Nixon, along with other Presidents, from a novel perspective which relies heavily on analysis of individual personalities. A provocative psychological study is Bruce Mazlish, *In Search of Nixon: A Psychohistorical Inquiry* (New York, 1972). Richard Nixon, *Six Crises* (Garden City, N.Y., 1962), is still the single most revealing estimate of the man—whether intentional or not. Earl Mazo and Stephen Hess, *Nixon: A Political Portrait* (New York, 1967), is a straightforward, basic biography written with sympathy but without adoration. Important revealing works on Nixon's White House, Watergate, and his resignation are Carl Bernstein and Bob Woodward, *All the President's Men* (New York, 1974); *The White House Transcripts* (New York, 1974); Dan Rather and Gary Paul Gates, *The Palace Guard* (New York, 1974); and Theodore H. White, *Breach of Faith* (New York, 1975).

Louis C. Hatch, as revised by Early L. Shoup, *A History of the Vice-Presidency of the United States* (Westport, Conn., 1970), is a reissue of the original work on the subject. Edgar W. Waugh, *Second Consul: The Vice-Presidency; Our Greatest Political Problem* (Indianapolis, 1956), focuses on the problems of succession but also concludes that the office is "a monumental failure" that deserves reexamination and upgrading. Irving G. Williams, *The American Vice-Presidency: New Look* (Garden City, N.Y., 1954), analyzes the office from the viewpoint of political science, offers case histories of performance in each of the Vice-President's varied roles, and proposes a solution to succession by disability. Williams's *The Rise of the Vice-Presidency* (Washington, D.C., 1956) is the best historical study of the office from its formation in 1787 to Richard Nixon's first term. A useful discussion of the Vice-Presidency and foreign policy is found in Williams's "The American Vice-Presidency and Foreign Affairs," *World Affairs* 120 (Summer, 1957), pp. 38–41. Donald Young, *American Roulette: The History and Dilemma of the Vice-Presidency* (rev. ed., New York, 1972), is a popular work with short sketches of each incumbent. Also useful is Paul T. David, "The Vice Presidency: Its Institutional Evolution and Contemporary Status," *The Journal of Politics* 29 (November 1967), pp. 721–48. Birch Bayh, *One Heartbeat Away: Presidential Disability and Succession* (Indianapolis, 1968), is an absorbing story of the framing, strategy, and ratification of the Twenty-fifth Amendment by the Senator most responsible for it. Richard M. Cohen and Jules Witcover, *A Heartbeat Away: The Investigation and Resignation of Vice President Spiro T. Agnew* (New York, 1974), will hardly be the last word on the subject, but it is a good first one by two responsible reporters. Michael V. DiSalle with Lawrence G. Blochman, *Second Choice* (New York, 1966), is an uneven study which deals mostly with the accidental successions. Ruth C. Silva, *Presidential Succession* (Ann Arbor, Mich., 1951), and John D. Feerick, *From Failing Hands: The Story of Presidential Succession* (New York, 1965), thoroughly discuss the legal aspects and problems involved. Richard H. Hansen, *The Year We Had No President* (Lincoln, Neb., 1862), discusses disability problems and suggests solutions. It is useful for its inclusion of colonial and state precedents. A biography that discusses Gerald R. Ford's political career through his short tenure as Vice-President is Jerald F. terHorst, *Gerald Ford and the Future of the Presidency* (New York, 1974).

KEY ISSUES

Critical historical overviews of the President's exercise of military power are contained in Arthur M. Schlesinger, Jr., *The Imperial Presidency* (Boston, 1973), and Jacob K. Javits, *Who Makes War: The President Versus Congress* (New York, 1973). For historical and constitutional background on the President's military power, the reader should consult Edward S. Corwin, *The President: Office and Powers* (rev. ed., New York, 1957). The most useful analysis of the Lincoln experience is found in works by James

G. Randall, particularly in his *Constitutional Problems Under Lincoln* (New York, 1926) and *Lincoln the President: Midstream* (New York, 1952). Eisenhower discussed the use of military power in his autobiography, *Mandate for Change* (Garden City, N.Y., 1963). The Cuban Missile Crisis is represented by a large bibliography, but the most useful accounts are in Elie Abel, *The Missile Crisis* (Philadelphia, 1966), and Robert F. Kennedy, *Thirteen Days* (New York, 1969). Bibliography is also plentiful on the Vietnam War. An analysis sympathetic to the Johnson and Nixon Presidencies is by the Assistant for National Security Affairs in the Johnson White House, Walter W. Rostow, *The Diffusion of Power* (New York, 1972). Studies critical of the Presidency are represented by David Halberstam, *The Best and the Brightest* (New York, 1972), and Townsend Hoopes, *The Limits of Intervention* (New York, 1969). For accounts of the President's efforts to control nuclear arms, see Robert Gilpen, *American Scientists and Nuclear Weapons Policy* (Princeton, 1962), and Adam Yarmolinsky, *The Military Establishment* (New York, 1971), which also provides further bibliography on the subject.

General analytical accounts of Presidential assistants and advisers may be found in Patrick Anderson, *The President's Men* (Garden City, N.Y., 1968), which covers major White House assistants from Franklin Roosevelt's Presidency to Lyndon Johnson's; and in Louis W. Koenig, *The Invisible Presidency* (New York, 1960), which examines the phenomenon for selected Presidencies between Washington and Eisenhower. The development of the Cabinet and its relation to the White House staff is treated in Richard F. Fenno, Jr., *The President's Cabinet* (New York, 1959). For particular Presidents and their White House assistants, the literature is extensive. Concerning Franklin Roosevelt, a study by one of his Brain Trusters is especially useful: Rexford G. Tugwell, *The Democratic Roosevelt* (Garden City, N.Y., 1957). The Truman era is best treated in his *Memoirs*, 2 vols. (Garden City, N.Y., 1955–1956), and *Truman Speaks* (New York, 1960). Eisenhower's approach is recounted by his chief of staff, Sherman Adams, in *First-Hand Report* (New York, 1961). Discussions of Kennedy and his staff are found in comprehensive studies of his administration by two staff members, Theodore Sorensen, *Kennedy* (New York, 1965), and Arthur M. Schlesinger, Jr., *A Thousand Days* (Boston, 1965). Lyndon Johnson's experience is presented by a Washington journalist, Charles Roberts, *L.B.J.'s Inner Circle* (New York, 1965), and by a member of the Johnson staff, Harry McPherson, *A Political Education* (Boston, 1972). Nixon's White House staff is discussed in Rowland Evans, Jr., and Robert D. Novak, *Nixon in the White House* (New York, 1971), and by two *Washington Post* reporters who first uncovered the Watergate scandals, Carl Bernstein and Bob Woodward, in *All the President's Men*

(New York, 1974). For dialogue between Nixon and his staff, see Staff of the *Washington Post, The Presidential Transcripts* (New York, 1974). One of the most insightful studies of the general functioning of the White House staff is by George E. Reedy, *The Twilight of the Presidency* (New York, 1970). The causes of the malfunctioning of the President's advisers in the Vietnam War and other crises are explored in Irving L. Janis, *Victims of Group Think* (Boston, 1972).

The racial attitudes and policies of earlier Presidents are covered in George Sinkler, *The Racial Attitudes of American Presidents from Abraham Lincoln to Theodore Roosevelt* (Garden City, N.Y., 1971), and Rayford W. Logan, *The Betrayal of the Negro: From Rutherford B. Hayes to Woodrow Wilson* (new enlarged ed., New York, 1965). A fine collection of essays discussing black Americans and the Franklin D. Roosevelt administration is Bernard Sternsher, ed., *The Negro in Depression and War: Prelude to Revolution, 1930–1945* (Chicago, 1969). The best examination of the Truman record on civil rights is found in Donald R. McCoy and Richard T. Ruetten, *Quest and Response: Minority Rights and the Truman Administration* (Lawrence, Kans., 1973). A discussion relating the Presidency to the civil rights movement is Ruth Morgan, *The President and Civil Rights: Policy Making by Executive Order* (New York, 1970).

There is not a single study on Presidential attitudes and policies toward city and suburb. Those interested in further reading should be prepared to peruse a wide variety of sources. A comprehensive coverage of federal legislation and its effect on city and suburb in the twentieth century is provided by Mel Scott in *American City Planning Since 1890* (Berkeley, 1969), while the specifics of various acts and programs can be found in an abbreviated form in the *Congressional Quarterly*. The New Deal's approach to experimental communities is examined in Paul K. Conkin, *Tomorrow a New World: The New Deal Community Program* (Ithaca, N.Y., 1959), and Joseph L. Arnold, *The New Deal in the Suburbs: A History of the Greenbelt Town Program, 1935–1954* (Columbus, Ohio, 1971). Timothy McDonnell, *The Wagner Housing Act* (Chicago, 1957), examines the background of the origins of public housing, while Richard O. Davies in *Housing Reform During the Truman Administration* (Columbia, Mo., 1966) offers insight into the politics behind the Housing Act of 1949. John Williams's *The Department of Housing and Urban Development* (New York, 1967) is a useful description of this agency, though somewhat dated. Douglas M. Fox, ed., *The New Urban Politics* (Pacific Palisades, Calif., 1972), contains an excellent collection of articles on the federal government and its relations with local governments. A useful assessment of urban housing and planning in the postwar era is provided by Charles Abrams in *City Is the Frontier* (New York, 1965). James Q. Wilson, ed.,

Urban Renewal: The Record and the Controversy (Cambridge, Mass., 1966), offers articles written with different points of view. Sam Warner, Jr.'s *Urban Wilderness* (New York, 1973) is an intentionally polemical interpretation of urban history, which contains much thought-provoking material on American values, institutions, and legislation and their effects on metropolitan structure and social organization.

James E. Pollard, *The Presidents and The Press* (New York, 1947), and his sequel, *The President and The Press: Truman to Johnson* (Washington, D.C., 1964), are the best overall studies on Presidential relations with the press. Other useful studies are Robert S. Harper, *Lincoln and the Press* (New York, 1951), and Harold W. Chase and Allen H. Lerman, eds., *Kennedy and The Press: The News Conferences* (New York, 1965). Elmer E. Cornwell, Jr., *Presidential Leadership of Public Opinion* (Bloomington, Ind., 1965), assays the techniques by which Presidents have tried to lead public opinion. Edwin Emery, *The Press in America* (3rd ed., New York, 1972), is not as complete as Frank Luther Mott's *American Journalism* (3rd ed., New York, 1962), but it is a good general history. Two excellent surveys the reader should consult are by John Tebbel, *The Media in America* (New York, 1974) and *The Compact History of the American Newspaper* (New York, 1963). Louis Filler, *The Muckrakers* (Chicago, 1968), is still the definitive work on the press in the progressive era. William A. Hachten, *The Supreme Court on Freedom of the Press* (Ames, Iowa, 1968), deals mainly with developments since World War I and Edward S. Hudon, *Freedom of Speech and Press in America* (Washington, D.C., 1963), covers events from the Constitutional Convention to the 1960s. The bibliography and references in this work are most helpful. The reader also should consult "First Amendment and The News Media" (Final Report, Annual Chief Justice Earl Warren Conference on Advocacy in the United States, June 8–9, 1973) which is an excellent survey.

VIEWS OF THE TOP

General works dealing with Presidential nominations and campaigns are Gerald Pomper, *Nominating the President: The Politics of Convention Choice* (New York, 1966); James W. Davis, *Presidential Primaries: The Road to the White House* (New York, 1967); James David Barber, ed., *Choosing the President* (Englewood Cliffs, N.J., 1974). Books that discuss various aspects of the McGovern campaign and the 1972 election are: Theodore White, *The Making of the President 1972* (New York, 1973); Richard Dougherty, *Goodby Mr. Christian: A Personal Account of McGovern's Rise and Fall* (Garden City, N.Y., 1973); Timothy Crouse, *The*

Boys on the Bus (New York, 1973); Sheila Hixson and Ruth Rose, eds., *The Official Proceedings of the Democratic National Convention, 1972* (Washington, D.C., 1972); and Carl Bernstein and Bob Woodward, *All the President's Men* (New York, 1974).

Arthur M. Schlesinger, Sr., conducted two polls in which he asked a number of experts to rate the Presidents. The polls appeared in *Life* 25 (November 1, 1948), pp. 65–66, and the *New York Times Magazine* (July 29, 1962). Criticism and commentary on these polls have been constant ever since their publication. For example, see C. A. Amlund, "President-Ranking: A Criticism," *Midwest Journal of Political Science* 8 (1964), pp. 309–15, or the more recent article by Gary M. Maranell, "The Evaluation of Presidents: An Extension of the Schlesinger Polls," *Journal of American History* 57 (June, 1970), 104–13. Other individuals have offered insights, and listings including H. S. Commager, "What Makes for Presidential Greatness," *New York Times Magazine* (July 22, 1945), and Morton Borden, ed., *America's Eleven Greatest Presidents* (Chicago, 1971). The best overall treatment is Thomas A. Bailey, *Presidential Greatness: The Image and the Man from George Washington to the Present* (New York, 1966).

For further elaboration of Arthur M. Schlesinger, Jr.'s ideas, see his *The Imperial Presidency* (Boston, 1973). In dealing with the expansion of Presidential power, the book to start with is *The Federalist Papers*, which is available in many editions. Also helpful are: Edward Corwin, *The President: Office and Powers* (New York, 1957); Marcus Cunliffe, *American Presidents and the Presidency* (London, 1969); Louis W. Koenig, *The Chief Executive* (New York, 1975); Richard Neustadt, *Presidential Power: The Politics of Leadership* (New York, 1960); Aaron Wildavsky, ed., *The Presidency* (Boston, 1969); Emmet J. Hughes, *The Living Presidency* (New York, 1973); and George Reedy, *The Twilight of the Presidency* (New York, 1970).

Watergate has again led us to consider the benefits of parliamentary government in comparison to our presidential system. Insight on this issue can be found in Arthur M. Schlesinger, Jr., *The Imperial Presidency* (Boston, 1973); Howard A. Scarrow's "Parliamentary and Presidential Government Compared," *Current History* 66 (June 1974), pp. 264–67, 272, is less comprehensive in its coverage of this topic. Woodrow Wilson in his essay entitled "Cabinet Government in the United States," *The International Review* 7 (August 1879), pp. 146–63, provides an interesting assessment of parliamentary and presidential government and considers the feasibility of altering the American constitutional system in the direction of the British parliamentary one. The parliamentary form of government is covered in *Parliaments: A Comparative Study of the*

Structure and Functioning of Representative Institutions in Forty-One Countries (New York, 1962). Produced by the staff of the Inter-Parliamentary Union, this comparative approach is based upon the information collected from forty-one parliaments. The comparative approach also is used in Leslie Wolf-Phillips, ed., *Constitutions of Modern States* (New York, 1968), which provides selected texts and commentary on the constitutions of twelve states including those with presidential as well as parliamentary systems. The volume by William Bennet Munro and Morley Ayearst entitled *The Governments of Europe* (4th ed., New York, 1954) offers an overview of the governmental systems of the major European powers. Herman Finer's *Governments of Greater European Powers* (New York, 1955) and Robert G. Neumann, *European and Comparative Government* (New York, 1955), also are classic works. For the American political background Leonard Woods Labaree's *Royal Government in America* (New Haven, 1930) traces the British input in the American colonies and particularly the role of the crown in shaping their constitutional history, while J. R. Pole's *Political Representation in England and the Origins of the American Republic* (London, 1966) concentrates on the forces which influenced the formation of the American Constitution.

The best works on the scope and limitations of Presidential power include James D. Barber, *The Presidential Character: Predicting Performance in the White House* (Englewood Cliffs, N.J., 1972) which is an original psychopolitical approach to predicting Presidential performance. Robert S. Hirschfield, ed., *The Power of the Presidency* (2nd rev. ed., Chicago, 1973), presents differing views of presidential power as expressed by early commentators, by Presidents themselves, by the Supreme Court, and by students of the Presidency. Works which emphasize constitutional limitations on Presidential power are: Raoul Berger, *Impeachment: The Constitutional Problem* (Cambridge, Mass., 1973); Alan F. Westin, *The Anatomy of a Constitutional Law Case: Youngstown Sheet and Tube Co. v. Sawyer* (New York, 1958); Leon Friedman, ed., *United States v. Nixon: The President Before the Supreme Court* (New York, 1974). Other valuable books are: Emmet John Hughes, *The Living Presidency* (New York, 1973); Louis W. Koenig, *The Chief Executive* (New York, 1975); Richard E. Neustadt, *Presidential Power: The Politics of Leadership* (New York, 1960); and Arthur M. Schlesinger, Jr., *The Imperial Presidency* (Boston, 1973).

CONTRIBUTORS

STANLEY BUDER is Associate Professor of History and Chairman of the Department at Bernard Baruch College of the City University of New York. He is the author of *Pullman: An Experiment in Industrial Order and Community Planning* and *Ebenezer Howard and the Rise of the Garden City Movement.* He was a consultant to the Chicago Historical Landmark Commission and is an Associate of the Columbia University Seminar on the City.

JAMES MAC GREGOR BURNS is Woodrow Wilson Professor of Government at Williams College. He is the author of *Congress on Trial, Roosevelt: The Lion and the Fox, John Kennedy: A Political Profile, The Deadlock of Democracy: Four Party Politics in America, Presidential Government: The Crucible of Leadership, Roosevelt: The Soldier of Freedom,* and *Uncommon Sense.* Dr. Burns has won the Pulitzer Prize as well as the Francis Parkman Prize, the National Book Award, and the Woodrow Wilson Foundation Award.

JOHN A. CARPENTER is Professor of History at Fordham University and author of *Ulysses S. Grant* and *Sword and Olive Branch: Oliver Otis Howard.* His articles have appeared in many journals including *The Journal of Negro History,* the *New York Historical Society Quarterly,* and *Civil War History.*

FRANK J. COPPA is Associate Professor of History at St. John's University. He has written and edited many books including *Planning, Protectionism and Politics in Liberal Italy, Camillo di Cavour,* and *Cities in Transition: From the Ancient World to Urban America.* Dr. Coppa's articles have appeared in many journals including *The Journal of Modern History* and *The Journal of Economic History.*

PHILIP C. DOLCE is Coordinator of Public Media Programming and Associate Professor of History at Bergen Community College. He has edited a number of books including *Cities in Transition: From the Ancient World to Urban America* and *Suburbia: The American*

Dream and Dilemma. He has also produced many radio and television series including "The American Presidency: The Men and The Office" (for CBS) and "Science and Society: A Humanistic View" (for CBS) and "The American Suburbs: Myth and Reality" (for NBC).

HENRY F. GRAFF is Professor of History at Columbia University. He is the author of many books including *The Tuesday Cabinet: Deliberation and Decision on Peace and War under Lyndon B. Johnson, American Imperialism and the Philippine Insurrection, The Adventure of the American People,* and *Bluejackets with Perry in Japan.* He has served as a member of the National Historical Publications Commission, the Historical Advisory Committee of the United States Air Force, and as a consultant to Time, Inc.

RICHARD HARMOND is Associate Professor of History at St. John's University. His work has appeared in the *Journal of American History, Journal of Social History,* and *New-York Historical Society Quarterly.*

ROGER HILSMAN is Professor of Government at Columbia University. He served as Director of Intelligence and Research at the State Department and as Assistant Secretary of State for Far Eastern Affairs in the Kennedy administration. He is the author of *To Move a Nation: The Politics of Foreign Policy in the Administration of John F. Kennedy, Strategic Intelligence and National Decisions, The Politics of Policy Making in Defense and Foreign Affairs,* and *Military Policy and National Security.* Dr. Hilsman's articles have appeared in numerous journals and books.

ROBERT F. HIMMELBERG is Associate Professor of History at Fordham University and author of *The Great Depression and American Capitalism* and *The Business Community and Anti-Trust Policy, 1919–1933: Origins of the NRA.* His work has appeared in *The Journal of American History* and *Business History Review.*

ROBERT S. HIRSCHFIELD is Professor of Political Science and Chairman of the Department at Hunter College. He is the producer of "Cityscope," a weekly television series, and author of *The Constitution and the Court* and *The Power of the Presidency.* Dr. Hirschfield's articles have appeared in *The Political Science Quarterly, The Nation,* and many other journals.

R. GORDON HOXIE is President of the Center for the Study of the Presidency. He has served as a consultant to the Department of Defense and the Department of State and is President of the Public Members Association of the Foreign Service. He is the author of many books including *John W. Burgess: American Scholar, The White House: Organization and Operations*, and *The Presidency of the 1970's*. Dr. Hoxie has been awarded the Meritorious Service Medal by the President of the United States.

ROBERT F. JONES is Assistant Professor of History at Fordham University and author of *The Formation of the Constitution*. His work has appeared in the *William and Mary Quarterly* and he is at work on a biography of George Washington.

LOUIS W. KOENIG is Professor of Government at New York University and author of *The Chief Executive, The Invisible Presidency, The Truman Administration, The Presidency Today*, and *Bryan: A Political Biography of William Jennings Bryan*. He has worked with many federal agencies including the Bureau of the Budget, the State Department, the National Resources Planning Board, and the Foreign Affairs Task Force of the First Hoover Commission. Dr. Koenig is a consultant to the Ford Foundation's Fund for the Advancement of Education.

HERBERT S. PARMET is Associate Professor of History at Queensborough Community College. He has written a number of books including *Eisenhower and the American Crusades, Never Again: A President Runs for a Third Term*, and *Aaron Burr: Portrait of an Ambitious Man*.

EDWARD PESSEN is Distinguished Professor of History at the City University of New York. He is the author of *Most Uncommon Jacksonians, New Perspectives on Jacksonian Parties and Politics, Jacksonian America: Society, Personality and Politics, Riches, Class, and Power Before the Civil War*, and *Three Centuries of Social Mobility in America*.

ROBERT V. REMINI is Professor of History at the University of Illinois at Chicago Circle and consulting editor for *The Papers of Andrew Jackson*. He is the author of many books including *Andrew Jackson and the Bank War, The Election of Andrew Jackson, Martin Van Buren and the Making of the Democratic Party, Andrew Jackson*, and *The Presidency of Andrew Jackson*.

ARTHUR M. SCHLESINGER, Jr., is Albert Schweitzer Professor of Humanities at the City University of New York. He is the author of many books including *The Age of Jackson, The Crisis of the Old Order, The Coming of the New Deal, The Politics of Upheaval, A Thousand Days: John F. Kennedy in the White House,* and *The Imperial Presidency.* Professor Schlesinger has won the Pulitzer Prize twice in addition to being awarded the Francis Parkman Prize, the Bancroft Prize, the National Book Award, and a gold medal from the National Institute of Arts and Letters. He was Special Assistant to the President of the United States and has held many important civic positions.

ROBERT B. SEMPLE, JR., is London Bureau Chief of the *New York Times.* Mr. Semple formerly served as White House correspondent and Deputy National Editor for the *New York Times.* His articles have appeared in numerous journals including *The New Republic, The New York Times Magazine,* and *Playboy.*

GEORGE H. SKAU is Professor of History and Chairman of the Department of Social Sciences at Bergen Community College. He is Vice Chairman of the Eastern Community College Social Science Association, and his articles have appeared in a number of journals including *Current History* and *Presidential Studies Quarterly.*

JOHN W. TEBBEL is Professor of Journalism at New York University. He is the author of many books including *The Media in America, A Compact History of the American Newspaper, The American Magazine: A Compact History,* and *Makers of Modern Journalism.* He has been a reporter for the *Detroit Free Press,* a feature writer and editor for the *Providence Journal,* and a staff writer for the *New York Times.*

RICHARD C. WADE is Distinguished Professor of History at the City University of New York. He has held important positions in every Presidential campaign from 1956 to 1972. Dr. Wade has served as a consultant to the National Advisory Commission on Civil Disorders, the National Commission on the Causes and Prevention of Violence, and the President's Task Force on Suburban Problems. He is the author of many books including *The Urban Frontier, Slavery in the Cities, Chicago: Growth of a Metropolis,* and *Cities in American Life.*

ROY WILKINS is Executive Director of the National Association for the Advancement of Colored People. He joined the staff of the NAACP in 1931 and has been Executive Director of the organization since 1955. He was a member of the National Advisory Commission on Civil Disorders and the Leadership Conference on Civil Rights.

IRVING G. WILLIAMS is Professor of History at St. John's University. He is the author of *The American Vice-Presidency: New Look*, *The Rise of the Vice-Presidency*, and *Government: Its Structure and Interpretation*. He received the Sylvania Television Award for his "See It Now" script, entitled "The Vice Presidency: The Great American Lottery."

INDEX

Page numbers of articles appear in boldface.